THE BUCKET LIST
WILD

Published in the United States of America in 2018 by
Universe Publishing, a division of
Rizzoli International Publications, Inc.
300 Park Avenue South,
New York, NY 10010
www.rizzoliusa.com

2018 2019 2020 2021 / 10 9 8 7 6 5 4 3 2 1

ISBN: 978-0-7893-3445-9

Library of Congress Control Number: 2018941597

Conceived, designed, and produced by
The Bright Press, an imprint of
The Quarto Group
Ovest House,
58 West Street,
Brighton, BN1 2RA
United Kingdom

Publisher: Mark Searle
Associate Publisher: Emma Bastow
Creative Director: James Evans
Managing Editor: Isheeta Mustafi
Senior Editor: Caroline Elliker
Project Editor: Angela Koo
Cover and design: JC Lanaway
Picture research: Katie Greenwood
Additional text: Dave Hall
Conservation consultant: Dr. Simon Dures

Printed and bound in China

A NOTE ON CONSERVATION
The protection of the natural world has
been treated as a priority with all of the
suggestions in this book, and where
species are at risk, this has been noted
in the text. However, conservation status
can change both rapidly and often,
so before embarking on any adventure,
check with an authority such as the
International Union for Conservation
of Nature (IUCN) for the latest
information and advice. The IUCN Red
List provides comprehensive listings
for both animal and plant species.

FRONT COVER: Photographing goats
above the fog in the mountains of
North America
Getty Images; John Mahan/Design Pics

THE BUCKET LIST

WILD

1000 ADVENTURES BIG AND SMALL
ANIMALS·BIRDS·FISH·NATURE

KATH STATHERS

UNIVERSE

CONTENTS

HOW TO USE THIS BOOK

This book is organized by the continents of the world. Within each chapter you will then find entries organized under individual countries—or in the case of the US and Canada, states, provinces, and terrritories. If you have a specific wildlife adventure in mind, simply turn to page 406 to search for it in the index.

A note about locations

Location details appear at the start of each entry. Sometimes these will lead you to a specific place. Where animals are widespread, or there are numerous possible sites to scout them out in nature, then broader details of geography and terrain are provided instead.

When to see nature

Some activities will be best done at certain times of year—in a dry season, when animals are breeding or migrating, when flowers are in bloom, and so on. Some animals are nocturnal, too, so this has also been noted.

Color code

Each entry number in the book has been given a color that relates to one of nine categories, as shown below, allowing you to select activities based on the type of animal, plant, or experience you are interested in.

Key to the color code

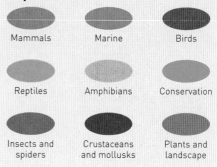

Mammals	Marine	Birds
Reptiles	Amphibians	Conservation
Insects and spiders	Crustaceans and mollusks	Plants and landscape

FOREWORD

I have spent my life studying and working to help conserve
the natural world, so it was both an inspiration and an honor
to be asked to review each of the 1,000 adventures you will
find within the pages of this book—each one both ethical
and amazing.

As a conservation biologist I have been fortunate enough
to undertake many adventures; however, it is not always easy
to know where to find the best nature has to offer. This book
does not prescribe adventure or guarantee that perfect
photograph, but it sets you up to discover for yourself what
our world has to offer. Its stunning photographs and inspiring
words will help you seek out beauty, majesty, tranquility,
excitement, and much more. You will find opportunities to
learn, to admire, to help, or simply to have your mind blown!
I will certainly be looking to experience some of the activities
suggested; kayaking with killer whales would be my current
number one, or perhaps the simple serenity of a flower
safari . . . there are so many wonderful ideas to choose from.

Above all, I hope that you find inspiration to help preserve
what you see so that future generations can be equally awed.
So wherever you choose to travel, please remember—take
only photographs and leave only footprints.

DR. SIMON G. DURES

INTRODUCTION

Nature is amazing, so it's no surprise that so many travel experiences
are based around seeing different species in their natural habitat.
With this as inspiration, this book brings together 1,000 of the most
incredible animals and plants in the world, and where to find them.

As you set off on your fabulous adventures, do bear in mind that
nature offers no guarantees. For every memory I have of toucans
in the Guatemalan jungles and elephants at Tanzanian watering holes,
I have a corresponding memory of staring into a murky Honduran lake
from a canoe in a fruitless search for manatees, or a fabulous trek in the
Indian hills that revealed plenty of long grass, but no tigers.

Yet even for these fruitless searches, I am grateful. Species are dying
out at a rate not seen since the time of the dinosaurs, and the terrible
part is, this time we are responsible. Whether through habitat loss,
climate change, or pollution, many species are in a battle to survive.
I have had the opportunity to search for some of these animals;
future generations might only be able to see them in pictures, movies,
and museums.

The best thing we can do to help halt or reverse this mass die-off is to
protect habitats and biodiversity at every level—reducing our demands
on the planet by cutting our consumption and emissions, looking after
local nature spots around us, or joining conservation programs to look
after particular species. If we all do what we can, we might just help
some of these species to make it. Meanwhile, enjoy the show!

Kath

KATH STATHERS

Sharing a sea turtle's ocean ree
home off Oahu in Hawa

CHAPTER ONE

NORTH AMERICA

Alaska • Seward
1 SEE A GREAT OCEAN TRAVELER
April to May

While it's impossible to rank whales from least to most lovable, it's certainly hard not to fall in love with the doleful eyes and laconic smile of the gray whale. The skin of these whales is covered with parasites, making them look lumpy and bumpy, as if they've been dwelling in the ocean for millennia. Thousands of gray whales make an annual 14,000-mile (22,530-km) migration from Alaska to breed in the warmer waters off Mexico, and back again. See them return to their Alaskan home in the company of an experienced guide.

Alaska • Kodiak Island
2 ADMIRE THE SPEED OF THE SEI WHALE
June to September

Despite its impressive 20-ton (18-tonne) weight, this whale can move through the oceans at up to 30 mph (50 kmh) as it twists and turns, scooping up mouthfuls of plankton as it goes.

Alaska • Steep Creek
3 MARVEL AT COLOR-CHANGING SALMON
July to October

As sockeye salmon swim back to the fresh water of their beginnings to spawn a new generation, their bodies change to a brilliant red and their heads a darkish green.

Alaska • Denali National Park
4 COUNT AN ALTERNATIVE BIG FIVE
Mid-May to mid-September

With wolves, moose, grizzly bears, caribou, and Dall sheep, Alaska has its very own Big Five to rival the African version (lions, leopards, rhinos, elephants, and buffaloes). This list has a long historical association with hunters, but happily the latest generation comes armed only with cameras and Instagram accounts. You'll find all of these creatures in the national park that surrounds Denali (formerly known as Mount McKinley), North America's highest peak. Dall sheep are particularly plentiful in the park's more mountainous regions, where they make use of the forbidding terrain to shelter from less nimble predators. If you get close enough, you can calculate a Dall ram's age by counting the rings on its curly horns.

1 | *The gentle smile of the gray whale*

Alaska • Prince William Sound
5 WELCOME BACK A KEYSTONE SPECIES
All year

Sea otters in Alaska used to be hunted for their fur, and
by 1900 were all but extinct. Thankfully there has been a
successful reintroduction campaign since then, and today
huge rafts of them can be seen in Prince William Sound, lying
on their backs and living life at sea—eating, sleeping, even
giving birth in the water. Take a boat cruise and you will
discover why they are nicknamed "teddy bears of the sea."

Sea otters are also what is known as a keystone species.
Without them, sea urchins (their favored food) would take
over and decimate the kelp, leaving a barren landscape,
bereft of the many species that rely on the kelp for food and
shelter. Studying the interactions of species is a fascinating
way to learn more about our natural world.

Alaska • Katmai
6 HAVE THE PATIENCE OF A BEAR
Late June to early September

To see brown bears use nothing but their mouths and
paws to catch fish is an awesome sight. As they need to
eat enough in six months to last them all year, covering the
hibernation period, they spend all day fishing—and it can
be easy to spend all day watching!

5 | *The endearing sea otter has made a comeback in Alaska*

Alaska • Seward

7 SEE MUSK-OXEN ADAPT TO THE COLD

All year

This shaggiest of ox has the perfect coat to survive the blizzards and freezing temperatures found on the Seward Peninsula. With its humped back raising its neck up higher than its head, it looks as if it's permanently hunkered up against the cold.

Alaska • Sitka

8 WATCH MILLIONS OF HERRING SPAWN

March to April

The arrival of spring on Sitka Sound is heralded each year by a phenomenon of nature that sees the sea turn a foamy, milky white with herring eggs. As the adult herrings make their annual visit to the shallows in order to spawn they are pursued by whales, seals, and fishermen.

Hawaii • Kapoho; tide pools

9 WATCH A FISH TAKE A STROLL

All year

Zebra blennies are little fish that are commonly found in rock pools, partly because of their ability to cross from one pool to another—sometimes traveling surprising distances—by leaping across the rocks. This behavior also explains their alternative name of "rockskippers."

Hawaii • Honaunau Bay

10 GO FOR A SPIN WITH SPINNER DOLPHINS

All year

Spinner dolphins are named for the high spinning leaps they perform. They are best watched in the mornings, playfully interacting with each other. The clear waters and white sands of Hawaii's bays make it easy for them to keep an eye out for predators—sharks mainly. As they have never been hunted by man here, they often approach boats, making for an even more interactive experience.

Hawaii • Oahu

11 FIND THE WONDERFULLY NAMED MEGAMOUTH SHARK

All year

This species was only discovered in 1976 when a research ship accidentally caught one off the coast of Hawaii. It was later studied and named *Megachasma pelagios* due to its large mouth. It is a filter feeder, and grows up to 17 ft (5 m) long, making it one of the larger shark species. However, with only 55 recorded sightings since its discovery, be aware that the chances of seeing one are slim.

7 | *Musk-oxen huddled against the cold*

Hawaii • Oahu

12 WATCH HAWAIIAN MONK SEALS AT PLAY

All year

Most seals seek out cold climates, but the endangered Hawaiian monk seal favors the warm waters of Northwestern Hawaiian Islands, where it spends most of its time darting around the reefs, catching food. See it while you still can.

Hawaii • Angler Reef

13 WONDER ABOUT THE DANGLER OF AN ANGLER

All year

Among favorite sightings here are species of frogfish (members of the anglerfish family), with prehistoric jaws and a rod-like attachment on their heads to help attract prey. They share this feature with anglerfish of much deeper waters.

Washington • Oahu Methow Valley

14 SPOT AN ERMINE IN ITS WINTER COAT

December to March

The beauty of an ermine in its white winter coat (with black tail tip) is one of winter's pleasures— unless you're its prey, which it hunts ferociously all year round. In summer its coat turns brown.

Washington • Puget Sound

15 BE DAZZLED BY AN ANNA'S HUMMINGBIRD

All year

The tiny male of this species has an iridescent green body topped with a pink head. Courting males fly up high, then plummet down toward a female, making a sound with their tail feathers.

Washington • Olympic National Park and Forest

16 ADMIRE A SLUG

All year

Few land slugs are quite as eye-catching as the banana slug, which is, as you'd imagine, bright yellow. It can grow up to 7 in (18 cm) long.

Oregon • Oregon Dunes National Recreation Area

17 SEE FUNGUS "BLOOD"

All year

Take a walk through a pine forest and look out for a bleeding tooth fungus nestling on the floor. It emits, or "bleeds," a thick red fluid through its pores.

Oregon • Willamette Falls

18 CHECK OUT A BLOODSUCKING EEL

All year

The mouth of a lamprey eel—a species as old as dinosaurs—is a gory disk full of horny plates. It feeds by attaching its mouth to fish and sucking their blood.

19 SALUTE A LEGEND OF THE DEEP
All year

The largest recorded giant octopus measured a
whopping 30 ft (9 m) across, but its more average
brethren tend to reach a mere 16 ft (5 m), with
a 30 ft arm span—still big enough, though, to
swap their regular diet of fish and lobster for
the occasional shark. They are known to be
exceptionally intelligent creatures and are
able to use camouflage to disguise
themselves as intricate pieces
of coral.

California • Sequoia National Park

20 BE AWESTRUCK BY A MIGHTY REDWOOD

All year

Nothing is quite as humbling as walking among the giant redwoods and sequoias of Sequoia National Park. In this giant forest there are more than 8,000 of these ancient trees, whose trunks stretch hundreds of feet into the sky. The largest tree on Earth (by volume) is here—General Sherman, which is more than 2,000 years old.

California • Sequoia National Park

21 FORGET GIANTS—ENJOY MINI BEASTS INSTEAD

December to May

One of the most enjoyable smaller species here is the Californian newt. Its vibrant orange coloring and plodding walk are attraction enough, but if you are around during the half year when a male and female are getting amorous, you'll see a charming dance that culminates with the male climbing on top of the female and rubbing his chin on her nose.

California • Elkhorn Slough

22 SEE PLOVERS ACT ON INSTINCT

April to May

A snowy plover's nest is a small depression on an open beach, leaving hatchlings vulnerable. Parents call out if they sense danger and the babies flatten themselves to the sand in an attempt at invisibility.

California • Humboldt and Del Norte Counties

23 GET TO KNOW YOUR ELKS

All year

The Roosevelt elk found in these counties is the largest of the elk subspecies in California, while the state's smallest is the tule. How to tell them apart? A tule has a white rump.

California • San Francisco Bay Area

24 SEE A CLEVER WASP

May to August

Even tiny and irritating creatures can be extremely sophisticated—take the rainbow-colored cuckoo wasp, for example. It gets its name from the cuckoo bird because it shares that bird's habit of laying its eggs in the nests of other species.

California • Carrizo Plain

25 FEEL BRAVE ON THE TRAIL OF A GIANT KANGAROO RAT

All year

You don't have to be all that brave. Despite its name, the giant kangaroo rat is one of the sweeter-looking rodents. It's only 6 in (15 cm) long and jumps around on its hind legs.

26 IDENTIFY SPRINGTIME FLORA
March to April

With the right weather conditions, California's wildflowers don't just
bloom at springtime, they superbloom, turning whole mountains into
a rich tapestry of color. With species including California poppies,
desert lilies, and lupins, the wildflowers here are so thickly packed
together that, seen from a distance, they turn whole mountainsides
into a rich palette of purples, yellows, and oranges. And they cover
such a huge area that you'll always be able to find a patch to enjoy
in perfect solitude. The density of flowers depends on winter rainfall,
with more rain generally leading to more flowers, and superblooms
happening about once a decade.

27 | *Humpback whales in a feeding frenzy*

California • Monterey Bay
27 WATCH HUMPBACKS GORGE ON ANCHOVIES
June to September

Once humpback whales have vacuumed up all the krill they can find in the waters of Monterey Bay, they switch to anchovies. This feeding frenzy brings them close to the shore, where the fish cluster together, which in turn creates fantastic whale-watching opportunities.

Arizona • Paton Center for Hummingbirds
29 HUM WITH A HUMMINGBIRD
May to September

Fall in love with the metallic green body and long, thin red bill of a hovering male broad-billed hummingbird. This bird feeds on nectar, which it draws from plants using its long, extendable tongue.

Arizona • Saguaro National Park
31 HUNT FOR A GILA MONSTER
All year

This lizard—measuring 2 ft (0.6 m) long—is the largest native to the US. It has dramatic orange and black colorings, but is tricky to see since it spends almost all of its time in an underground burrow and can go for months between meals.

California • Yosemite National Park
28 SEE AMERICA'S SMALLEST BEAR
Mid-April to November

Black bears are North America's smallest and most common bear—yet no less appealing for that. In Yosemite there are only black bears, and despite their name, many of them have brown coats.

Idaho • Craters of the Moon National Monument and Preserve
30 LISTEN FOR LOVE
Early March to mid-May

When it comes to the mating season, the sage grouse knows how to put on a show. The males strut around their leks—the breeding grounds that generations return to year after year—fanning their tail feathers and puffing out two neck sacs that then deflate with whooshing air, pops, and whistles.

Utah • Fishlake National Forest
32 SEE A TREE THAT MAKES A FOREST
All year

Quaking aspens reproduce asexually by sprouting new trees from the same root. This has resulted in Utah's Pando, or the Trembling Giant—107 acres (43 hectares) of quaking aspen, all genetically identical and connected to the same root system.

33 | *Listen out for the call of the great gray owl*

Utah • Snowbasin
33 IDENTIFY THE CALLS OF OWLS
January to May, at night

The aspen groves of Utah are a rich hunting ground for forest owls. Sit out at night and listen to their calls: a low-pitched *boop* for a flagellated owl, a staccato Morse code for the whiskered screech owl, a high-pitched *too-too-too* for the northern saw-whet owl, and a low-pitched, resonating *hoo* for the great gray owl.

Wyoming • Red Desert
34 CATCH AN AMERICAN ORIGINAL
All year

The pronghorn has roamed the sagebrush steppes of America for thousands of years. The secret of its success? It can travel great distances—around 30 mph (50 kmh)—and reach 50 mph (80 kmh) when it accelerates. While commonly mistaken for an antelope, it is, in fact, more closely related to the giraffe and the smaller central African okapi.

Yellowstone National Park
35 DISCOVER THE INTRICATE BALANCE OF NATURE
All year

In 1995, gray wolves were reintroduced here. Because they hunted the elk, not only did elk numbers drop, but gangs also began to move more. This allowed more plant growth along the riverbanks, which in turn created the right habitat for beavers to flourish; a single colony was in place at the time, and now there are several. Many more layers of ecosystem changes like these—"trophic cascades"—were brought about by the wolves, making this a fascinating study.

Yellowstone National Park
36 HOWL WITH WOLVES
All year

The Mackenzie Valley wolf is a subspecies of gray wolf, also known as the northwestern wolf or northern timber wolf. It feeds primarily on elk, and occasionally bison or deer. Conveniently, if you visit Yellowstone and are keen to hear its howl, you won't have to wait for a full moon; the wolves do it all year round to defend their territory—and even in response to a human howl. But remember to keep your distance: the size of their prey is a very clear indication of what their strong jaws are capable of!

35 | *Gray wolves at home in Yellowstone*

Yellowstone National Park

37 BEWARE OF GRIZZLIES

April to November

The head and shoulders of a grizzly emerging from the grass of Yellowstone's meadows is a sight that will make you catch your breath—if you are lucky enough to see one. For a large and dangerous carnivore, grizzlies are very endearing: it's down to their lolling stride, curious faces, and nurturing ways with their young. The grizzly is a subspecies of brown bear, but because the hair on its back and shoulders is often tipped with white, it looks grizzled—and the name has stuck. As with most nature spotting, there's no guarantee of seeing one, but if you do, never approach it—just back away slowly without running. Always be careful around these wild and dangerous animals.

38 | *Photographing a coyote as it hunts for food*

Yellowstone National Park

38 SEE THE FOOD CHAIN IN ACTION

All year

Coyotes were once confined to the Great Plains. As settlers moved in, built on the coyotes' natural hunting ground, and introduced a new food source in the form of domestic animals, coyotes changed their behavior and range. They are adept hunters. To see one follow the burrow of a rodent under the snow and plunge in for the kill is a treat.

Yellowstone National Park

39 HEED THE SCREECH OF THE GROUND SQUIRREL

April to June

The Uinta ground squirrels of Yellowstone (also known less glamorously as "potguts") might not be the wildlife that people flock to the park to see, but it's still worth listening out for the loud *tsew-tsew-tsew* that these animals make to ward off nosy intruders.

Yellowstone National Park

40 SEE OSPREYS RETURN TO THEIR NESTS

April to September

Ospreys build their nests close to lakes and rivers so that they can go out hunting for fish. It's a magnificent sight to see these majestic birds with their 6 ft (2 m) wing spans, soaring back to their nests to feed their young. And the good news is that their numbers are increasing at Yellowstone.

Missouri • Mark Twain National Forest

41 BE DAZZLED BY A MOTH

All year

With its fabulous lime-green color and delicate flowing shape, the luna moth is one of the must-sees of the moth world. It's also one of the biggest moths found in North America, with a wingspan of up to 4.5 in (11.5 cm).

Dakota • Custer State Park

43 IMAGINE THE PRAIRIES OF OLD

All year

Bison on the prairies is a scene that has seen many changes since the time of the founding fathers. They were almost wiped out in the nineteenth century, going from millions to a few hundred, but their numbers are thankfully starting to increase.

South Dakota • Wind Cave National Park

42 FERRET OUT A MUSTELID

July to October

There is only one species of ferret in the US—the rather charming black-footed ferret. These speedy little hunters feed almost entirely on prairie dogs.

North Dakota • Badlands

44 SPOT A BADGER IN THE BADLANDS

All year

The striped face of this omnivorous mammal peers out of its sett around dusk. They're sometimes seen teaming up with coyotes to share strengths and hunt together.

New Mexico • Carlsbad Caverns

45 WATCH BATS SWARM FROM A CAVE

May to October

Nothing can quite prepare you for the sight of half a million bats all exiting from the mouth of a cave for their evening feed. Enjoy the spectacle from a custom-built amphitheater at the cave's mouth.

Nebraska • Platte River valley

46 LISTEN TO CRANES WARBLE

Late February to early April

The sight of huge migrating flocks of sandhill cranes is stunning, but their loud, gurgling call is even better. A bottleneck in their travel patterns brings half a million birds to this stretch of river.

Texas • Trans Pecos Wildlife District

47 SEE DEER AND ANTELOPE PLAY

All year

If you're looking for that special place where the deer and pronghorn antelope play, you might be lucky enough to find them both here in a single field—and you might then start to sing about it.

50 | *Mexican free-tailed bats emerge from under South Congress Bridge for their nightly feed*

Texas • Rio Grande Valley

48 SPOT A GOOFY-LOOKING CORMORANT

All year

The double-crested cormorant is not one of nature's most beautiful birds. It has two large tufts on either side of its head and when it grunts (there's no other word for its strange sound), a large yellow skin flap under its bill gives it that goofy look.

Texas • Rockport

49 BRING CRANES BACK FROM THE BRINK

September to March

Tall, elegant whooping cranes strutting along the coastal marshes of Texas is a stunning sight, and one we're lucky to still be able to see: conservationists have brought the number of birds up from just 15 in the 1940s to around 300 today.

Texas • Austin

50 INDULGE IN AN URBAN NATUREWATCH

All year, at night

When civil engineers planned the South Congress Bridge that spans Lady Bird Lake in Austin, they could not have imagined that its crevices would become home to a one-million-strong colony of Mexican free-tailed bats. The nightly emergence of the bats is now a top tourist attraction in the city, where sightseers armed with smartphone cameras line the bridge to catch the magic of the swarms.

Texas • Rio Grande Valley
51 WATCH AN ARMADILLO JUMP
All year, at night

Armadillos are mainly found in Central and South America, but the nine-banded armadillo has made such a success of life in the US that it is now the state mammal for Texas. These cat-sized animals come out at night to forage for insects, and when threatened can jump 3 to 4 ft (1 m) into the air to startle their predators before dashing away.

Texas • Great Trinity Forest
52 IDENTIFY A BIRD BY ITS TAIL
May to September

Often seen perched on fences and telegraph wires, it is the tail of the scissor-tailed flycatcher that is so distinct. It is about twice as long as the small bird itself and held in a pronounced forked shape that gives the bird its name. This bird is sometimes also referred to as a "Texas bird of paradise," but it's no true relation to the colorful Asian bird family of that name.

Louisiana • Arcadiana Park Nature Station
53 CHOOSE THE MOST OWL-LIKE OWL
All year

For many, the barn owl wins hands down at being the most owl-like owl, due to its distinctive, white rounded face and dark eyes. It's only its call that disappoints—not a hoot but more of a rasping scream. The Arcadiana nature center offers around 8 miles (13 km) of hiking trails to explore, and well over 100 other types of birds, too.

51 | *The state mammal for Texas, the nine-banded armadillo*

54 | *A northern flicker takes flight*

Alabama • Gunter Hill Park
54 WATCH A FLICKER FLY
All year

Related to the woodpecker, the northern flicker is pretty enough when on the ground pecking for ants, its tawny plumage covered with neat black spots. But see one take to the skies, and you will be treated to a dazzling display from beneath its wings. Different flickers have different colors under their wings.

Alabama • Tulip Tree Springs
55 STEER CLEAR OF THE BOMBARDIER
All year

As beetles go, the bombardier looks much like many others. However, make the mistake of threatening it, and it'll release its bomb: a pungent chemical spray that can reach temperatures of 200°F (100°C) when fired from its abdomen. That's one way to see off your predators.

Alabama • Monroeville
56 HEAR A MOCKINGBIRD
All year

It's hard to think of these attractive gray-and-brown songbirds without thinking of Harper Lee's novel *To Kill a Mockingbird*. She used the bird to portray innocence, but it is also known as a great singer and a skilled mimic of other birds' songs.

Oklahoma • Black Kettle National Grassland
57 BE THANKFUL FOR WILD TURKEYS
All year

Puffed up, male wild turkeys are one of the most splendid birds to see in the US. They strut around woodlands, searching for acorns and gobbling in a fantastic manner. They travel in flocks, so if you see one turkey, you'll likely see many more. The male bird is known as a "tom" or a "gobbler" and its gobble is so loud it can be heard from a mile away. Although ground-nesting birds, they sleep in trees.

All along Route 66
59 ON LONG DRIVES, PLAY "SPOT THE RED-TAILED HAWK"
All year

Identify the most common hawk in the United States by its fan-shaped tail and rounded wings.

Wisconsin • Fox River Valley
60 ADMIRE A NATIONAL SYMBOL
January

Since 1782 the bald eagle, with its soaring sense of freedom, has been the symbol of the US, and even before that, it held spiritual significance for Native Americans, as it still does. It is a majestic bird, with a distinctive chocolate-brown body, bookended with a white head and a white tail.

Wisconsin • Lake Mendota
58 DISCOVER THE BUFFLEHEAD
October to May

Male bufflehead ducks are a striking black and white, while females are brown with a white patch on their cheeks. They dive under water to feed before bobbing back up to the surface. And that name? Apparently it's because their overlarge head resembles that of a buffalo.

Bald eagles survive even the harshest winters

Ohio • Kent
61 SEE BLACK SQUIRRELS
All year

At Kent State University in Ohio, the squirrels found
around the campus are black—a genetic mutation
of the usual gray. It is thought there used to be far
more black squirrels in the wild when the US was
more densely forested. These ones, however,
originated from a handful that were brought
over from Canada in the 1960s.

Illinois • Suburban Chicago
62 JUST ONCE, SMELL A SKUNK
All year, at night

The name "Chicago" may come from the
Menominee Indian word *Shikako*, or "skunk
place"—so where better to sniff out this stalwart
of children's stories. Skunks spray a foul oil from
their anal scent glands when they feel threatened.

Maine • Manure piles on farmland
63 STUDY THE HABITS OF A BEETLE
All year

Animal dung has to go somewhere, so the fact
that dung beetles are willing to roll it away and
consume it provides a neat solution.

Connecticut • Rocky Neck State Park
64 SPOT A BOBCAT UP A TREE
All year, at night

There are as many as one million bobcats in the United States, yet very few will ever have seen one. They are only occasionally spotted during the day since they hunt at night, creeping up silently before making a final "death pounce" on an unsuspecting rabbit or squirrel from as far away as 10 ft (3 m). They have also been known to catch salmon in rivers. Bobcats are about twice the size of a domestic cat, although similar in color to many tabbies. They have distinctive tufted ears and a short tail—from which they get their "bobbed" name.

Connecticut • The Last Green Valley
66 COUNT HOW MUCH WOOD A WOODCHUCK CAN CHUCK
March to November

Technically a woodchuck wouldn't chuck much wood since it would rather eat nice succulent plants such as clover, alfalfa, or newly sprouted flowers. If it's not your flowers that it's digging up, it's a cute animal to spot, with its little legs, short tail, and tiny ears. There are more woodchucks in Connecticut today than there were in colonial times, so they are relatively easy to spot.

Virginia • Shenandoah National Park
67 START A BIRD-WATCHING HOBBY
All year

It's a joy that the eye-catching northern cardinal is so easy to see. The male's bright red body and bill are a regular sight in this park.

North Carolina • Croatan National Forest
65 WATCH A FLYTRAP
March to November

The carnivorous Venus flytrap, renowned throughout the world, originates in the coastal bogs of North and South Carolina. It is a small plant with a hinged "mouth" at the end of its stem. The mouth sits open, waiting to be triggered by a passing insect or spider—then snap! It closes, swiftly trapping the plant's prey inside, ready to be digested.

West Virginia • George Washington National Forest
68 FIND A HAIRY CATERPILLAR
June to September

There are many types of hairy caterpillars to be found in this West Virginian forest reserve, but few are quite as good as the spotted apatelodes. Look out for the long yellow hairs on this chap, as well as the striking red boots on its feet. It is often found munching on ash, cherry, and maple plants.

West Virginia • Canaan Valley

69 SEE A CHIPMUNK FILL ITS CHEEKS

March to October

These sweet striped rodents are even sweeter with cheeks stuffed with seeds, nuts, and berries (to be later stored in their burrows). See them in wooded areas.

Woodlands throughout the US

70 HANG A SHEET AND SEE WHAT FLIES IN

All year

Spread a white sheet between two trees and leave a flashlight on at its base. As moths fly in, put them in jars to see what you've got. In central and eastern states, you might get the black-and-white giant leopard moth, which measures 2 in (5 cm) across. Be sure to release them when the viewing's done.

Great Smoky Mountains National Park

71 WITNESS THE WORLD OF FIREFLIES

May to June

To see tiny lights flashing on and off in a forest is a magical view—as if fairies were roving around with little flashlights. It's no less magical when it's discovered to be the bioluminescence of fireflies switching their lights on and off to attract a mate. One species of firefly in this park flash synchronously, making a wonderful natural lightshow.

71 | *Fireflies fill the forest floor*

New Hampshire • Purgatory Falls

72 BE CHARMED BY A FUNGUS

August to November

Look closely at a bear's head tooth fungus growing on a decaying log; it looks just like white icicles hanging from the roof of a cave. It's part of the *Hericium* genus of edible fungi and said to taste wonderful when fried with garlic. Some equally flamboyant names of its close relatives include: comb tooth, lion's mane, and old man's beard.

Maryland • Baltimore

74 ENJOY THE COLORS OF AN ORIOLE

April to June

The Baltimore oriole is the sound of springtime. Its joyful chirping rings out from high up in the treetops. The male is a beautiful bright orange bird with a black head.

Maryland • Patuxent Research Refuge

75 SEE THE USA'S PRETTIEST MOTH

April to September

With its pink and cream markings, the candy-colored rosy maple moth is surely America's prettiest of all?

New Hampshire • White Mountains

73 CATCH FALL COLORS AT THEIR PEAK

Late September to late October

That leaves on deciduous trees change color each year and fall off is something so commonplace that we don't always take the time to admire the wonderful beauty it brings to the landscape. New Hampshire, with its rolling hills and many lakes, offers dramatically beautiful fall scenery year after year. Get up high on the Auto Road in the White Mountains for views over miles and miles of orange-hued trees. Look for a place to take the perfect photo of trees reflected in water in the Lakes region—Squam Lake offers outstanding views—or enjoy being on foot among the vibrant colors while taking a hike on Mount Kearsarge. The whole state is pretty amazing at this time of year.

Maryland • Schooley Mill Park

76 SEARCH FOR CADDISFLY LARVAE

All year

For disguise and protection, caddisfly larvae build themselves protective cases, which they stud with stones and plants, or whatever is close to hand. The French artist Hubert Duprat is well known for providing caddisfly larvae with gold and precious stones in order to procure natural works of art.

73 | *New Hampshire, resplendent in the fall*

Maryland • Chesapeake and Ohio Canal
77 HEAR A BARRED OWL
All year

"Who cooks for you? Who cooks for you all?" is said to be the cry of this forest owl.

Vermont • Mount Philo State Park
78 HEAR A WOODPECKER PECK
All year

The hammering of the pileated, or red-headed, woodpecker is a sure way to identify this bird.

Vermont • North Branch Nature Center
79 FIND A GOLDEN BEETLE
May to July

Scientists think that the light bouncing off a golden tortoise beetle may enable it to confuse predators.

New York • Constitution Marsh
80 ADMIRE THE LARGE HOOD OF THE SMALLEST AMERICAN MERGANSER
All year

The hooded merganser is the smallest of its kind in North America, and the only species of merganser that can be found only on this continent. Both sexes sport fancy headwear, their defining feature. The male's is white, with black edges matching his body feathers; the female's has a cinnamon tone to go with her mid-brown body.

New York • Sunken Meadow State Park
81 SPOT A SNAPPING TURTLE
All year

This freshwater turtle is found in much of the US. It grows up to 20 in (50 cm) long and uses its beak to break off vegetation or to catch frogs or mammals.

Pennsylvania • Appalachian Trail
83 MARVEL AT THE MINUSCULE
All year

There are more than 12,000 different types of plant hopper—a prevalent group of insects that are invariably camouflaged to enable them to blend in with their environment. Some hoppers are a rich green color; others are speckled like bark, with long, twig-like protuberances.

New York • Montauk
82 SEE AN AQUADYNAMIC SHARK
All year

With its slender body and pointy nose, the blue shark can be one of the fastest fish in the water, although it mostly favors a far slower pace.

Georgia • Okenfenokee National Wildlife Refuge

84 SEE THE LONGEST SNAKE IN THE US

All year

Found in pine forests throughout the eastern United States, the bluish-black eastern indigo snake is North America's longest snake, growing up to 9 ft (3 m) long. Despite its fearsome length, it is nonvenomous. It is also an essential predator in its habitat, keeping the ecosystem balanced.

Florida • Felts Audubon Preserve

85 ADMIRE A BUNTING

May to September

With its blue head, yellow back, green wings, and red chest, a male painted bunting looks like someone got overenthusiastic with a paintbrush. It's also clear why its French name is *nonpareil*—"without equal"! They're often spotted at bird feeders, with thick, stubby bills perfectly honed to crack seeds.

Florida • Everglades

86 TELL YOUR GATORS FROM YOUR CROCS

All year

The Everglades is an amazing subtropical wilderness and home to a huge amount of wildlife. It is also the only place where both American alligators and American crocodiles are found. If you need a clue to telling them apart: crocodiles have pointier, V-shaped snouts, while alligators' are broad and U-shaped.

86 | *The broad snout of an American alligator*

Florida • Three Sisters Springs
87 BE SOOTHED BY THE SERENE MANATEE
All year

The manatee is surely one of the world's most lovable species. It's blubbery and peaceful and has a very distinctive face. Large numbers of Florida manatees are present along the southeastern coasts of Florida all year, but in winter seek out warmer waters, offering better viewing opportunities for nature lovers.

Florida • Greenwood Urban Wetlands
88 SPOT FLORIDA'S OFFICIAL BUTTERFLY
All year

Although found in parts of Texas, you are most likely to see a zebra longwing in Florida, where it is a common garden visitor. It has longer wings than many butterflies; black with white or yellow stripes. The caterpillars live on passion vines, which contain a toxin, cleverly making adult butterflies poisonous to many predators. This is the only butterfly species known to eat pollen (as well as nectar), which could explain its six-month-long life span—a rarity in the butterfly world.

Florida • Everglades
89 ERECT A NEST FOR KESTRELS
All year

The southeastern American kestrel's numbers are in decline as its habitat disappears. It likes to nest in tall, dead trees with old cavities, but failing this, human help is possible—a nesting box positioned in the right place will make this species feel at home.

Florida • Everglades
90 DISCOVER THE TOE-BITER
All year

Also known as a giant water bug, this freshwater insect can grow up to 4.75 in (12 cm) in length. The largest examples in the US are found in Florida, where they are also known as alligator fleas. Be careful not to get too close if you spot one—they will give you a very nasty nip.

Florida • St. Augustine Beach
91 RESIST THE URGE TO PRESS THE "BLUE BUTTON"
All year

"Blue button" is the common name given to a tiny sea creature called *Porpita porpita*. Although it looks like a jellyfish, the blue button is, in fact, a colony of hydroids (jelly-like creatures) that look like blue tentacles, attached to one organism.

Florida • Coconut Creek
92 WATCH A BUTTERFLY EMERGE FROM A COCOON
All year

If you'd like to witness this small miracle of nature, then why not cheat with a visit to Butterfly World in Florida's Coconut Creek—the largest butterfly park in the world, and home to thousands of live butterflies year-round.

Florida • Blue Heron Bridge
93 SPY A STARGAZER—UNDER THE SEA
All year

Despite the northern stargazer's romantic name, it is in fact a fairly ugly fish whose features face upward rather than forward. This allows the fish to hide buried in the sand, waiting for prey, which it then pounces on when it passes overhead.

Florida • Tosohatchee Wildlife Management Area
94 SEE A CHICKEN TURTLE
All year

Although it sounds like an image from a Dr. Seuss book, this little turtle with a striped yellow neck more likely earned its moniker from the taste of its flesh.

Florida • Florida Keys
95 FIND A HIDING LOBSTER
March

Lobsters like to hide in rocky holes and crags, sometimes covering themselves with stones to put off predators. It is wonderfully satisfying to win the game of hide-and-seek and find these colorful crustaceans while snorkeling.

| *Lemon sharks—not as fearsome as they might appear*

Florida • Jupiter

96 DISCOVER NOT ALL SHARKS ARE GRAY

All year

It's quite convenient for the lemon shark to have a yellowy brown to olive color, since it helps camouflage itself against the sand in shallow waters. Its preferred hunting grounds are the shallow areas around coasts and islands, coral reefs, mangroves, and even river mouths—although it doesn't venture far into fresh water.

Like all sharks, it uses electric impulses—along with a keen sense of smell, which makes up for its extremely poor eyesight—to track its prey. Because it favors shallow waters for hunting, and hunts by day, divers have a very good chance of seeing lemon sharks. They are also not known to be aggressive toward humans. Scuba diving at Jupiter, off the east coast of Florida is a good way to spot them.

Florida • "Ding" Darling Wildlife Refuge

97 UNDERSTAND THE SPOONBILL'S NAME

All year

The roseate spoonbill is—as its name suggests—bright pink, just like a flamingo, but you'll be able to tell them apart because the spoonbill has a very different bill. It is wide and flat at the end, just like a spoon, and the bird uses it to strain small food out of the water.

98 KAYAK WITH KILLER WHALES

June to October

Watching orcas in their natural environment is an exhilarating enough experience, but to do it from a kayak in Canada's Johnstone Strait is one of life's must-have adventures. This narrow bit of water between Vancouver Island and mainland Canada is home to two different subspecies of resident killer whales: the Northern Resident Community and the Southern Resident Community. As a result, sightings are highly likely, and there is a great deal of knowledge about these animals' behavior, such as the way offspring stay with their mother for all their adult life. The Northern Residents display their very own particular behavior—beach rubbing. They come close to shore and swim alongside it, rubbing their bellies on the pebble beaches. Scientists think that they do this purely for a pleasurable massage.

British Columbia • Smithers

99 HOLD YOUR BREATH WHILE WATCHING GOATS

June to October

As mountain goats leap from one tiny foothold to the next on near vertical cliffs, it is almost impossible not to hold your breath. Although they don't look athletic, they are very narrow-shouldered, which is what helps them stick so closely to cliff walls.

99 | *Capturing a mountain goat teetering on the edge*

British Columbia

• Vancouver Island

100 BE FREAKED OUT BY A WOLF EEL

All year

Wolf eels sport a massive head, and a body that can reach up to 8 ft (2.4 m) long. Despite their snake-like appearance, wolf eels are actually fish. Their huge mouths allow them to crush the sea urchins that make up the main part of their diet. They can be very sociable around human divers and are not vicious, despite their name.

British Columbia

• Ryder Lake

101 MARVEL AT THE TIMING OF TOADLETS

June

Western toads live in forests but breed in ponds. Each year, once the new generation of tadpoles has turned into toadlets, they migrate back up to the forests— en masse. Whole roads are closed as, over the course of a couple of days, up to 800,000 toadlets make their first journey into the forest. Sadly, though, many of them do not survive.

British Columbia

• Cypress Provincial Park

102 SPOT THE BLUE OF A STELLER'S JAY

All year

There are many beautiful birds to be found in British Columbia, but it was the Steller's jay that won a popularity contest in 1987 to be voted the province's official bird. The Steller's jay is widespread throughout the region, and its vibrant blue-and-black coloring, and impressive head crest, can be seen regularly in forests, parks, and backyards.

British Columbia

• Princess Royal Island

103 BE MESMERIZED BY A SPIRIT BEAR

May to September

Spirit bears are a rare subspecies of black bear, with a gene that predisposes them to white fur; they are considered sacred by the indigenous people. Spirit bears have more luck catching salmon in the daytime, when their coloring makes them harder to spot from below the water.

British Columbia • Whistler

104 WATCH A BEAVER AT WORK

All year

These web-footed, flat-tailed semi-aquatic rodents are amazing creatures. If they don't like the bit of river that they're living on, they simply fell trees to create dams and change it. And their lodges can be ninja-worthy constructions that are only accessible via underwater entrances.

British Columbia

• Kootenay National Park

105 BE AWED BY A BIGHORN'S HORNS

All year

Bighorn sheep are the largest wild sheep in North America— and the males have the horns to go with it. Firm and solid, they curve from the top of the head around in an almost complete circle to the eye. The Little Bighorn River (site of the battle) is named after them.

British Columbia

• Campbell River

106 GET A FISH-EYE VIEW OF A SALMON RUN

July to September

It's one thing to see a river teeming with thousands of salmon heading back to breed at the site of their birth, but imagine donning a snorkel and experiencing the journey with them. The crystal clear water of the Campbell River makes for ideal viewing.

British Columbia

• Kootenay National Park

107 STUDY OWLS' EARS

All year, at dusk

The great horned owl is the most common owl in North America, identified by its size, fabulous ear tufts ("horns"), and deep hoot, which has earned it the name "hoot owl." It has the most diverse prey of any American bird, including jackrabbits, fish, insects, and reptiles.

British Columbia • Victoria

108 RENAME THE SURF SCOTER

December to April

As is often the case in the bird world, the female surf scoter is a plain-looking brown sea duck, while her male counterpart is much more distinctive—black all over, with white patches on its head. As a result, it is sometimes known as the skunk-headed coot. Could you possibly improve on that?

106 | *Snorkeling with salmon*

Alberta • Waterton Lakes
National Park
109 JOIN A BISON REWILDING CAMPAIGN
All year

In the nineteenth century, the
wild bison of Canada were
almost wiped out, thus upsetting
the ecosystem forever. However,
a single herd was saved and then
moved to Elk Island National
Park, to reestablish this majestic
animal in the wild again. From
there, a tiny herd was brought
to Waterton Lakes in the 1950s.

Alberta • Banff National Park
110 MEASURE A HARE'S SHOESIZE
All year

The back feet of the snowshoe
hare are big—bigger than its
ears. They help the hare to run
across the top of snow and to
leap 12 ft (3.6 m) in one go. The
hare's fur changes completely
twice a year—from a dusky
brown in spring to a well-
camouflaged white in winter—
as does its diet, which in winter
includes birch twigs and willow.

Alberta • Jasper National Park
111 SPOT A MOOSE WITH ANTLERS
April to December

You can see moose in Canada
all year round, but if you want to
see males with their antlers, you
will need to make sure that you
time it properly—they grow their
antlers each April in time for the
mating season and then lose
them in the winter. Moose are
the largest member of the deer
family and can grow to be as big
as horses.

Alberta • Edmonton River
112 STUDY A BUTTERFLY'S TRAVELS
May to October

The painted lady is a salmon-
pink butterfly with wonderfully
complex black-and-white
markings across its wings.
Occasionally its numbers soar,
and there is a mass migration
to Alberta. Scientists are keen
to know more about their habits,
and have urged the public to
report any mass sightings.

Saskatchewan • Fields
113 SEE A SNOWY OWL IN WINTER
December to March

This most beautiful of owls—
which is either completely white
feathered (the males) or dappled
white and black—only travels
south of the Arctic during the
winter. Perhaps as a result of
the 24-hour daylight of the
Arctic summer, this owl is not
nocturnal, so can be spotted
hunting at any time.

Manitoba • Hudson Bay
114 BE CAPTIVATED BY BELUGA WHALES
Mid-June to mid-September

Most beluga whales live around
Arctic waters, then migrate south
when it gets colder. The largest
population arrives in Hudson
Bay once the ice breaks up there,
which provides the opportunity
to see tens of thousands of
these white giants. They're very
vocal, making a range of clicks,
whistles, and chirps.

Manitoba • FortWhyte Alive

115 SEE A BURROWING OWL MAKE ITS HOME

April to September

The burrowing owl doesn't dig its own burrows but moves into those left by ground squirrels, badgers, and foxes. Look for parents on guard outside a burrow's entrance.

Manitoba • Churchill

116 STUDY CLIMATE CHANGE ON THE ARCTIC'S EDGE

June to October

To know what the actual effects of climate change are involves a huge range of monitoring and studying. Join a volunteer expedition that counts animals or studies plant growth in order to be an active part of the solution rather than a passive part of the problem.

115 | *Burrowing owls on high alert*

Manitoba • Narcisse

117 SEE 100 SNAKES WRITHE AS ONE

Early May

At the end of spring, red-sided garter snakes emerge from their dens—to mate. Alarmingly, one female is likely to be engulfed by up to 100 males.

Ontario • Boreal forests

118 LEARN ABOUT THE FEMALE CARIBOU

Early August

The female caribou is the only deer species that grows antlers like the male. Males lose their antlers in winter, but females keep theirs until spring.

Ontario • Algonquin Provincial Park

119 HEAR A LOON WAIL

All year

A loon's cry echoes eerily across lakes, and sounds more like the wail of a wolf than a bird. Four distinct calls are used to communicate with each other.

| *A wapiti, one of the world's largest species of deer*

Ontario • Bancroft
120 IDENTIFY A WAPITI
All year

Wapiti is another name for elk (*Cervus canadensis*)—American elk, at least. In Europe "elk" is the name given to the animal Americans call a moose (*Alces alces*). *Wapiti* is the original Cree and Shawnee name for this huge deer, which helps clear up all the confusion in one fell swoop. It refers to the "one with a white rump."

Quebec • Lake Mistassini
121 WATCH GOLDENEYES DIVE
May to September

Common goldeneyes often dive for food as a flock, leaving a temporarily empty patch of pond. Look out for their telltale yellow eyes.

Quebec • Îles de la Madeleine
122 SAVE OUR SEALS
January to May

Harp seals need solid sea ice to give birth to their young, and so could be at risk from future climate change—as well as the annual Canadian seal hunt.

Quebec • Ottawa River
123 LEARN ABOUT THE MILK SNAKE
April to November

Because milk snakes were often spotted around barns, it was erroneously thought that they drank milk. In fact, dairy barns simply provide good hunting grounds for the real prize—mice.

Quebec • Gulf of St. Lawrence
124 GO BEYOND THE BLUE— SPOT NUMBER TWO
May to September

The fin whale is the world's second-largest mammal and has a very distinct lower jaw: creamy white on the right side and mottled black on the left.

Quebec • Gulf of St. Lawrence
125 SEE ONE OF NATURE'S SHOW-OFFS
March to April

Male hooded seals have a remarkable party trick of inflating their nostril cavity into a pink balloon that they use to ward off other males and attract a mate.

Quebec • Lac Saint-Pierre in Montreal
126 WATCH 5,000 HERONS
April to December

In spring, thousands of herons come to nest
here, building huge platforms in the silver maples
around the lake and hunting for fish. Each spring
the area floods, cleaning away the acidic excrement
that would otherwise destroy plant growth.

Prince Edward Island
127 STUDY CHICKADEES AT LENGTH
All year

The black-capped chickadee is comfortable
enough around humans that you can watch it for
hours. It will happily take seeds from a feeder and
bury them to eat later.

Throughout Canada
128 WHEN IN CANADA,
LOOK OUT FOR A CANADIAN GOOSE
June to September

This large goose with a pale brown body and black
neck is a frequent visitor to any nice expanse of
lawn or park. They can also be seen flying in a
perfect V formation.

128 | *Canadian geese are a graceful vision in flight*

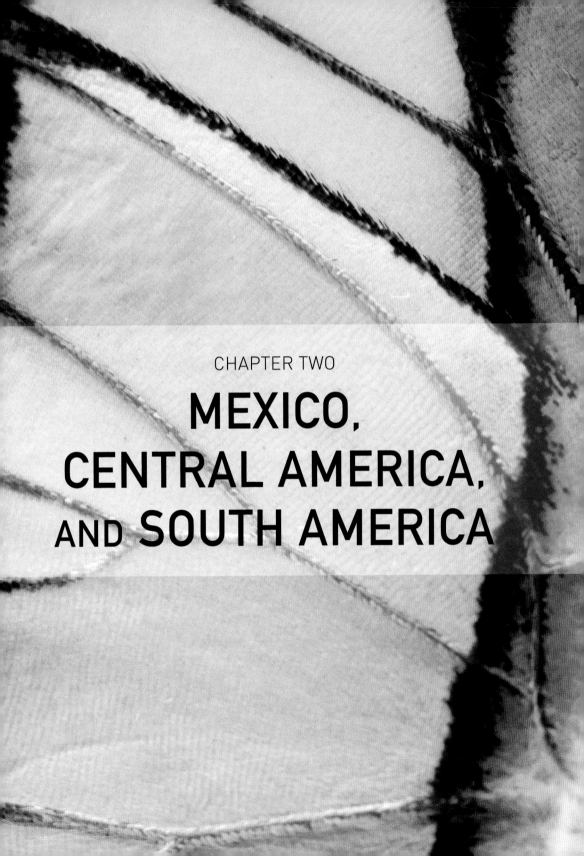

CHAPTER TWO

MEXICO, CENTRAL AMERICA, AND SOUTH AMERICA

Mexico • Sonoran Desert
129 SEE A DESERT ICON
All year

The saguaro truly is the king of the cacti family. It can live for up to 200 years and grow to be as tall as 60 ft (18 m). To see its long trunk rising up from the desert scrub with its curved branches silhouetted against the blue sky is an iconic image of the desert. Yet for all that, the saguaro only grows in a very particular desert—the Sonoran Desert, which straddles Mexico, Arizona, and California. And even here, the plant only grows where winter temperatures don't drop below freezing.

Saguaros seem to have made the practice of reproduction particularly tricky. Each year between April and June, they produce crowns of large white flowers that open for one night and then close up the following afternoon. That short window is their only chance to be pollinated. For the flowers that do get pollinated, a fruit grows with a bright red fleshy interior containing hundreds of seeds. When these seeds are eaten by a coyote or a cactus wren, they pass through the animal and get distributed around the desert, allowing new seedlings to grow.

Mexico • Islas Marietas National Park
130 ADMIRE SEAHORSE MATING RITUALS
All year

During their reproduction season, male and female seahorses get very close. They begin the day with a dance, swimming side by side, imitating each other's movements and color changes. And then they swim off and do their own thing—only to reunite the following morning.

129 | *Saguaros tower over a human visitor
to their Sonoran Desert home*

131 | *Exploring the giant aquarium that is the Sea of Cortez*

Mexico • Baja California

131 REVEL IN A MARINE MAMMAL PARADISE
All year

Nestled between the Mexican mainland and the peninsula of Baja California is the Sea of Cortez. It is one of those areas where the most benign of boat trips is likely to find itself with an escort of dolphins. Trips out to the islands will reward you with Californian sea lions, blue-footed boobies, and ospreys, while the chances of seeing great fish such as marlin and yellowfin tuna leap out of the water are high. At certain times of the year, humpback, gray, and even blue whales appear, as well as whale sharks—all of them drawn to these waters by the rich source of plankton.

The sea is home to 900 fish species and 32 types of marine mammal, so it's no wonder that Jacques Cousteau called it the world's aquarium.

Mexico • Chihuahuan Desert

132 SEE A HOPPER HEAT UP AND COOL DOWN
July to October

The black-and-yellow western horse lubber grasshopper is quite a handsome beast, but it also has a very clever survival strategy. It uses the black coloring of its body to draw in the sun's heat and maintain an optimum body temperature of around 97°F (36°C), even if the temperature of the surrounding desert is lower.

Mexico • Central region; volcanic slopes
133 LISTEN FOR A VOLCANO RABBIT
All year

The volcano rabbit earns its dramatically explosive name from the fact that it lives only on the slopes of volcanoes—and only four specific volcanoes in Mexico at that: Popocatépetl, Iztaccíhuatl, El Pelado, and Tláloc. It is rare but very sweet, being one of the smallest rabbits in the world, with short, little rounded ears and hardly any tail. Instead of thumping its foot as other rabbits do when it senses danger, it emits a high-pitched squeak. It makes its burrows in the undergrowth of the volcanoes, usually at elevations of over 1,000 ft (3,000 m). Sadly, the volcano rabbit is endangered since its habitat is being lost to encroaching human populations that use the volcano slopes for grazing and often start deliberate fires to promote the regrowth of brush.

Mexico • Michoacán
134 STUDY A POCKET GOPHER
All year

The pocket gopher is so called because of the large pouches in its cheeks. Unlike a hamster's, these pouches are external to the gopher's mouth, and the animal uses them to store the roots and tubers that they burrow underground to find. When it burrows, it seals its lips with its big digging teeth still on the outside.

Mexico • Monarch Butterfly
Biosphere Reserve

135 SEE A MASS OF MONARCHS ALL AT ONCE
Mid-November to March

The annual migration of monarch butterflies is one of the phenomenons of nature. Every year they breed in the US and Canada before taking to the sky in their millions to fly to overwinter in Mexico—a journey of 1,800 miles (2,900 km). They head to the same 200 square miles (520 sq km) every year, navigating using the time of day, based on their own circadian rhythm and the sun's position. Their arrival in this reserve is a spectacular sight: thick carpets of monarchs line the ground and cover trees. And then, come March, they leave again.

Mexico • Interior highlands;
Baja California

136 SPOT A DUCK WITH A BLUE BILL
November to March

After seeing ducks with the usual black or brown bills, it's disconcerting to spot the male ruddy duck with its bright blue bill—like a textbook doodle come to life. The bill changes to blue in the spring; it's a dull gray for the rest of the year.

Mexico • Central, eastern, and northern regions
137 JUDGE IF ROADRUNNERS LIVE UP TO THEIR NAME
All year

These birds have earned the name of roadrunner—as well as their legendary status. They can reach speeds of 26 mph (42 kmh) for short sprints, or jog along for a while at 15 mph (24 kmh). In fact, they are better on the ground than in the air and tend to fly only for short periods if they really have to. They are usually found in pairs—they mate for life—in fairly barren land, such as deserts and canyons, where they will patrol their territory, leaving clear X-shaped footprints behind them: they have two toes that point forward and two that point backward.

Mexico • Gulf of California
138 COUNT THE WORLD'S RAREST MARINE MAMMAL
All year

The vaquita (which means "little cow" in Spanish) is a small and stocky porpoise that lives only in the north end of the Gulf of California. Its very existence is threatened by illegal fishing using gill nets in the area. The vaquita is now critically endangered, and scientists believe that there are as few as 60 individual animals remaining here. They are often seen in shallow waters, and usually solo, and they will swim away if approached. So if you do happen to be lucky enough to spot one, make sure you report it in order to help monitor the species' survival.

Mexico • Mexico City
139 WONDER AT THE WEIRD AXOLOTL
All year

The axolotl is a kind of salamander that keeps some of its larval characteristics (such as frilly gills) in adulthood, giving it a strange appearance. It has a gelatinous texture and short little legs. This wonderful creature is critically endangered and was only recently rediscovered in the wild, in 2014.

Mexico • Mexico City
140 SOAK UP JACARANDA FLOWERS
March to April

Every spring the streets of Mexico City turn purple with the flowers of the jacaranda tree. It might not receive nearly as many likes as the Japanese city of Kyoto and its famous cherry blossom, but it should—the city has thousands of the trees, and it's a beautiful sight to behold.

Mexico • Central region

141 SEE A TINY SCAVENGER TAKE ON A MIGHTY VULTURE

All year

The crested caracara is an attractive red-and-white beaked scavenger. While its wingspan can reach up to 51 in (131 cm), it is still a dwarf compared to the turkey vultures with whom it competes for carrion, so it's a thrill to see them stand up to the vultures and steal their meat for themselves.

Mexico • Oaxaca

142 STAND BESIDE THE WORLD'S WIDEST TREE

All year

Dwarfing the church it stands next to, the Árbol del Tule holds the honor of being the world's widest tree. It is a Montezuma cypress—or ahuehuete— with a trunk that is 31 ft (9.4 m) across. Local legend claims that it was planted 1,400 years ago by Pecocha, the Aztec god of the wind.

143 | *The calm waters of the Xochimilco wetlands*

Mexico • Xochimilco wetlands

143 LOOK AFTER A PIECE OF MEXICO
August to October

To the southeast of Mexico City lie the stunning canals and islands of Xochimilco. They were created as a farming system by the Aztecs around 500 years ago and are now a hugely important wetland area both for wildlife and for agriculture. But the area is in danger from pollution and rapid urbanization. Join a trip to monitor the water quality and wildlife of these wetlands and help preserve the area for future generations.

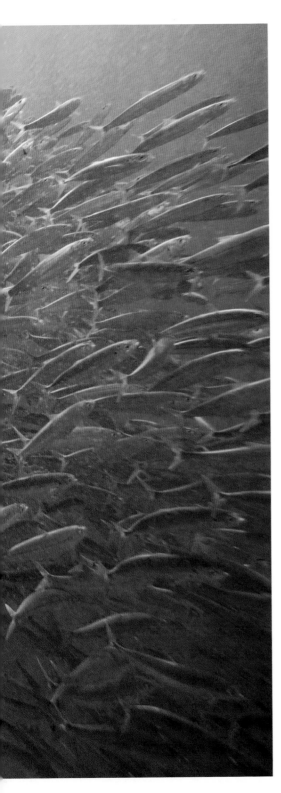

Mexico • Cancún
144 WATCH SAILFISH HUNT FOR SARDINES
February to April

With their long sword-like bills and beautiful arching dorsal fins, sailfish are one of the most distinctive fish in the sea. They are also prolific hunters. They form packs when they hunt and round up shoals of sardines, driving them toward the surface. They put their bills into the midst of the shoal and rapidly slash them back and forth, injuring individual sardines which they then pick off and eat. Each sailfish in the pack takes turns to go into the sardines, reducing any risk that their long bills will damage each other. Tours from Cancún look for circling seabirds to know a hunt is underway, and it's possible to watch this amazing sight with just a mask and snorkel.

Mexico • Cozumel Island
145 DEBATE THE COZUMEL THRASHER'S NAME
All year

Quite how this critically endangered member of the mockingbird family got its name is up for debate. It could be because it looks like the similarly named "thrush," or it could be as a result of its twitchy tail.

144 | *A sailfish slashes through sardines*

Mexico • Gulf of Mexico
146 ADMIRE THE RESILIENCE OF A TURTLE
March to September

The Kemp's ridley sea turtle is the bearer of several superlatives. It is the smallest of the sea turtles—only growing to 2 ft (0.6 m) long—and also the most endangered of all sea turtle species. Footage dating back to the 1940s shows 40,000 females clambering ashore to nest on a single beach in Mexico in just one day, but overharvesting of their eggs in the past century has led to a severe drop in numbers.

There are still enough turtles that arrive at protected beaches to form quite a spectacle, and to see the tiny vulnerable babies emerge from their nests around 45 days later and scramble to reach the waves is to feel the true battle for survival that this species has to endure.

Mexico • Gulf of Mexico
147 SEE A SEA THAT'S MORE JELLYFISH THAN WATER
All year but sporadically

A sea containing more jellyfish than water (up to 100 jellyfish per cubic meter) is not pretty, but it's amazing—as long as you don't dip your toes in. Scientists think numbers may indicate increased pollution, overfishing, or climate change, which jellyfish, unlike other creatures, are immune to.

152 | *The giant rock iguana of the Bahamas*

Mexico • Gulf of Mexico
148 WATCH THE SEA TURN RED
All year but sporadically

The "red tides" that occasionally turn the sea orangy red are caused by algal blooms. The sight can be impressive, but take care as they can be toxic.

Mexico • Southeastern region
149 SEE A TURTLE SCALE THE RAPIDS
All year

The Central American river turtle, or hickatee, is known for its fast swimming—and for being able to swim up rapids. It leaves the water only to lay eggs.

Bahamas • Andros and isolated islands
152 GET CLOSE TO AN IGUANA
All year

There are several subspecies of Bahamian rock iguanas, each of them equally gnarly, with thick leathery skin and spikes down their backs that are used in territorial displays to make them look larger. They are a type of lizard, the largest of which can grow to around 6 ft (2 m). They are plant eaters and cold-blooded, so depending on the temperature, can be found warming up in the sunshine, or keeping cool in the shade of a cave retreat.

Bahamas • Tiger Beach
150 DARE TO SWIM WITH TIGER SHARKS
October to January

It's quite a feeling to swim with a striped 5 ft (1.5 m) apex predator. Stripes give the shark its name.

Bahamas • Big Major Cay
151 SEE A WILD PIG SWIM
All year

The population of feral pigs on this island likes to swim out to meet arriving boats.

153 | *Curious reef sharks circle round divers*

Bahamas • Tiger Beach

153 LEARN TO LOVE SHARKS, NOT FEAR THEM

All year

There is a certain movie that is perhaps single-handedly responsible for giving sharks a bad name. But if you get the opportunity to swim alongside Caribbean reef sharks with a professional guide, or watch them patrol the sea bottom in their natural way, you can't help but be awed by their streamlined efficiency and sense of majesty. If you also consider that far more people are killed by dogs than sharks each year, you will realize that a fear of these fish is misplaced. Cultivate a healthy respect for them instead.

Bahamas • Abaco and Great Inagua Islands

154 BE DAZZLED BY THE VIVID BAHAMIAN PARROT

All year

There's nothing like seeing an animal in the place it takes its name from. The Bahamian parrot—or to give it its full scientific name, the *Amazona leucocephala bahamensis*, a white-headed Amazon from the Bahamas—also has a red throat and cheeks (reminiscent of a watermelon), and bright blue flashes under its wings when it flies. The species used to live on seven Bahamian islands, but that is now down to just two. It is particularly vulnerable to predators and natural disasters because it builds its nests on the ground.

Cuba • San Diego de los Baños
155 ENJOY CUBAN BIRDSONG
All year

Discover that not all Cuban music comes in the form of *salsa* and *son*. The national bird of this country is the Cuban trogon, and it is famed for its constant singing—to the sound of *toco-toco-tocoro-tocoro*. It's a very distinctive bird, too, with a white chest, blue-and-green back, red belly, and black-and-white graphically patterned wings. The Cuban trogon is usually spotted perching in trees on wooded hillsides, but it is also an accomplished hoverer.

Cuba • Valle de Viñales
156 CATCH A GLIMPSE OF A CUBAN TODY
All year

Todies look like birds that never grew up. They have large heads on their tiny, colorful bodies, and a compact shape. Cuban todies are prolific throughout the island but they can be tricky to spot since they favor dense vegetation, often next to rivers where there are plenty of insects. These birds can catch two insects a minute and hunt all day long. Look out for the nesting tunnels that they excavate into embankments or tree trunks.

155 | *A Cuban trogon displays its unique plumage*

Cuba • Valle de Viñales
157 TAKE NOTE OF GASTROPODS
All year

Cuba is home to 1,400 species of snails, many with wonderfully bright shells.

Cuba • Eastern region
158 DISCOVER THE SOLENODON'S SECRET
All year

This small, rat-like furry mammal, native to Cuba, is known for its extremely long nose. Once thought extinct, it remains endangered. And its secret? Poisonous saliva.

Cuba • Alejandro de Humboldt National Park
159 WONDER AT THE ORIGINS OF THE HUTIA
All year

There's something charming about a Cuban hutia—it looks like a guinea pig with a tail, but four times a guinea pig's size. It weighs up to 19 lb (8.5 kg)!

Cuba • Playa Larga
160 GET A BUZZ FROM A BEE HUMMINGBIRD
All year

The perfection of a bee hummingbird at such a tiny scale is mesmerizing. Just 2.5 in (6 cm) long, and perfectly formed, this is the world's smallest bird.

Cayman Islands
• Brac Parrot Reserve
161 FIND A WILD BANANA ORCHID
April to May

What's not to love: a fabulous name; abundant, scented flowers tipped with purple; and funny, yellow banana-shaped petals.

Cuba • Lomas de Banao Ecological Reserve
162 MAP THE BIODIVERSITY OF CUBA
March to November

Cuba is one of the world's biodiversity hot spots, with around 20,000 species of animals and 7,500 species of plants within its shores. However, for a number of years it has been cut off from international research, and little is known about the current state of play of many of these species. Join scientists to document this magnificent island and know that you're part of protecting species for the future.

Jamaica • Coasts and mountains
163 SEE JAMAICA'S MOST BEAUTIFUL BIRD
All year

The red-billed streamertail is a stunner. Both sexes have a bright red bill and iridescent green body, but the male also sports long, glossy black tail feathers that are twice the length of its body. Being a type of hummingbird, it is a picture to behold it hovering in front of flowers or feeders, searching out the sweetest nectar. Its beautiful appearance has also earned it the names of "scissortail" and "God bird."

Jamaica • Montego Bay
164 BE IMPRESSED BY A GIANT ANOLE'S DEWLAP
All year

The Jamaican giant anole, or crested anole, is a lizard that is only found in the West Indies. You will want to make sure that you see one when it is bright green in color since it is a stunning sight—but some do turn brown. The males have large, loose pouches of skin in their necks called "dewlaps," which they puff out to attract females and to indicate their territorial boundaries.

Jamaica • Central forest reserves
165 HEAR A FROG SNORE
All year

The sound that is made by the wonderfully named Jamaican snoring frog clearly needs no explanation. Sadly its numbers are in decline due to habitat loss.

164 | *A giant anole puffs out its dewlap*

Jamaica • Falmouth
166 CREATE A GLOW IN THE SEA
All year

There are very few places in the world to reliably witness the phenomenon of bioluminescence, and the aptly named Luminous Lagoon is one of them. Trail your hand in its waters by night and watch it leave a path of sparkles and light behind it. This stunning, natural phenomenon is caused by millions of tiny microorganisms called "dinoflagellates," which thrive in the blend of salt and fresh water created as the Martha Brae River flows into the lagoon. When the water is agitated, it gives off an eerie but spectacular glow.

Jamaica • Forests
167 HEAR A CHESTNUT-BELLIED CUCKOO
All year

This pretty gray bird with a white chest and eponymous chestnut belly is found only in Jamaica. You'll more likely hear it than see it—its distinctive song is described as a series of deep, guttural croaks.

Jamaica • Negril Watershed Protection Area
168 IDENTIFY A YELLOW WARBLER
November to March

There are 40 species of different warblers found in the Caribbean, so learning how to identify one is a handy skill to have. The vivid little yellow warbler is the most entirely yellow of them all, with stripes of black through its lower wings and tail. Listen out for its six-note song, which provides a soundtrack to gentle spring and summer mornings; it seems to say "Sweet, sweet, sweet, I'm so sweet."

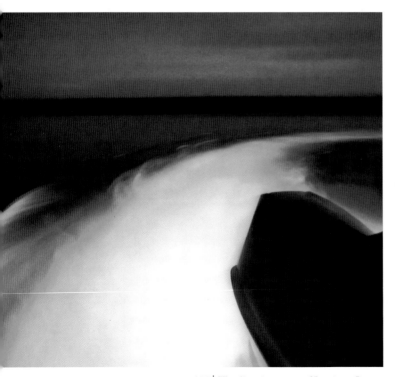

166 | *The glistening waters of Luminous Lagoon*

169 | *The impressive shell of the queen conch*

Turks and Caicos • Coastal waters
169 SPY A SEASHELL ON THE SEAFLOOR
All year

The shell of the queen conch is surely the royal highness of all seashells, with its beautiful, pink interior and fabulously horned exterior. It also reaches majestic sizes of around 14 in (35 cm) in length. The shell is formed by the conch snail that lives inside it. Sadly, because of the beauty of the shell, and its popularity, it is now threatened in certain areas.

Bonaire • Shallow coastal waters
170 SPOT AN OCTOPUS IN DISGUISE
All year

The Caribbean reef octopus can completely change its color (using special color cells on its body called "chromatophores") and blend in with any background. Of course, that does make it tricky to see. It is most active in the late afternoon and at night, in shallow rather than deep water. If you see empty shells, that could indicate there's an octopus nearby since it uses them to disguise its lair. It preys on clams, snails, and other crustaceans, and in turn, is preyed on by large fish and sharks. It squirts out a cloud of ink when it needs to escape in a hurry. Not only does this hide it from predators, it also tastes foul.

Antigua and Barbuda
• St. Marys in Antigua; hills
171 SEE DONKEYS IN THE WILD
All year

The last sugar factory on Antigua closed in the 1970s. With it the last of the sugar plantations' working donkeys became unemployed and were put out to live freely on the island's tropical slopes and plains. While captive donkeys have existed on the island since they were first brought there in the 1630s, large populations of feral animals now live and breed in the wild on the island and have become a familiar sight, entertaining tourists while frustrating farmers, for whom the pickup has long been the preferred beast of burden. Life in the wild is tough, and many of the donkeys end up in sanctuaries where they are nursed and protected.

Antigua and Barbuda • Wherever there are trees

172 TRACK THE SOUND OF THE CARIBBEAN

All year

The distinct sound of nighttime in the Caribbean is a repetitive, high-pitched *gleep, gleep*—the sound of Caribbean tree frogs. There are several different species, often brown or green in color, and usually very small—no more than 1.2 in (3 cm) long. Look to the ground, since they descend at night to search for ants and spiders.

Antigua and Barbuda • Guana Island

173 HEAR A DUCK WHISTLE

All year

The West Indian whistling duck may not be the most spectacular duck in the world—long legs and a brown-and-black body, but it is unique in the sound it makes. Instead of the regular quack, this duck makes a shrill whistling sound—*vis-i-see, vis-i-see*—hence its name. It lives around ponds and mangroves but is usually seen high up in the trees rather than on the water. Keep an eye out around dusk since that's when it's most active.

Antigua and Barbuda • Barbuda Island

174 DON'T MISS THE BARBUDA WARBLER

All year

This pretty little yellow-and-gray bird is the only bird endemic to Barbuda. It hops around all types of vegetation looking for insects, with its tail feathers cocked up, piping a warbled song.

Antigua and Barbuda • Great Bird Island

175 SEE IF THE RACER SNAKE LIVES UP TO ITS NAME

All year

In short it can't—it is quite a slow mover. In the 1990s only 50 Antiguan racers remained on this island (victims of mammals introduced in the 1800s), but happily, numbers are now over 1,000.

St. Vincent and the Grenadines • Western and eastern ridges

176 SPOT A PARROT ON HOME TURF

All year

The St. Vincent parrot is more muted than many: a bright tail kept in check by a yellowish brown body.

Barbados • Eastern forests

177 BLINK AND MISS THE WORLD'S TINIEST SNAKE

All year

As thin as a piece of spaghetti, the tiny Barbados threadsnake could coil itself up on a coin.

Barbados • Northeastern woodlands

178 NOD HELLO TO A BARBADOS GREEN MONKEY

All year

It's not green like grass, but the fur of the Barbados green monkey does have a definite green tinge. These monkeys are found all over the island, but are most common in vegetation around the northeast coast. Unlike their parents, babies have a bluish appearance due to a lack of fur. They are often seen clinging to their mothers' stomachs.

Barbados • Andromeda Botanical Gardens

179 ENJOY HUNDREDS OF EXOTIC PLANT SPECIES

All year

This hillside botanical garden in St. Joseph parish was established in the 1950s. It offers winding paths through 6 acres (2 hectares) of tropical plants, including trees not found anywhere else in the Caribbean. There are hundreds of different plant species here to witness at your leisure, including orchids, heliconias, bougainvilleas, and ginger lilies.

Grenada • Carriacou; leafy scrubland

180 ADMIRE A RED-FOOTED TORTOISE

All year

Search for these guys in scrubland—with their red, spotty legs, they're worth the effort. Their looks have made them popular as pets and emblems on stamps, but they're best seen in the wild.

Grenada • Mountainous interior of the island

181 CHECK OUT THE CHEEKY MONA MONKEYS

All year

Brown-backed, white-bellied, and with a stripe of black in between, mona monkeys are often seen storing food in their cheeks.

Grenada • Coasts

182 CONVERSE WITH A RED-FOOTED BOOBY

All year

The distinctive blue bill of this colorful-footed bird looks as if it is made for chatting.

Grenada • Coastal waters

183 SEE THE PYGMY RIGHT WHALE

All year

Small for a whale, the pygmy right whale is still around 19.5 ft (6 m) long and is a year-round resident of Grenada's waters.

184 | *The ocelot is top cat on Trinidad*

Trinidad and Tobago • Trinidad; forested areas

184 MONITOR OCELOTS

November to December

Very little is known about the local populations of these wild cats, which are around twice the size of domestic cats. However, the island of Trinidad, where ocelots are not overshadowed by other bigger cats, offers a perfect place to study them.

Trinidad and Tobago
• Tobago; forested highlands

185 HEAR A COCRICO

All year

You can't deny that the pheasant-like cocrico, or chachalaca, has a fabulous name. You will hear it more than see it with its loud *cocrico* chorus ringing out at dawn and dusk.

Trinidad and Tobago
• Caroni Swamp

186 COUNT ALL THE IBISES YOU CAN

April to August

Most plentiful in the breeding season, scarlet ibises are a wonder to behold. Together with the cocrico, they are Trinidad and Tobago's national bird.

Guatemala • Mountainous tropical forests

187 WORSHIP A QUETZAL

All year

Often described as the world's most beautiful bird, the resplendent quetzal was worshiped by the Mayan and Aztec people.

Guatemala • Rain forest floors and in decaying wood

188 SEE A GOD OF THE INSECT WORLD

All year

The Hercules beetle is aptly named—the biggest specimens can reach around 7 in (17.5 cm) long, including the horn.

Guatemala • Rain forests

189 SEEK LOST SPECIES

All year

The Search for Lost Species campaign has already had one success: discovering that the "golden wonder" of Jackson's climbing salamander is still in existence in Guatemala.

Guatemala • Throughout; near water

190 DISCOVER A BASILISK'S NICKNAME

All year

When the brown basilisk is fleeing from a predator, it can run on top of water, hence its other name—Jesus lizard.

Guatemala • El Mirador
191 LISTEN TO A DAWN CHORUS
All year

As if climbing to the top of the ancient ruins at El
Mirador wasn't already enough of a wonder, do it
as dawn breaks over the jungle and be treated to a
cacophony of sounds—parrots chattering, howler
monkeys howling, Guatemalan turkeys gobbling.
It starts as isolated sounds that get more frequent
and louder as the sun comes over the horizon and
ever more birds join in. The area is fabulous for
wildlife, and once dawn has broken, you will see
all the animals that you may have heard in the dark.

Belize • Cockscomb Basin
Wildlife Sanctuary
192 WHOOP WITH A BLACK HOWLER
All year

If you spend time in the
Cockscomb Basin Wildlife
Sanctuary, you're sure to hear
the whoops of howler monkeys.
Disease, hunting, and hurricanes
had wiped them out by the late
1970s, but in the early 1990s,
a program was undertaken to
reintroduce them to the area,
and now a population of several
hundred is thought to live in the
sanctuary. Look for the dark
shapes of their black furry
bodies up in the canopy, listen
out for their throaty roars, or
even have a sniff—their urine
has a very distinctive smell.

Belize • Cockscomb Basin
Wildlife Sanctuary
193 SPOT A JAGUAR IN THE WILD
June and July

Go in the rainy season and at
night for the best chance of
seeing a jaguar.

192 | *A juvenile black howler monkey*

Belize • Corozal

194 LISTEN TO THE GRUNTS OF A PECCARY

All year

It's not an animal we hear about often, but the peccary is a pig-like mammal that grows to about 3 ft (1 m) long and is found in the rain forests of much of Central and South America. They live in herds of around 15 and have poor eyesight, so keep in regular communication with a range of sounds, from barking, grunting, woofing, coughing, and purring, as they root around the undergrowth looking for roots and tubers. The Shipstern Conservation and Management Area in northeast Belize offers a good chance of spotting one of these fascinating creatures.

195 | *The tayra's claws make it a strong climber*

Belize • Southern forests

195 SEE A TREE-CLIMBING OTTER

All year

The tayra is, in fact, a weasel, but it's called the "tree otter" due to its climbing capabilities.

Belize • Chaa Creek

196 TAKE A JUNGLE WALK AT NIGHT

All year, at night

By night the jungle is alive with the sights—and sounds—of nocturnal animals.

Belize • Rain forest trees and floors

197 SEE THE WORLD'S MOST LETHAL SNAKES

All year

From the fer-de-lance to the Mayan coral, Belize is home to some very venomous snakes.

Belize • Glover's Reef atoll

198 SEE TORTOISESHELL WHERE IT BELONGS . . .

All year

. . . on the beautiful (and sadly, highly sought-after) carapace of a now critically endangered hawksbill turtle.

Belize • Rain forest fruit trees

199 FIND A TOUCAN ALTERNATIVE

All year

The collared aracari is a toucan and has the big bill you expect of these birds. Listen for its loud *pseek* ringing out in the forest.

Belize • Dense forest canopy
200 TICK OFF ANOTHER STUNNING BIRD
All year

With a long tail, scarlet stomach, and green head and throat, the male slaty-tailed trogon is a stunner. It often spends long periods perching motionless on a branch.

Belize • Forests, riverbanks, and clearings
201 GLIMPSE A BAIRD'S TAPIR
All year, at night

Known also as the "mountain cow," the Baird's tapir is an iconic and beloved species of Belize, and the country's national animal. Hunting this endangered mammal is illegal, and large forest reserves exist to protect it. It has a wonderful drooping nose, almost like an anteater's, although it is, in fact, more closely related to the rhinoceros. Baird's tapir is a herbivore—like a cow—and spends most of its time hunting for food.

Belize • Belize Barrier Reef
202 APPRECIATE ELKHORN CORAL
All year

Coral is proving very vulnerable around the world as our climate changes, and none more so than elkhorn coral, which in 2006 was designated a threatened species. However, evidence on the Belize Barrier Reef—the second-largest barrier reef in the world—seems to indicate that the elkhorn coral is recovering. Its flat, fungal-like growths are spreading out into new areas and thereby affording a vital ecosystem for the many species that rely on these reefs.

Belize • Belize Barrier Reef
203 HANG OUT WITH A JACKFISH SCHOOL
All year

Diving is an activity that is full of many different experiences, particularly in the complex diversity of a coral reef. As well as spotting the more impressive creatures, however, there is also the experience of swimming among more common species. Jackfish are often found in large shimmering shoals, and to swim among them is to blend into ocean life and to feel the full force of nature going about its business around you.

Belize • Shark Ray Alley
204 SNORKEL WITH A SHARK
All year

Swimming with sharks is an amazing experience. These animals are sleek, powerful, and beautiful. Those who don't scuba dive might think that this is an experience too wild for them, but at this location in Ambergris Caye, off Belize, you can swim with the resident nurse sharks with just a mask and snorkel. These 10 ft (3 m) long bottom feeders have small mouths and feed infrequently since they use very little energy.

201 | *A Baird's tapir foraging among the leaves*

Belize • Lowland forests and forest borders

205 **DELIGHT IN A VIVID TOUCAN**

All year

No bird can rival the keel-billed toucan for having the most spectacular bill. It is green, blue, orange, and red, and if you see it close up, it has a black outline where it meets the toucan's body, which is mainly black with a yellow front and green around its eye. If you see one toucan, you'll often see more; they congregate in flocks of around six birds on the edges of forests where they use their large bills to pick and eat fruit from the trees.

El Salvador • Forest edges

206 **LOVE THE EQUALITY OF THE TURQUOISE-BROWED MOTMOT**

All year

Both sexes of El Salvador's national bird, the turquoise-browed motmot, get to have a beautiful blue racket-tail. Look out for their elaborate wag-displays with this tail, used to warn predators to keep away.

Honduras • Starfish Alley

207 **WISH UPON A STARFISH**

All year

Not far out from the beach, and in among the seagrass that they feed on, are hundreds of red, yellow, orange, and beige cushion starfish, slowly creeping about on the seafloor.

205 | *The vibrant keel-billed toucan*

Honduras • Cuero y Salado Wildlife Refuge

208 CANOE WITH MANATEES
All year

Quietly paddle around the mouth of the Salado River, and you could be lucky and come across the rare and endangered West Indian manatee. Around 50 are thought to live here, snuffling around the mangrove roots, but they are very elusive.

Honduras • Rus Rus Biological Reserve

209 SEE RED AS A SCARLET MACAW FLASHES BY
All year

With its scarlet body and blue-and-yellow wings, the scarlet macaw is a distinctive member of the parrot family. It likes to go high up in deciduous trees in its hunt for nuts.

Honduras • Throughout; scrubland and forests

210 COUNT THE BANDS ON AN ARMADILLO
All year

The conveniently named nine-banded armadillo is surely one of the most unique mammals out there. Its body is like an overgrown woodlouse, with a tiny head and long tail.

Honduras • Arid valleys in the northeast

211 SPOT THE JEWEL IN THE CROWN
All year

One of Central America's rarest birds, the Honduran emerald is a turquoise hummingbird only found in certain valleys in the country's interior—the Valle de Telica and the Rio Aguán and Agalta Valleys. It lives in dry thorn forests, feeding on the nectar of cacti and air plants.

Honduras • Around Lago de Yojoa
212 WATCH A TAMANDUA FORAGE
All year

The northern tamandua is definitely the best-dressed anteater subspecies—honey-colored with a black body and bands like a black vest around its shoulders. It uses its long, sticky tongue to root out ants and termites. You're as likely to see it foraging on the forest floor as climbing trees.

Honduras • Pico Bonito National Park
213 SEE A HAIRY DWARF PORCUPINE
All year, at night

Despite its name, the Mexican hairy dwarf porcupine (or tree porcupine) is sizable enough—between 19 and 31 in (50 and 80 cm) long, brown and furry, concealing 3 in (8 cm) quills. These detach if it comes into contact with prey, and embed themselves in flesh. Spot it up in the trees.

215 | *Hammerheads congregate at Cocos Island*

Honduras • Rain forests along the Caribbean coast

214 IDENTIFY A HONDURAN BAT

All year

The tiny Honduran white bat feeds on fruit, and it would be easy to mistake the bat itself for a berry—it measures less than 2 in (5 cm) in length and lives in the crook of the leaves of the heliconia plant.

Costa Rica • Cocos Island

215 SEE HAMMERHEAD SHARKS MASS TOGETHER

June to October

As if seeing one of these fabulously odd-headed sharks wasn't enough, in the rainy season they gather in their hundreds at this island off the coast of Costa Rica for the nutrient-rich upwellings in the sea.

Costa Rica • Corcovado National Park

216 TREK IN A WILDLIFE HAVEN

November to April (dry season); avoid October.

The nature and wildlife of this national park is like nowhere else on Earth—2.5 percent of the world's biodiversity in one place. The park is a fabulous mixture of the power of nature with just enough tracks, bridges, and boardwalks to make it accessible for trekking, yet with wildness all around. You're almost guaranteed to see at least two species of monkeys, but you could also spot a Baird's tapir, northern tamandua, coati, turtles, brightly colored tree frogs, and all manner of beautiful butterflies and birds. May to September is wetter, but some animals are more active then.

Costa Rica • Manuel Antonio National Park

217 BE CHARMED BY A THREE-TOED SLOTH

All year

Everybody loves a sloth. Nothing can hurry these tree-dwelling mammals, which can sleep for up to 20 hours a day. They move slowly, eat slowly, and metabolize slowly. They have very weak hind legs, and interestingly, although cumbersome on the ground, they move very well in water.

216 | *The lush forest of Corcovado National Park*

Costa Rica • Santa Rosa National Park

218 MARVEL AT JUMPING AGOUTIS

December to April

The agouti is a fairly common mammal throughout the different forest types of Costa Rica, but you will be sure to see one in this national park. It is a rodent, reddish brown in color, about 16 to 32 in (40 to 80 cm) long, but with a very tiny tail. It is a little like a guinea pig—if guinea pigs had longer legs and a discernible neck. Agoutis forage for food (seeds and fruits) on the forest floor. One of the more surprising things about them is their ability to jump. This tends to happen when males, being highly monogamous and fiercely protective of their own patch, are asserting their territorial borders. From a standing start, two males may jump an astounding 6 ft (2 m) into the air before kicking at each other with their hind legs.

Costa Rica • Humid forests

219 ADMIRE ABUNDANT TREE FROGS

All year

Costa Rica has more than 150 species of frogs and toads, 43 of which are tree frogs. They are usually so tiny that their weight can be supported by leaves, and they generally have large fingers and toes with pads at the end for gripping twigs. The red-eyed tree frog is one of the most striking examples— bright green with yellow feet and bulging red eyes. It sleeps through the day and is active at dusk when it begins its distinct, loud call. Not all tree frogs sleep through the day. Poison dart frogs rummage in damp soil and leaf litter in the daylight. Although most species are poisonous, they don't have darts. This part of the name comes from the practice many local tribes had of dipping the tips of their arrows in the poisonous venom of these frogs.

Costa Rica • Guanacaste

220 TAKE THE FAMILY ON A CONSERVATION TRIP

February to June

It's never too soon to get children involved with conservation work. Turtles are a great species to study. They return to the same beaches each year, yet climate change is affecting the waters they live in. Conservation work usually involves monitoring turtle nests and offering protection to hatchlings so they can reach the sea.

Costa Rica • Monteverde Cloud Forest Reserve

221 STUDY THE WINGS OF THE GLASSWING BUTTERFLY

All year

There is something mesmerizing about the wings of the glasswing butterfly. The edges are in color, but the centers are transparent panes separated by black, as if they were a colorless stained-glass window. It doesn't affect their function, though. Glasswings can travel 7.5 miles (12 km) in one day when they're migrating.

219 | The red-eyed tree frog of tropical rain forests

Costa Rica • Inland tropical lowland forests

222 BE SURPRISED BY THE FACE OF A VULTURE

All year

The king vulture doesn't look like other vulture species. It has an elegant two-toned body and a vibrantly colorful face and neck, with a bizarre-looking fleshy caruncle on its beak. It's just as foul as other vultures, though—eating dead carcasses and keeping its nest rank-smelling to ward off predators. This species of vulture has one extra questionable trick—it defecates on its own legs as a cooling mechanism.

Costa Rica • Pacific coast

223 SEE A REAL FALSE KILLER WHALE

All year

Although similar to a killer whale when seen from above, the false killer whale—or pseudo orca—rarely has the distinctive white markings, and is actually a dolphin. Costa Rica has one of the largest populations of these creatures. They are playful and will happily approach boats.

222 | *The unforgettable look of a king vulture*

Costa Rica • Tree trunks in lowland rain forests

224 HEAR THE WORLD'S NOISIEST BUTTERFLY

All year

A noisy butterfly sounds like an oxymoron, but the variable cracker butterfly snaps its wings to make a snapping sound.

Costa Rica • Cordillera de Talamanca; rain forests of the lower slopes

225 TELL TOUCAN SPECIES APART

All year

The chestnut-mandibled toucan is larger than its keel-billed cousin, and has a two-toned bill of chestnut and yellow.

Costa Rica • Foothills on the Caribbean coast

226 FIND THE ELUSIVE SNOWCAPPED HUMMINGBIRD

All year

This tiny hummingbird is just 2.5 in (5 cm) long and lives in a very specific—and sadly fast-disappearing—range of lowland forest where it favors the porterweed bush. Find porterweed at places such as Rancho Naturalista and in the Tenorio National Park, and you'll likely see a bright white blur buzzing around. That is the snowcap crown that tops this bird's beautiful burgundy body.

Costa Rica • Braulio Carillo National Park

227 SEE THE RED LEGS OF A RUSSET-NAPED WOOD RAIL

All year

Make the distinctive *ponay, ponay* call to see if you can attract this ground bird into a clearing in this Central Volcanic Conservation Area national park.

Costa Rica • Lowland forests and foothills

229 BE AWED BY THE FLASH OF A HONEYCREEPER

All year

The female green honeycreeper is a joy to see, its bright green plumage flitting around feeders and fruiting bushes in many gardens and forest walks. But then the male appears with its beautiful turquoise feathers and black-capped head, and once again, in the world of birds, the female is outshined. They are often seen in mixed-species flocks, so keep an eye out for other beautiful gems.

Costa Rica • Lowland forests

228 FEEL THE WISDOM OF A SPECTACLED OWL

All year, at night

With its dark face and bushy white eyebrows, the spectacled owl has the archetypal "wise owl" appearance. It is most vocal on moonlit nights.

234 | *Costa Rican plant life attracts key pollinators*

Costa Rica • Puerto Jiménez
230 LOOK AFTER THE BIRDS AND THE BEES
June to August

Agriculture and climate change are rapidly taking their toll on the rich biodiversity of Costa Rica—a country that has, in addition to other creatures, more than 400 species of bee. Projects helping to mitigate these effects are planting what are known as mini "agroforests" in pastureland and arable fields. These will recreate the lost habitat for important pollinators such as bees, in addition to butterflies, and hummingbirds. Join a project and help scientists learn more about the threats facing pollinators.

Costa Rica • Rivers in dense forests and mangrove swamps
231 SIZE UP A PYGMY
All year

A large bill and a tiny body give the American pygmy kingfisher a very top-heavy look. Look out for a hint of turquoise and reddish brown concealed in the trees alongside rivers.

Costa Rica • Lowland gardens
233 RATE THE RED-LEGGED HONEYCREEPER
All year

You'd think a stunning blue bird with bright red legs would be a rare sight, but this guy is surprisingly common.

Costa Rica • Carara National Park
232 SEE THE HORNS OF A CRESTED OWL
All year

This owl's impressive white eyebrows flow into equally impressive ear tufts that stick out a good couple of inches from the side of its head.

Costa Rica • San Luis Adventure Park
234 CATCH A CRIMSON-COLLARED TANAGER
All year

This black-and-red bird is sparrow-like in size, but a little more racy in appearance.

Costa Rica • Northwestern tip; edges of lowland forests

235 MARVEL AT THE NESTS OF THE MONTEZUMA OROPENDOLA

January to May

This bird has thought long and hard about its nests. It likes to construct them in large trees that stand alone in a clearing—so troops of monkeys are less likely to swing in. It even chooses trees with wasps nests to provide an added deterrent. The nests are intricately woven hanging baskets that are up to 70 in (180 cm) long, made from twigs and banana fibers. There can be as many as 40 in one tree.

Panama • Isla de Escudo de Veraguas; red mangrove forests

236 LOCATE THE PYGMY THREE-TOED SLOTH

All year

Over thousands of years, these sloths have evolved to be smaller than those found on the mainland. They generally grow to around 20 in (50 cm) long. They are critically endangered since they are only found in a tiny 1.7 square mile (4.4. sq km) area.

Panama • Throughout

237 DISCOVER HOW COLORFUL BEES CAN BE

All year

Orchid bees are not all black and yellow. Some are glossy green and others a wonderful array of blue, green, red, and gold. They are found around many species of orchid from which the male collects different scents in sacks in his back legs—probably to entice a female.

Panama • Pacific coast; coastal rain forests and mangrove forests

238 SEE A CRAB WITH TWO NAMES

All year, at night

Since it is a nocturnal crab, it's easy enough to understand how *Gecarcinus quadratus* earned its common name of moon crab. But the nickname of Halloween crab? That is almost certainly due to its eye-catching orange-and-black coloring—but it may also have been inspired by its slightly ghoulish orange legs.

Colombia • Forest floors

239 RESPECT THE LEAF-CUTTER ANT

All year

You might find yourself looking down on Colombia's leaf-cutter ants as they march in their long lines across forest paths, but make sure you stop and give them the respect they deserve. These tiny insects—although some can be over 0.3 in (1 cm) long—can carry up to 50 times their own bodyweight. That's equivalent to a human carrying a van.

239 | *Leaf-cutter ants on the march*

Colombia • Caribbean coast

240 DELIGHT IN THE SIGHT OF WILD BOUGAINVILLEA

All year

The bright colors of bougainvillea light up many an urban street, with their hues of pink, purple, orange, and red. But see this stunner in the wild, and it seems even more magnificent. The colors aren't actually the flowers, but the bracts around small, simple white flowers.

Colombia • Lowland forests

241 WATCH THE MATING DANCE OF THE MANAKIN

March to August

With its black body, red head, and fluffy yellow legs, the red-capped manakin is a fabulous sight at any time of the year. But catch it when it's courting (March to August) and you'll be treated to a fabulous dance where the male shimmies up and down a tree branch as if it were moonwalking.

Colombia • Southern cloud forests

242 IDENTIFY A "NEW" CARNIVORE

All year, at night

The olinguito is a member of the raccoon family and wasn't discovered until 2013—probably due to its nocturnal foraging habits and the density of the cloud forest where it lives.

Venezuela • Canaima National Park

243 FACE THE WORLD'S HEAVIEST SPIDER

All year

The goliath birdeater—a member of the tarantula family—is the world's heaviest spider. With a leg span of 11 in (28 cm), it is also the second biggest (after the huntsman).

Venezuela • Lowland forests

244 REVEL IN THE RUBY REDNESS OF A COTINGA

All year

There aren't many birds that have such a dark, rich-red plumage as the pompadour cotinga. Add in the snowy white wings, and it's pretty unmistakable. Which is just as well—it's also mostly silent.

245 | *The stunning blue morpho butterfly*

Venezuela • Rain forests

245 SEE A BUTTERFLY THE SIZE OF A BIRD
All year

Blue morpho butterflies can be up to 8 in (20 cm) across, with iridescent blue wings. They live in tropical forests but love the light, which means they are often found in clearings. Pilots have reported seeing groups of blue morphos basking in the sunshine above the jungle canopy. On the underside their wings are brown, so as they fly they flash from blue to brown, which can make it very tricky for predators to track them. As caterpillars they're red and yellow.

Venezuela • Lowland to midlevel rain forests

246 CATCH SIGHT OF A BINGO WINGER
All year

There is a fabulous black-and-white butterfly that will surely bring you luck if you spot it— it has a very clear "88" in the markings on its wings.

Venezuela • Southern and eastern tropical forests

247 SEE A WHITE-FACED SAKI SELECT FRUIT

All year

These monkeys live in the lower part of the jungle canopy—look out for their bright white faces set against black bodies (males only; females are grizzly brown). They specialize in eating the seeds of unripe fruits, so find a tree that has fruit yet to ripen for the best chance of finding them.

Venezuela • Lowland forests and woods

248 SPOT VENEZUELA'S NATIONAL BIRD

All year

Venezuela has selected the Venezuelan troupial as its national bird. It's a handsome choice, with a golden body, a black head, and black wings with a white stripe. They do not build their own nests, but instead find a vacated one—or, failing that, steal one.

Venezuela • Rain forest canopies

249 LEARN ABOUT ANOTHER ANTEATER

All year, at night

The silky anteater is golden in color but not easy to see since it is small, nocturnal, and hunts for ants and termites in the canopy of trees. It is the smallest of the anteater subspecies, at just 14 to 17 in (36 to 45 cm) long. You'll know it by its luminous fur, and the red soles of its feet.

247 | *A male white-faced saki and his plainer mate*

Venezuela • Lowland forests and woodlands

250 LISTEN FOR A GREAT POTOO

All year, at night

At night in the jungle, make a point of listening for a low growl coming from the treetops. It's not a jaguar as you might expect, but a great potoo—a large bird with a long tail and a rounded head. They are notoriously difficult to see, since by day their mottled plumage blends in with the tree bark and they look like broken branches. At night, though, they leave their perches in order to catch large insects and, occasionally, bats.

Venezuela • Llanos wetlands

251 CHOOSE YOUR FAVORITE JACAMAR

All year

Jacamars are birds that, to the untrained, could be described as a bit like a cross between a kingfisher and a hummingbird. They are small, with a long, pointed bill, a long tail, and usually beautiful iridescent colors. There are at least 18 species to discover, but one of the most beautiful is the rufous-tailed jacamar, with its shimmering green body with hints of a dark reddish bronze. Look out for them on the edges of woodlands.

Guyana • Swamps and rivers

252 SNIFF OUT A HOATZIN

All year

The hoatzin has another name—the stinkbird. This is, as you might imagine, because it smells somewhat stinky. Its digestive system ferments its vegetarian diet, leading to a distinctive odor. It lives in trees along lakes and rivers, and is about the size of a pheasant, with an impressive crest on its head. It is a noisy bird that croaks, hisses, and grunts, yet despite all this, it is handsome, which is perhaps why Guyana has chosen it as its national bird.

Ecuador • Galápagos Islands

253 STUDY THE BEAK OF DARWIN'S FINCH

All year

Follow in the footsteps of Charles Darwin. Noting the varying beaks of the finches on these islands helped lead to his theory of evolution.

Ecuador • North Seymour, Galápagos Islands

254 WATCH A BLUE-FOOTED BOOBY DANCE

June to August

A female blue-footed booby will select a mate on the brightness of its feet, so males show them off with high-stepping dances.

Ecuador • Galápagos Islands

255 SPOT A RED-LIPPED BATFISH

All year

Batfish are best known for their bright red lips, but they are worth spotting regardless—they don't swim well, but walk on their pectoral fins on the ocean floor.

Ecuador • Galápagos Islands
256 HEAR AN IGUANA SNEEZE
All year

Marine iguanas are a species of iguana
that are only found on the Galápagos, and
they're the only species that forage under
water. They have strange squashed faces
with wide-set eyes, and although not pretty,
they have adapted perfectly to marine life—
right down to a habit of sneezing to expel
the salty water after their dives.

Ecuador • Galápagos Islands
257 SALUTE THE ANIMAL THAT LIVES FOREVER
All year

Giant tortoises are extraordinary creatures. Not only can they live, in some cases, for more than 250 years, but they can go for a year without food or water, due to supplies of water stored in their necks. And look at them! They can grow to weigh up to 919 lb (417 kg) and can walk at a speed of around 0.17 mph (0.27 kmh). (Maybe the last fact isn't quite so impressive.)

It's sometimes thought that these venerable reptiles emerged as a result of "island gigantism," the process by which isolated communities of animals become larger across the generations in the absence of any predators or competitors. In fact, in the case of the giant tortoise, this is not strictly true. Giant tortoises evolved from more familiar-looking relatives about 80 million years ago and were once common across all continents. They were already massive when they reached their island homes. It was only about 100,000 years ago that they began to become extinct on the mainland, and today, only a few populations survive in small island groups, the most famous of which is, of course, the Galápagos.

Ecuador • Galápagos Islands
258 SEE A PENGUIN NORTH OF THE EQUATOR
All year

The world's second-smallest penguin is also the only one to be found in the wild, swimming north of the equator, thanks to the cool ocean currents that surround the hub of biological curiosity that is the Galápagos Islands. To protect its eggs and chicks from the heat of the sun, it buries them deep in the rocks, and to protect itself it pants like a dog, to cool its throat and airways.

Ecuador • Galápagos Islands
259 SEE A SALLY LIGHTFOOT AGE WITH STYLE
All year

Named (perhaps) after a once-famous Caribbean dancer, this crab grows more fabulous as it ages. Beginning life a demure brown, it is peppered with just a few red spots, hinting at what is to come. As it ages, it grows more nimble, has less need for camouflage, and, as successive shells molt, the little spots become an allover array of vivid red, blue, and yellow.

257 | *The venerable Galápagos giant tortoise*

Ecuador • Coca

260 BIRD-WATCH IN A CLOUD FOREST
All year

Ecuador's cloud forests are situated high in the Andes, where the hot damp air from the Pacific causes everything to squelch as it condenses. They are an accessible drive from the country's capital, Quito, making them a destination for some of planet Earth's most exotic day trips. The hundreds of species of birds on view are a highlight: trogons, toucans, tanagers, cotingas, and multitudes of hummingbirds.

Bird-watching tours are organized by expert guides and are always an eye-opening experience. You can also venture out onto a viewing platform in a kapok tree, around 130 ft (40 m) above the ground, so that you can look up to the skies above, or survey the forest below your feet. When you're back down on the ground, look out for the wealth of sloths, howler monkeys, jaguars, pumas, coati, tayras, spectacled bears, and butterflies to be found here, too.

262 | *A pelican dives, bill first*

Ecuador • Yasuni National Park

261 SEE A PLANT GROWING ON AIR

All year

Your botanical education is not complete until you've taken the time to appreciate an epiphyte. These need neither soil nor standing water to survive, but instead climb up another plant, getting all their nutrients from air, rain, and falling debris. Colorful bromeliads, hanging from branches, are one example.

Ecuador • Western coast

262 WATCH PELICANS DIVE-BOMB

September to March

Peruvian pelicans, which are also found in abundance in neighboring Ecuador, along with closely related brown pelicans, are the only species of this well-known bird family to plunge-dive for their food. Whole squadrons of them can be seen hovering above the water's surface, watching for a cluster of fish, their massive wings—over 6 ft 8 in (2 m) wide—holding them on the breeze. When the moment is right, they dive. As they enter the water at full speed, their mouths open, and the massive gular pouches on the lower parts of their bills fill like balloons with water and fish. As they drain out their bills following a successful catch, seagulls are often spotted stealing fish right out of the pelicans' mouths—and even standing triumphantly on the larger birds' heads as they gulp down their stolen treats.

Ecuador • Throughout
263 TALLY UP HUMMINGBIRD SPECIES
All year

And the prize for the greatest diversity of hummingbird species in the world goes to . . . not Brazil or Mexico, but the relatively small territory of Ecuador, which is said to be home to at least 130 different species. The smallest birds are tiny—less than 2 in (5 cm) long.

Ecuador • Northeastern rain forests
264 ADMIRE THE WARMTH OF A MONKEY
All year

The adorable brown woolly monkey is found in the Andes. As the name suggests, its fur is thick, as if it has been crossed with a poodle. Sadly, its appealing looks have also made it popular as a pet, so it is now highly endangered.

Ecuador • Andean foothills
265 SEE A PACARANA FLUTTER ITS WHISKERS
All year

This chunky, cat-sized rodent with a thick, furry tail lives in the tropical forests of Ecuador. Its long blond whiskers flutter back and forth when it gets excited. The name "pacarana," which means "false paca," comes from its similarity to a paca (an unrelated type of rodent).

Ecuador • Yasuni National Park
266 SEE A FIG STRANGLE A TREE
All year

Below the canopy of the tropical forest, light can be scarce, but light is what plants need to grow, and so some have developed more aggressive and competitive approaches than others to get a start in life and soak up some sunshine. The strangler fig takes no prisoners, beginning as a seed growing in crevices high up on a host tree—often the result of having been dropped by a passing bird. The growing fig then slowly envelops the host tree with its roots as the plant grows downward, until, in some cases, the host dies and its strangler lives on as a hollow ghostly skeleton.

Ecuador • Andean foothills
267 BEHOLD THE MOST STRIKING HUMMINGBIRD OF ALL
All year

The velvet-purple coronet's striking plumage comes from intense iridescence—meaning its feathers refract light rather than reflect it, thereby producing its colors. As a result, in low light it can appear almost black. But when the sun shines, its indigo front, green-blue back, green upperwing feathers, and red-brown underwings dazzle in shimmering waves. And of course, being a hummingbird, it shimmers at a rapid rate, its wings making dozens of figure eight movements per second.

Ecuador • Central cloud forests

268 MARVEL AT THE SWORD-BILLED HUMMINGBIRD'S BEAK

All year

This hummingbird has evolved alongside the *Passiflora mixta*, a species of passionflower with a long, nectar-filled tube that can only be accessed with the bird's specialized apparatus. Its bill is longer than its body, with a tongue inside to match.

Ecuador • Andes Mountains

269 SEE A WHITE-BOOTED RACKET-TAIL

All year

The defining characteristic of this elegant, long-tailed, mostly green hummingbird is—you guessed it—its fluffy white foot coverings, which hang below it like ski boots while in flight. At the tips of its tail are two deep blue teardrop-shaped feathers like tennis racket heads.

Ecuador • Andes Mountains

270 BE AMAZED BY A TORRENT DUCK

All year

This is one of just a few duck species to have adapted to the raucous environment of fast-flowing mountain streams. The male and female look entirely different (a property known as "diamorphism") but are equally spectacular. Males have black-and-white–striped heads with bright orange beaks; females are nut brown and charcoal.

Ecuador • Northwestern cloud forests

271 KEEP AN EYE OUT FOR A GLISTENING-GREEN TANAGER

All year

Tanagers account for 4 percent of the world's bird species and come in a vast array of colors and patterns. The glistening-green tanager will often join up with mixed-species flocks, but you won't lose sight of one—its feathers almost glow with an unnaturally bright emerald green.

Ecuador • Western coast

272 ADMIRE THE STATELY BLACK-FACED IBIS

All year

With a total length of around 30 in (75 cm), these impressive and elegant (if noisy) birds can be spotted on high Andean puna grasslands.

Peru • Florida

273 SEE A TRULY MARVELOUS BIRD

All year

The endangered male marvelous spatuletail has two long racket-shaped outer tail feathers that end in large violet blue disks or "spatules," which it waves about as part of its courtship display.

Peru • Swamps and forests

274 SPOT A LONG-BILLED WOODCREEPER

All year

They may not be the most flamboyant birds in Amazonia, but these charming red-brown–plumed insect eaters are still worth spotting. They have exceptionally long bills that are one quarter the length of their bodies, and are one of the largest of the uniquely South American woodcreeper family, growing to 14 in (35 cm). They hold their bodies vertically against tree trunks, gripping the bark with their claws, and climb by flexing their legs and hopping up the trunk. With their poise, they seem oblivious to gravity, and they might sometimes give the impression that a picture has simply been turned on its side. They are not endangered, but their numbers are falling, so a sighting is worth treasuring.

Peru • Colca Canyon

275 WATCH THE CONDORS OF COLCA CANYON
May to December

Not far from the "White City" of Arequipa, the world's second-deepest canyon is also one of the best places to see condors close-up in the wild. Colca Canyon is 13,650 ft (4,160 m) deep and is full of life—human, wild, and farmed. Terraces built to break up the steep slopes date back to 800 BCE, when the first humans came here to farm.

Tours on foot or the back of a mule will take you to the heart of the canyon, where you can see these vulture-like birds soaring gently on thermals next to the cliffs. They are not pretty, but with wingspans of 10.5 ft (3.2 m), they are certainly awe-inspiring.

277 | *The regal whiskers of the emperor tamarin*

Peru • Western coast
276 ADMIRE A FULL-THROATED FRIGATEBIRD
March to June

Beautiful and fast, with a penchant for flying fish, the frigatebird can reach speeds of 95 mph (153 kmh), but just as impressive as this are the male bird's courtship displays. It cranes back its neck to show off its inflated crimson neck pouch to any females circling above. If a female likes what it sees, it will descend and engage with the male in an odd dance, with both birds twisting their heads in unison. It all takes place away from the mainland on a few remote Pacific islands.

Peru • Eastern rain forests
277 COVET THE WHISKERS OF A MONKEY
All year

The bearded emperor tamarin apparently got its name from a resemblance to the German emperor Wilhelm II. Look for them in groups in the trees.

Peru • Coastal areas
279 GET HIPSTER CHIC WITH AN INCA TERN
All year

With a red beak, black feathers, and a long, white, curly mustache below the eyes, what's not to love?

Peru • Eastern cloud forests
278 FEEL THE PEACE OF AN ANGEL BUTTERFLY
All year

With transparent wings refracting a kaleidoscope of color, sylphina angel butterflies will keep you company on the trek up to Machu Picchu.

Peru • Andean slopes
280 SEE THE DISPLAY OF A SUNBITTERN
All year

When threatened, the sunbittern will open its wings to display a pattern of two large red eye spots on a yellow background.

Peru • Andean cloud forests

281 PAY ATTENTION TO AN ANDEAN COCK-OF-THE-ROCK

All year

The unofficial national bird of Peru is quite a looker. Nature has bestowed on the male of the species a bright orange plumage on its upper quarters, set off by its jet-black tail and wings. The orange feathers continue up from the top of its forehead into a fabulous semicircular crest. The males are, in fact, somewhat preoccupied with showing off their plumage. At certain hours of the day, groups of males will form, from which pairs will split off to take each other on *mano a mano* in displays of bowing, jumping, flapping, squawking, and grunting—all to get a female's attention.

Peru • The puna

282 DISCOVER ALL THE BIRDS OF THE PUNA

All year

The puna is a spectacular sprawling grassland region above the treeline and before the snow in the Andes. It begins in Peru and continues down into Argentina and Chile, encompassing foothills and plateaus, with some areas wet, and others drier or desert. It is a habitat for vast numbers of bird species, many of whom have been named after the region. They include the puna ibis, puna teal, rhea, tinamou, plover, thistletail, miner, and canastero: incredibly diverse birds that are associated with this breathtaking rolling landscape. See how many you can spot.

281 | *The dazzling male cock-of-the-rock*

283 | *A yellow-tailed woolly monkey in its treetop home*

Peru • Amazonas; San Martin

283 SEE PERU'S LARGEST MONKEY

All year

Once thought to be extinct, the yellow-tailed woolly monkey is even woolier than other monkeys in its family, with denser and longer fur that is adapted to life at higher altitudes. Its body is brown but its extremely long, bushy tail turns paler near the tip, and is capable of supporting the animal's entire weight as it hangs from branches to feed and explore.

Peru • Throughout

284 TOUCH A TOUCH-ME-NOT

All year

Not just the name of a cocktail, mimosas are also a family of plants renowned for their rapid and decidedly unplant-like movements. Some, like the *Mimosa pudica*, also known as the "shy plant" or "touch-me-not," respond not only to changes in light but to touch or vibrations. These little plants curl their leaves in a fascinating domino-like sequence at the slightest stimulation.

Peru • Cloud forests; paramos

285 WATCH A WOOLLY TAPIR TAKE A SIESTA

All year

At home in the forests or on the paramo plateaus, where winter temperatures can fall below freezing, this sleepy herbivore loves to nap.

Peru • Andean slopes

286 TRACK DOWN PADDINGTON BEAR

All year

South America's only bear species, the spectacled bear of Paddington fame, has white markings around its eyes and a short, thimble-like snout.

Brazil • Amazon rain forest

287 SEE A JAGUARUNDI IN THE FOREST

All year

Jaguarundis can be red or gray and were once thought to be two different species. These sleek wildcats are common across both rain forest and plains.

Brazil • Amazon rain forest

288 DON'T WALK—RUN FROM GIANT ANTS

All year

They may not eat you alive but at 1.5 in (4 cm) long, giant Amazonian ants will certainly give you a fright.

Brazil • Western Amazon basin

289 SEEK OUT THE WORLD'S SMALLEST MONKEY

May to June

The pygmy marmoset won't come to you so you'll have to go to it, far up near the western origins of the Amazon River. it is fast-moving, sharp-clawed, and alien-looking, as if it were the result of a malfunction in a shrinking machine. It has developed a method of farming tree sap, which is its main food.

Brazil • Amazon rain forest

290 GET FAMILIAR WITH THE SQUIRREL MONKEY

All year

All male South American monkeys are colorblind. The most commonly found is the squirrel monkey, and they are no exception to the rule.

Brazil • Atlantic rain forest

291 HELP PRESERVE AMAZON WILDLIFE

All year

Join a nonprofit organization that transforms tourists into "citizen-scientists," offering a fulfilling and fascinating alternative to downtime spent on a beach. Travelers who share their vision of a healthier planet can take part in expeditions that include studying jaguars, pumas, and their prey in Brazil's Atlantic rain forest, an area known as the "jaguar corridor."

Brazil • Amazon rain forest

292 DON'T BE TEMPTED BY A SNAKE

All year

Beautiful but dangerous, the emerald tree boa is a powerful six-footer that comes in vivid green, decorated with subtle, off-white lightning bolts. They don't have or need venom; like all boas, they envelop their prey—mostly small tree-dwelling mammals—and fatally constrict their ability to breathe. If you feel yourself being drawn in by their hypnotic beauty, you'd better snap out of it, fast.

Brazil • Amazon River

293 TAKE AN AMAZON MYSTERY TOUR

All year

Canoeing and kayaking offer the most magical ways to experience the peace and grandeur of the Amazon River. Guided tours of several nights will take you deep into the forest, where you'll feel less like a tourist and more like an adventurer, exploring this unspoiled wilderness. With an itinerary of land- and water-based activities, you'll see tarantulas, snakes, bats, vultures, caimen, and dolphins along the way.

Brazil • Amazon rain forest

294 SEE MAHOGANY IN ITS NATURAL HOME

All year

Famous around the world as a luxury hardwood for furniture and flooring, mahogany is of course also a living tree, and a majestic one at that. Big-leaf mahogany is the variety found in the Amazon, and the leaves can be 20 in (50 cm) long. Its sweet-smelling, flaky bark and delicate white flowers make these canopy-topping giants a delight to encounter up close. Sadly it remains threatened by the timber trade.

Brazil • Amazon rain forest

295 CATCH A FIRST-NIGHT FLOWER

All year

Like something straight from a fairy tale, the giant water lily grows in the shallow waters of the Amazon basin, as well as in slow-moving streams and certain lakes in Brazil. With floating leaves that grow to twice the area of a king-size bed, it can support the weight of a person or two. The flowers, which can be 16 in (40 cm) in diameter, are white the first night they open and become pink as soon as they are pollinated.

293 | *The majestic Amazon River*

Brazil • Amazon rain forest

296 SWERVE AROUND A MIGHTY NUT TREE

January to March

Wild brazil nut trees are under threat in the country with which they share a name, where it is illegal to chop one down, wherever it may be growing, be it a back garden or in the path of a road. The trees are massive and live up to 1,000 years by some reckoning, taking 125 years just to reach maturity. The nuts we eat fall in the wet season in dangerously heavy, coconut-sized clusters, so look out for falling objects!

Brazil • Amazon rain forest

297 LOOK INTO A PACU'S MOUTH

All year

Few things you'll see swimming in the Amazon are as unsettling as the pacu, a medium-sized gray fish that is a relative of the piranha. But while piranhas have razor-sharp teeth and are a genuine menace with a fierce bite, the much larger pacu is relatively benign. So what makes them so perturbing? Are they poisonous? No, they simply possess what appears to be a spookily perfect imitation of human teeth.

Brazil • Northern-central forests

298 HOLD A BUG THE SIZE OF YOUR HAND

All year

Titan beetles are not for the fainthearted. The largest measured specimen was 6.5 in (16.7 cm) in length, yet nobody has ever seen their larvae. It's believed they burrow inside wood for years, before forming a pupa and transforming into an adult beetle. Boreholes have been found that could have been formed by just such a larval titan, measuring 2 in (5 cm) across and 1 ft (30 cm) long.

299 | *The giant otter is perfectly adapted to an aquatic life*

Brazil • Amazon and Pantanal
299 SEE A GIANT OTTER FISHING
All year

Giant otters reach sizes similar to that of small humans, making these Amazonian carnivores the largest (and noisiest) of their kind. They are formidable killers of catfish and partial to crabs, turtles, snakes, and even small alligators.

Brazil • Chapada do Araripe
300 SPOT AN ARARIPE MANAKIN
All year

This critically endangered bird, with white feathers on the male's body and a neat little red "helmet" (earning it the name "little soldier" in Portuguese), now numbers fewer than 1,000 birds. Thanks to conservation efforts, however, this is rising.

Brazil • Central to southern regions;
river meadows

301 KEEP ON THE RIGHT SIDE OF A RED-LEGGED SERIEMA

All year

Found south of the Amazon basin, these long-legged, flight-shy birds run faster than a human and are fierce fighters, going in with two feet while they hover in the air. Local poultry farmers use them as guards to protect their flocks from predators.

Brazil • Throughout

303 SEE THE RECORD-BREAKING GREEN ANACONDA

All year

This snake reaches 17 ft (5.2 m) in length and 154 lb (70 kg) in weight, making it the heaviest (but not quite the longest) in the world.

Brazil • Central and northern rain forests

304 KEEP YOUR DISTANCE FROM A POISON DART FROG

All year

This frog's varied bright colors are a classic warning sign to predators, saying "stay away" loud and clear (even though some species aren't poisonous at all). The name comes from the use of their poison in native Amerindians' blow darts.

Brazil • Chapada dos Veadeiros
National Park

302 WATCH RHEAS WINDSURF

All year

The largest bird in South America is the flightless rhea, a distant relative of the ostrich and emu, which roams the continent's grasslands in flocks of 20 or so animals. The best place to see them (outside Germany, where an escaped population has gone feral) is in one of Brazil's spectacular national parks. While they don't use their wings for flight, they have developed alternative uses for them: when running in line with the wind, they hold them out and use them as sails, and when fleeing, they run in a zigzag, holding alternate wings out to steer.

Brazil • Iguaçu National Park

305 HEAR THE SNUFFLE OF A RING-TAILED COATI

All year

This relative of the raccoon looks like a cross between a ring-tailed lemur and a badger. It has a long, squidgy nose that can snuffle its way into hard-to-reach places, searching for insects or fruit to eat. It also has a long, fluffy tail that is held upright when foraging. Another trick is its ability to reverse its ankle joints to run down trees. Ring-tailed coatis are found throughout Brazil, but you will be assured a sighting at this national park.

Brazil • Amazon River

306 HEAR THE CHATTER OF PINK DOLPHINS

All year

A unique, slightly pink, species of dolphin patrols the vast Amazon River basin, its narrow but extended fins giving it great maneuverability in the rivers and swamps, where it must negotiate knotty tree roots. They communicate with whistling tones, sending messages to one another under water along the bends of rivers, pointing their podmates toward sources of food.

Brazil • Throughout

307 AVOID THE BITE OF A VAMPIRE BAT

All year, at night

There are three types of vampire bat: the hairy-legged, the leaf-nosed, and the white-winged. All share the trait unique in mammals—with the exception of humans—of feeding on blood. Vampire bats hunt in the dead of night using a combination of sonar and thermal imaging (some can "see" heat), and they will suck the blood of any large, sleeping mammal or bird.

Brazil • Ilha de Santa Catarina

308 PHOTOGRAPH THE WORLD'S SMALLEST ORCHID

September to November

Found on the island of Santa Catarina, the *Campylocentrum insulare*'s perfectly formed flowers are 0.2 in (0.5 mm) in diameter.

Brazil • Amazon and Orinoco basins

309 SEE AN ELECTRIC EEL STUN ITS PREY

All year

A brief 860-volt shock is all it takes for this creepy-looking, electricity-delivering fish to stun anything from small fish to rats into submission.

Brazil • Western Amazon basin

310 LEARN HOW A RED HOWLER MAKES A PROTEST

All year

You'll know when you've gone a step too far with the red howler monkey—it's not above throwing its poop when it feels threatened!

Brazil • Far north; rain forest canopy

311 SEE ONE OF SOUTH AMERICA'S LARGEST PRIMATES

All year

Red-faced black spider monkeys have long, gangly arms and faces the color of watermelon flesh poking out from their shaggy black fur.

312 DIVE IN AN ECOLOGICAL PARADISE
September to March

To Brazilians, the archipelago of Fernando de Noronha is a byword for paradise on Earth, a jewel in the nation's crown to which few have ever been, as only a few hundred visitors are ever allowed here at any given time (and many of those, inevitably, are wealthy international honeymooners). The 21 islands that make up this national marine park are a UNESCO World Heritage Site and a haven for sea turtles; spinner and spotted dolphins; humpback, pilot, and melon-headed whales; albatrosses; and hundreds of other species on land and sea, many unique to these islands. Sadly the Portuguese nobleman after whom the islands were named in 1504 never even got to make a visit himself.

Brazil • Eastern rain forests
313 LOOK OUT FOR A LION TAMARIN
All year

These little guys share their namesake's golden mane but at 12 in (30 cm) tall, not its mighty roar. They are endangered, but conservation efforts are ongoing.

Brazil • Ilhéus
314 SEE SLOTHS SWIMMING
All year

In Ilhéus, an oasis for these friendly faced emblems of apathy takes in rescued and donated animals from across the country.

Brazil • Pantanal
315 MARVEL AT PIRANHAS IN A FRENZY
All year

Drop some raw meat in the river and you'll see the water come alive with the furious motion of these voracious fish in a feeding frenzy.

Brazil • Pantanal
316 CATCH A HYACINTH MACAW
July to December

The world's longest parrot—head to tail, 3 ft (1 m)—is very rare, but a ravishing deep blue charmer if you do spot one in this paradise for bird-watchers.

Brazil • Pantanal
317 SEE AN ANTEATER SNIFF OUT ANTS
All year

Giant anteaters are wonderful to watch and listen to as they go about the extraordinary business of sucking up insects. They can eat up to 30,000 ants a day.

Brazil • Pantanal
318 WATCH HERDS OF GIANT RODENTS
All year

The capybara—sheep-sized and the largest of all rodents—spends its time in and out of rivers and streams, and can live in groups of up to 100 members.

Brazil • Rio de Janiero
319 SEE CAPUCHIN MONKEYS IN A CITY
All year

Marauding gangs of these little monkeys cause mischief across the city, but you can surely forgive the occasional fruit theft for the entertainment they give.

Brazil • Southeastern region
320 SEE MORE THAN YOU'D EXPECT OF THE GLASS FROG
All year

Green on top and transparent underneath, the internal organs of this tiny amphibian—including the heart, liver, and intestinal tract—are visible through its skin, which reflects light only at infrared wavelengths. There are about 50 species, of varying sizes and distributions, but all are defined by this unusual physical trait.

Bolivia • La Paz

321 SEE POTATOES GROW BY LAKE TITICACA

All year

Imagine how the early Amerindian settlers would have felt as they stumbled on the versatile and sustaining potato plant for the first time. Did they bake it, boil it, or fry it? This tuber, brought back by Spanish explorers, and now cultivated and enjoyed in every corner of the world, still grows wild high in the Andes, in the countryside where it was first found.

Bolivia • Beni

322 SEE 12 SPECIES OF MACAW IN ONE PLACE

June

Bolivia has the most species of macaw of any country—12 in total, including the blue-throated and red-fronted macaws, which are only found in this landlocked nation, and are faced with extinction. Specially organized tours will take you through nature reserves to spot as many of these colorful and talkative birds as you can, and also to take in a wealth of other wildlife.

Bolivia • Manique River

323 SPOT SOME TWISTED MONKEY TAILS

All year

The white-eared, or Bolivian, titi monkey has a charming habit. Groups of these fluffy, small-faced gray monkeys huddle together on branches in the evenings and, as they snooze, their tails entwine like the strands in a rope, quietly cementing the bonds of family and friendship within the group, without a word ever being spoken among them.

321 | *Tending potatoes by Lake Titicaca*

Bolivia • Throughout

324 SEE CACTI IN BLOOM

September to October

From the wetlands in the east to the dry, rugged Andes in the west, you'll find cacti thriving all across Bolivia, but they are most abundant on the hills and mountains of the west, and in particular around Lake Titicaca, 12,500 ft (3,800 m) up. Tours run all through the winter dry season, which take hikers through the deserts and grasslands to enjoy the rich and diverse plant and animal life to be found there. But go in the spring, and the stern, leafless cacti begin to turn festive. Flowers of every color emerge from the tips of the stems, with each species delivering its own unique bloom.

At ground level look out for the rebutia, a small globe-shaped cactus that produces many colors of flowers, creating a bouquet bigger than the body of the cactus itself. Or look higher and see San Pedro cacti, which can grow to be 40 ft (12.2 m) tall, and are among many species with psychoactive properties harnessed in traditional medicine. Their beautiful white flowers only open at night and can be 9 in (23 cm) long and 8 in (20 cm) in diameter.

Bolivia • Throughout

325 CLIMB HIGH TO SEE A LONELY PALM TREE

All year

On the steep rocky slopes of the Bolivian Andes, one close relative of the coconut palm has managed to thrive. The *Parajubaea torallyi*, or Bolivian mountain coconut, is found at altitudes of up to 11,200 ft (3,400 m) and is incredibly tolerant of a cool, dry climate, surviving temperatures well below zero. These slender, isolated trees protrude from the landscape, stretching up to 79 ft (24 m) tall. Locals eat the fruit of the wild trees, which can also be found in markets.

326 | The vicuña's fur protects it in the high alpine areas of the Andes

Bolivia • National Wildlife Ulla Ulla Reserve

326 CELEBRATE THE RETURN OF THE VICUÑA

All year

In 1974, only about 6,000 of these wild ancestors of the domestic alpaca remained, mostly due to hunting. Today the story is very different, with over 350,000 individuals now roaming the grassy plains of the Andes. In Incan culture, it was illegal for anyone but royalty to wear garments made from the wool of the vicuña, which is exceptionally fine. It fetches a high price today; the animals must be caught in the wild, shorn, and released. This practice has been key to their survival, since the substantial sums raised by the sale of the wool has been put back into efforts to sustain the populations of these gentle creatures.

Bolivia • Throughout

327 SEE THE STORY OF LIFE IN A SNAKE'S SPURS

All year

Common tree boas, like all the members of the boa family, betray the evidence of an evolutionary link to other lizards in the form of "spurs" protruding from the rear of their bodies on either side. These are actually the remnants of back legs, and they are connected to pelvic bones buried deep in their thick muscles. Try not to get too close—they will spray you with a skunk-like stink.

Chile • Atacama Desert

328 ADMIRE THE DESERT IN FLOWER

Every five to seven years

This desert is one of the driest places on Earth, so it may come as a surprise, if you find yourself there following one of its rare drenchings, to see it suddenly carpeted with wildflowers. The seeds of over 200 species of plant are buried in the dry earth at any given time, simply waiting for the rains to come, when they will germinate then flower, then sink back into the earth to wait for the process to begin again.

Chile • Chiloé Island

329 SEE A CHILOÉ FOX ON ITS ISLAND HOME

All year

With only a few hundred remaining, mostly on the island of Chiloé, this small canine is critically endangered. Sometimes known as Darwin's fox, it is, in fact, a closer relative of the wolf, but since it was first identified by the great Charles Darwin, few have bothered to argue the point. It is small and dark gray, lives in forests, and feeds on just about anything it can find.

332 | *A Juan Fernández seal pup at rest on the rocks*

Chile • Juan Fernández Islands
330 LEARN ABOUT A FUR SEAL
November to December

Not much is known about these solitary seals, who spread out around the Pacific waters off mainland Chile and return to the Juan Fernández Islands at intervals to mate and give birth to their young. They are among the smallest seals in the world, but are relatively stocky. The males are black and larger than the light brown females, but both reach the size of an average human.

In the 1960s these seals had been hunted almost to extinction for their fur, with only a few hundred remaining. Nowadays, numbers are much healthier—up to an estimated 32,000 around the start of the twenty-first century.

Chile • Easter Island
332 FOLLOW UNDERWATER DISCOVERIES AS THEY'RE MADE
All year

The kiwa crab was only discovered in 2005, and it was dubbed the "yeti crab" on account of its shaggy covering of long filaments of yellow bacteria. The bacteria are actually its food, and it cultivates them by wafting the filaments in front of thermal vents. You will need to hitch a ride on a research sub to see one though, as they live 7,200 ft (2,200 m) down.

Chile • Juan Fernández Islands
331 ADMIRE THE JUAN FERNÁNDEZ FIRECROWN
All year

On Isla Róbinson Crusoe, second largest of the three islands that make up the remote Juan Fernández archipelago, and erstwhile home of Alexander Selkirk, the inspiration for the famous fictional castaway, you'll find a small hummingbird that exists nowhere else in the world. The two sexes are the most unalike of all hummingbirds: the males are red, and the females, bright green.

Chile • Atacama Desert
333 SEE GRACE IN A DESERT
All year

The Andean avocet is an incredibly graceful wading bird that can be found in the lakes that lie at the fringes of the world's driest desert.

Chile • Tierra del Fuego
334 LOCATE KING PENGUINS IN PATAGONIA
All year

This Patagonian island hosts the only American breeding colony of these regal seabirds and is the most accessible place to see them in the wild.

Chile • Offshore islands

335 FEEL THE LOVE WITH MACARONI PENGUINS

October

In eighteenth-century speak, a "macaroni" was someone who was flamboyant when it came to accessorizing their attire. These crested birds, with yellow feathers on the tops of their brows, are guilty as charged. (The feather-capped Yankee Doodle was another offender.) They form pairs that mate for life, reuniting each year on crowded breeding colonies after 11 months at sea. It's a wonder of nature they can always seem to find each other.

Chile • Southern region; Chiloé Island

336 DISCOVER THE WORLD'S SMALLEST DEER

November to January

It isn't all about size when it comes to spotting deer. The dwarfish pudu has a fairy-tale air to it, making an encounter with these terrier-sized forest creatures all the more magical. They are solitary animals that shelter in dense underbrush and bamboo thickets, and only interact with one other to mate. If you see one, it may be at twilight, when they come out to feed. A warning: their fawns are born in late spring and are unbelievably cute.

Chile • Valdivian temperate forests

337 TRACK DOWN CHILE'S NATIONAL FLOWER

December to April

The *copihue*, or Chilean bellflower, grows in the Chilean south. It is very rare and unique to one small area of this long country. Still, its delicate, drooping pink petals, shaped just like bells, have earned it renown and the status of national flower. This climber can reach heights of 33 ft (10 m) when attached to a suitable tree or shrub and takes its Latin name, *Lapageria rosea*, from Napoléon's wife, Marie-Joseph Rose de Tascher de la Pagerie.

Chile • Tarpaca

338 SEE THE WORLD'S SIX FLAMINGO SPECIES, STARTING WITH THE CHILEAN

December to April

We are fortunate to share our planet with six distinct species of flamingo, three of which can be found in Chile: the Chilean, Andean, and St. James. (For the greater, lesser, and American flamingos, you'll have to keep trekking.) The Chilean can be identified by its long gray legs with pink patches over the knees. It builds its nest out of mud in the shape of a pillar, and lays just one egg, which the parents take turns to incubate.

Chile • Andean slopes
339 ENTER A FOREST OF MONKEY PUZZLE TREES
All year

Considered a "living fossil" becuse of its ancient evolutionary lineage, the monkey puzzle tree does look like it has emerged from some other world. Tall and perfectly round, with "reptilian" branches made of thick, spiky, spiraling evergreen leaves, you may have seen one in a garden but the impact of these curiosities is multiplied when you see them en masse in the wild.

Chile • Southern and central regions; Chiloé Island
340 HUNT FOR A MOUNTAIN MONKEY
October to May, at night

This misnamed miniature marsupial is, in fact, not a monkey at all, and you might mistake it for a mouse, but the *monito del monte* (which mates monogamously and munches mistletoe in summer) is much more of a possum. Look out for them hiding in thickets of bamboo in the forests of the southern Andes, where these curious rascals come out at night to catch insects.

339 | *The primeval vista of a monkey puzzle forest*

Chile • Los Flamencos National Reserve

341 WATCH FLAMINGOS THROW SHAPES

April to May

What does a female flamingo look for in a partner? It's all in the complexity of the dance moves, apparently. Studies have shown that male flamingos possess a battery of 136 moves that they can reach for in their efforts to attract a lady (a statistic that is as great a credit to the birds as it is to the researchers who counted them), and that the more moves the male can pull off in a short space of time, the more likely it is to bag a mate. They will stay together for the duration of the mating season, then the male returns again the following year to entice a new partner.

Chile • Savanna and woodlands

342 AVOID THE BREATH OF THE CRAB-EATING FOX

All year

This dark-furred distant relative of domestic dogs and wolves (there are, in fact, no true foxes in South America) is an omnivore, but it lives on a diet of crabs and other crustaceans in the wet season. It digs the crabs out from the mudflats. Some locals keep them as pets.

Chile • Throughout

343 SEE A STUNNING BLACK-NECKED SWAN

October to March

So stark is the contrast between the pure white feathers on the body of the largest waterfowl in South America and the deep black of its neck, it looks like it has plunged its head into a puddle of oil. Chile is thought to be home to the largest population of these birds.

Chile • Atacama Desert

344 FIND A MOUNTAIN VISCACHA

All year

In the barren heat of the Atacama Desert, keep an eye out for this red-brown rabbit-eared rodent sunbathing among the rocks that will provide it cover if a mountain cat comes near. Food here is far from plentiful, but it gets what it needs from grass, moss, and lichens.

341 | *St. James's flamingoes—one of three species in Chile*

Argentina • Low-lying shrubland
345 CATCH A PATAGONIAN MARA'S MANY WAYS OF MOVING
All year

Imagine the head of a rabbit on the body of a deer, and you'll have a picture of this hoofed rodent. As the situation dictates, a mara may move by walking, hopping like a rabbit, galloping like a horse, or stotting— bouncing on all four legs at once.

346 | *Sea lion pups are easy prey for an orca*

Argentina • Punta Norte

346 WATCH ORCAS HUNT SEA LIONS

March to April

Killer whales need to consume about 175 lb (80 kg) of meat every day to sustain themselves, so a sea lion pup or two makes a tasty proposition. To anyone who has only seen these majestic animals performing in captivity, watching them hunt in their wild habitat is a thrilling revelation, and there are few better locations than this nature reserve on the Valdes Peninsula. Orcas, to give them their proper name, are present in this area all year round, but sightings are more common during a brief period in the spring, a few months after the unfortunate sea lion pups are born.

Argentina • Patagonia

347 SEE FOUR SPECIES OF AMERICAN PENGUIN

December to January

Magellanic, gentoo, rockhopper, or macaroni—with varying degrees of effort, you can catch a glimpse of all four of these species of penguin in colonies on the islands of Patagonia. Magellanics can be seen at rookeries in Punta Tombo and Puerto San Julián, where more than a million come to breed. Gentoos can be seen at Ushuaia via organized tours, some of which will take you ashore. For the rockhoppers and macaronis, however, you're on your own; you'll need some serious commitment to reach their isolated colonies.

348 | *The cougar is a solitary and stealthy survivor*

Argentina • San Guillermo National Park
348 MAKE A DATE WITH A COUGAR
All year

In this national park in San Juan province, cougars pick off vicuñas from their herds at night, earning their reputation for meanness and stealth. They're also known as "mountain lions," and though they can growl, hiss, and scream, a cougar doesn't have the vocal chords to roar. You might know them as "pumas" or "panthers" or one of many other names. In fact, this species holds the record for having the greatest number of common names: around 40 of them. This is testament to how this species has spread out and adapted to many varied habitats across both American continents.

Argentina • Throughout
349 IDENTIFY A LLAMA, ALPACA, GUANACO, AND VICUÑA
All year

These four South American animals are all classed as camelids—relatives of the camel and dromedary found in the deserts of Africa and Asia. Guanacos and vicuñas are the wild varieties. The former are found in the south of the continent, including the scorching Atacama Desert; the latter are smaller and more delicate and are found farther north, in the central Andes. Llamas are a domesticated form of guanacos and alpacas, a domesticated vicuña. Both are widely farmed for wool and meat. Of all the species, llamas are by far the largest.

Argentina • Northwestern mountains
350 CUDDLE THE WORLD'S SOFTEST ANIMAL
All year

A chinchilla has the densest fur of any land animal, so it feels like velvet to touch. Popular as pets, they have also inevitably been hunted extensively for their fur. By 1953, reports of their extinction turned out to be exaggerated, but they remain endangered.

Argentina • Throughout
351 SPOT A COYPU WHERE THEIR STORY BEGAN
All year

Coypu are found invading river systems around the world, sometimes causing hysteria about "giant rats" (they're not—they're supposed to be that size), but they are native to South America, and they are, in fact, playful, charming creatures.

Argentina • The puna
352 DO A DOUBLE-TAKE AT THE EYE OF A MORENO'S GROUND DOVE
All year

This dove, native to Argentina's puna grasslands, has some very peculiar markings. Surrounding its small black eye is a bald orange oval, just the shape of a human eye. You'll have to look again to see what's really going on.

Argentina • Northeastern grasslands
353 SEE THE MIGHTY MANED WOLF
All year

The tallest wild dog on the continent is a fierce and formidable predator, with long legs adapted to stalking through tall grasses, and a taste for fruit and meat. It has a black mane of longer hair around the scruff of its neck, which can stand on end to enlarge its appearance when threatened.

Argentina • Northern and central forests
354 SEE THE HOME OF AN OVENBIRD
August to December

Rather than build a nest from twigs that might leave them open to attack, red ovenbirds have instead settled on clay as a preferred building material, building up nests protected on all sides, like an igloo, or the centerpiece of a very tiny pizzeria.

Argentina • Mendoza; Rio Negro; Buenos Aires
355 SPOT THE COOLEST ARMADILLO
All year, at night

The pink fairy armadillo has a bullet-shaped body, with a pinkish shell covering the upper half. You'll be lucky to spot one even in their native habitat: they keep cool in the desert by burrowing, and only ever come out at night.

South Georgia • Salisbury Plain

356 SEE A PENGUIN INCUBATE
AN EGG ON ITS FEET

November to December

Some 60,000 king penguins come to Salisbury
Plain on South Georgia to breed every year. The
females lay a single pear-shaped egg, which they
and their mates take turns to incubate, taking on
the crucial task for a week or two at a time,
keeping it up for around 55 days in total until
the eggs hatch.

CHAPTER THREE

EUROPE

Greenland • Davis Strait
357 SEE A MIGHTY NARWHAL TUSK
October to March

Narwhals are a type of whale—close relatives of
the beluga, but with one unmissable feature that
distinguishes them: incredibly long spiraled tusks,
present on all males and some females. These
tusks are, in fact, fantastically extended canine
teeth, and they keep growing all the way through
an animal's life, reaching up to 10 ft (3 m) in length
and 22 lb (10 kg) in weight. Centuries of debate
have surrounded the actual purpose of these tusks,
but recent drone footage has shown at least some
narwhals use them to stun fish with a rapid blow
before eating them. About one in 500 narwhal
males is a two-tusker, but the last time a two-tusked
female was recorded was way back in 1684.

Greenland • Northeast Greenland National Park
358 SPOT A WOLF IN THE SNOW
April to June

Like the Arctic wolf in Canada, the Greenland wolf
is a white-furred subspecies of the same wolves
found farther south. Their camouflage makes them
hard to spot and even harder to count. They feed
on caribou—deer many times their size—so their
disguise comes in handy.

357 | Narwhals—the "unicorns of the sea"

359 LISTEN TO THE DIN OF WALRUSES

April to June

While the walrus is recognizably a cousin of the seal and the sea lion, there is no mistaking it for its svelter counterparts. Only the equally monstrous elephant seal grows to a similar size, with adult male walruses coming in at 2 tons—heavier than a hippo and twice the size of the largest horse. You'll be familiar with their formidable appearance, with tusks and whiskers. Less familiar but equally memorable—especially when you hear them in person—are the many sounds they make, both above and below water: snorts, roars, whistles, grunts, barks, clicks, and rasps. They are noisier than any similar species, and when they come together, as they often do in their twice-yearly migrations, the din is almost fearsome.

Once hunted extensively for their tusks, which were valued alongside elephant ivory, they are now protected, and their numbers have increased. Although the Pacific boasts the largest populations, in the seas around Greenland, you will still see many thousands of these powerful sockfuls of blubber and muscle foraging for shrimp, crabs, and clams.

Greenland • Thule

360 CATCH A SUMMER FESTIVAL OF AUKS

May to September

In the height of summer the population of little auks in the Thule area reaches some 30 to 50 million. The skies become dappled with swarms of the squat black birds, and the barren earth becomes so well fertilized by their droppings that grasses begin to grow, attracting musk-oxen and hares.

Iceland • Hornstrandir Nature Reserve

361 WATCH A FOX CURL INTO A BALL

November to February

Arctic foxes don't even start to shiver until it's colder than you'll find anywhere else on Earth, −94°F (−70°C), thanks to their thick fur, furry feet, and ability to roll into a perfect ball. They are white in winter and brown in summer, when they shed a third of their body weight in fat.

Iceland • Lake Myvatn

362 SEE THE WORLD'S BIGGEST FALCON

All year

Myvatn offers a breathtaking backdrop to the sight of a majestic gyrfalcon. Females are larger and more fearsome than males, with wings spanning over 5 ft (1.5 m) when outstretched. They have virtually no natural predators and are entirely fearless, with reports of them even attacking brown bears.

Iceland • Húsavík

363 AVOID A MINKE WHALE'S BREATH

March to December

You won't appreciate the smell of a "stinky minke"—its breath reeks of the half-digested krill slowly fermenting in its belly. The odor can be detected from a boat, which is the one downside of observing these small and streamlined whales up close. They're noisy, too, so if you don't smell them, you will hear them.

Iceland • Thjorsarver

364 GO ON A WILD GOOSE CHASE

May to September

Pink-footed geese spend their summers in this protected wetland nature reserve in the central highlands of Iceland, where the birds establish huge breeding sites containing tens of thousands of pairs. During migration, large groups of loud honking geese can be almost deafening as they pass overhead.

Iceland • Laxárdalur Valley

365 VIEW TROUT IN CRYSTAL WATERS

May to August

Flashes of energetic brown trout in the crystal clear waters of Iceland quicken the heart of nature lovers and anglers alike. The species has been introduced to rivers and lakes around the world, but here, where the waters of Lake Myvatn flow into the Laxárdalur Valley, it is a bona fide native.

Iceland • Snaefellsnes Peninsula
366 SEE KITTIWAKES ON A CLIFF
All year

Small black-legged kittiwakes are seabirds that
perch high on basalt cliffs here, surveying the
drama of Iceland's rugged volcanic coastline.
They make their nests and rear their young on
these precarious rocks, from which they launch
themselves into the waves in search of fish. It's
an invigorating place for intrepid tourists to visit,
with views of the sea, and many volcanoes and
beaches on offer in the area. The name of these
birds comes from their call—a raucous and gutsy
kittee-wa-aaake!

Iceland • Skjálfandi Bay
367 WITNESS PIRACY ON THE HIGH SEAS
April to September

The Arctic skua's best-known trait might also
be its least endearing. These gray-black seabirds
(also known as "jaegers") are renowned fish thieves,
aggressively approaching other birds like seagulls,
puffins, fulmars, and terns and stealing their
hard-earned food. As well as the Arctic skua, the
larger great skua—also common in Iceland—will
attack larger birds, including the great black-backed
gull. Skuas may not be pretty, but they are thrilling
to watch, and who doesn't like to root for a baddie?

366 | *Kittiwakes in their precarious cliff home*

Northern Ireland • Ballynahone Bog
368 BE AWED BY A HERON'S NEST
All year

In the birch woodland surrounding this raised bog where herons come to feed, you'll find nesting spots where generations of birds have come to construct huge, scraggly, precarious bundles of sticks and twigs amid the treetops.

Scotland • Solway Firth
369 SEE AN ANCIENT SHRIMP
All year

Tiny tadpole shrimps, the oldest living animal species—220 million years and still going strong—can be found swimming in quiet temporary pools. Their eggs can lie undisturbed for up to 27 years before hatching when it's wet.

Scotland • Highlands
370 SPOT A PTARMIGAN IN BOTH OF ITS COLORS
All year

Ptarmigans are a type of grouse that have adapted to snowy wilds like the Scottish Highlands. Their plumage is seasonally camouflaged: snow white in winter and gray brown in summer. With few predators to share their habitat with, these birds are often friendly and approachable.

Scotland • Falls of Shin
371 SEE SALMON LEAP UP A RIVER
October to November

No image is quite as iconic of this unique landscape as that of scores of salmon leaping heroically up mountain streams to spawn.

370 | *A ptarmigan blends into the winter snow*

372 | *Red deer stags lock horns in the Scottish Highlands*

Scotland • Highlands
372 WATCH RUTTING DEER STAGS
October

Around 400,000 red deer live wild in Scotland's Highlands and islands. Every fall, the males face off violently, for the chance to impress a female. Their weapons are their antlers, which begin growing in spring ready for the season to come. Testosterone causes the growth, and it reaches a peak at the beginning of mating season, generating maximum aggression. Watching from a safe vantage point, it's perfectly possible to see every stage of the drama unfolding as two males size each other up, then engage in a cacophonous bout from which one clear victor will eventually emerge—and take the prize. By winter their antlers will be discarded, their hormones will have settled, and all animosity will be forgotten.

Wales • Anglesey
373 SEE A SQUIRREL'S EAR TUFTS
All year

Red squirrels are revered in the British Isles to the same extent that gray squirrels can be loathed. The grays—foreign invaders from North America—began their ascendancy in the 1870s when they were first introduced, and now outnumber their rust-brown cousins by a factor of 250:1, so the Brits can be forgiven for being a little peeved. On the Welsh island of Anglesey, however, grays have recently been eradicated in a deliberate effort to boost numbers of the native reds that otherwise struggle to compete for food. Their numbers have boomed in this rural idyll, so it's worth the trip. Grays are more intelligent, better at finding food, and more resistant to disease, but the reds are indisputably cuter.

Wales • Forest ponds
374 SPY A GREAT CRESTED NEWT IN A POND
April to September

The largest newt in Europe is strictly protected by UK laws, making it illegal to capture or harm one of these warty but adorable little amphibians.

Wales • Red Kite Feeding Station
375 SEE A TRIUMPH OF CONSERVATION
All year

Red kites had been virtually eliminated from South Wales by the start of the twentieth century, mostly due to fears these scavengers would rob precious food and livestock from farms. Only a handful of pairs remained, but in recent years, breeding pairs have been brought in from England, Scotland, and Scandinavia, and numbers are well up in the hundreds. Visitors to this center in Llanddeusant can take their seats in the bird blinds at the same time every day to see these majestic birds competing for the meat left out for them.

375 | *Red kites are on the rise in Wales*

376 | *A basking shark off the Cornish coast*

England • Cornwall
376 BASK WITH A BASKING SHARK
May to September

The largest animals in Britain are as big as an iconic double-decker bus and twice the size of the great whites made famous in *Jaws*. Basking sharks are docile creatures, however—harmless to humans and quite unfazed as they approach divers and swimmers along the coasts in the warmer months of the year.

England • Northumberland
377 SEE THE WORLD'S BEST-TRAVELED BIRD
April to September

A tiny 4 oz (100 g) Arctic tern that was tagged at the Farne Islands nature reserve holds the record for the longest recorded migration of any bird: a 57,000 mile (91,000 km) round trip to the Antarctic and back. Thousands arrive to nest along the coast here before leaving in September for warmer shores.

England • London
378 SPOT PARAKEETS IN A CAPITAL CITY
All year

Nobody quite knows how these exotic green-feathered central African birds ended up thriving in great flocks in London's suburban parks, but they are an incredible sight. One theory even credits rock star Jimi Hendrix for releasing a breeding pair of them back in the 1960s, thereby establishing a feral population.

England • London
379 TAKE CHILDREN MINIBEAST HUNTING
April

It's easy to forget that there is a miniature world of invertebrates lurking right in our midst, filled with vibrant and diverse animal populations to rival any safari park. Lift a rock in a garden or public park and this world is yours to explore.

If you want to explore it in more depth, you and your family can be guided by experts well versed in the intricacies of this beastly and fascinating other world. At the London Wildlife Trust's Centre for Wildlife Gardening, for example, to celebrate the first day of spring, children can take part in an outdoor learning session that will open their minds to the array of creatures lurking in the undergrowth. Elsewhere in the city, such as the green expanses of its many parks, little explorers need only seek out a space, bring along a magnifying glass, and get ready to get their hands dirty. Specialist kits containing tweezers, brushes, collecting jars, and traps make great gifts. Paired with a good guidebook they might just inspire in a child a lifelong love of nature.

England • Throughout
380 RECOGNIZE GARDEN BIRDS BY THEIR SONGS
All year

British gardens are visited regularly by dozens of bird species, and while it's one thing to identify them all by sight, you will develop a whole new appreciation for them when you learn to listen closely to their distinctive individual songs. Comprehensive guides are available online.

379 | *Exploring the undergrowth in one of London's many green spaces*

England • The New Forest

381 SEE PONIES IN THE WILD

All year

A wild population of ponies (currently around 4,500) have been living in the New Forest, a national park area on England's south coast, since they were introduced in 1066 by King William the Conqueror. Along with pigs (that also vacuum up acorns, which are poisonous to other grazers) and cattle, they are responsible for maintaining the wild rolling landscape by feeding constantly on grass and herbs, earning them the moniker "the architects of the forest."

England • Throughout

382 SURVEY A COUNTRY'S BIRDLIFE

January

The Big Garden Birdwatch is the world's largest garden wildlife survey, orchestrated by the Royal Society for the Protection of Birds since 1979, but carried out by regular members of the public. Taking part couldn't be easier: you simply need to sit in a garden for an hour and count how many birds of each species you see. With half a million people taking part regularly, and decades of accumulated data, the results are an invaluable resource for conservationists.

381 | *A New Forest pony grazes on ancient grounds*

England • Dorset
383 COUNT BUMBLEBEES
June to August

The Bumblebee Conservation Trust organizes the BeeWalk, a monitoring scheme that's also a great way to help conserve this vital pollinator while spending time in the outdoors and generally feeling good about yourself. Volunteers walk the same route each month and count the bees they find.

England • Wicken Fen Nature Reserve
384 SEE A STUNNING METAMORPHOSIS
June to August

At the Dragonfly Centre on Wicken Fen, where 22 species of these beautiful, elegant, acrobatic insects can be spotted, it's fascinating to find out about the two years some species spend underwater living as nymphs before they emerge transformed for a few brief weeks in summer.

England • Throughout

385 RECONSIDER THE APPEAL OF WEASELS

All year

Britain's smallest carnivore gets a bad press, no thanks to *The Wind in the Willows*. See them in woods, grassland, hedgerows, heaths, and moors and learn to appreciate them again.

England • English Channel

386 SEE A FISH THAT SUCKLES ITS YOUNG

December to February

The European eelpout's young suckle while still inside the mother—the larvae suck nutritious fluid from the walls of her ovaries, and then emerge as grown fish.

England • Slimbridge Wetland Centre

387 WATCH A DUCK WITH ITS TAIL IN THE AIR

All year

Many freshwater ducks have a curious habit of "dabbling"— pointing their rear ends skyward. They are, in fact, feeding on plants just below the water level.

England • Southern coast

388 WATCH A HERMIT CRAB MOVE HOUSE

All year

Many species of hermit crab can be found in rock pools around the coasts of England. The most common, *Pagurus bernhardus*, is also the largest, growing to 6 in (15 cm) across. Famously they do not possess shells of their own so instead have to rely on the discarded shells of other creatures that they find (and often jealously fight over) in their travels. Their soft bodies allow them to adapt to a range of different homes, and no two ever look quite the same.

England • Throughout

389 ADMIRE (BUT DON'T TOUCH) BIRD EGGS

All year

Blackbird eggs are an exotic bright blue, a gem to spot in an English garden.

Norway • Lovund

390 WATCH PUFFINS HATCH

April

On April 14 every year, local people flock to see hundreds of thousands of hatchlings, "the day the puffins come."

Norway • Gjesvaerstappan Islands

391 SEE THREE MILLION BIRDS ON ONE TRIP

June to September

Almost one million puffins— in addition to hundreds of thousands of cormorants, northern fulmars, kittiwakes, guillemots, and gannets— occupy the remote cliffs on a few small islands off one of the most northern points in mainland Norway. Take a specially chartered boat on a unique bird safari and see them in their multitudes during nesting season. Hot drinks and warm coats are provided!

Norway • Svalbard

392 SPOT A POLAR BEAR IN THE MIDNIGHT SUN

May to September

Witness the midnight sun shine on the otherworldly polar landscape of this remote island as you join a boat trip to head out in search of polar bears. Some voyages see 20 or more individual animals, often surfing on icebergs, watching you watching them. Hunting of these beautiful animals was outlawed in 1973, when only 1,000 animals remained on the island, and their numbers have been slowly growing ever since.

Norway • Andenes

393 SEE THE WORLD'S BIGGEST PREDATOR

June to August

Weighing in at over 56 tons (50 tonnes), a sperm whale is the undisputed heavyweight champion of the sea. Whale watching takes place all year here, but your best chance is in summer when they follow the herring north to colder waters.

Norway • Svalbard

394 ADMIRE THE BEAUTY OF THE EIDER

May to September

Renowned for their soft and highly insulating feathers, which are harvested from their nests after the ducks themselves have left them, the eider is a large sea duck, identifiable by the wedge-like shape of its bill and its stocky neck.

395 WITNESS A STARLING MURMURATION

March, April, September, and October, at night

In fall and spring, starlings perform one of the most astonishing rituals in the natural world every night before sunset, around the marshes of Jutland—a murmuration, or black sun (*sort sol* in Danish). While these individual birds may be small, their aerial ballets are mighty—hundreds of thousands of birds moving as if they were mere components of a single massive organism. Theories differ as to why they do it; it is no better understood than the human habit of dreaming. It surely confuses and wards off predators, important for these traveling birds, who are merely passing through on their migratory routes, but some hypothesize that they also communicate and share information through their movements.

396 SNAP AN OYSTERCATCHER'S BILL

March to September

The Eurasian oystercatcher is the national bird of this small, self-governed Danish archipelago. The bird is a charmer, with black-and-white plumage and a long red-orange bill. It protects its nest from predators so effectively that smaller bird species often move in beside it as a safety measure.

395 | *Thousands of starlings take to the sky at sunset*

Denmark • Forests
397 BE TAKEN ABACK BY A GIANT ANTHILL
All year

If you go down in the woods today . . . you might just come across a red wood ant nest: an unruly, domed pile of twigs that may be as tall as a single-story building. Intriguingly studies have found that the nests are eight times more likely to be found next to tectonic fault lines, but nobody is quite sure why.

Sweden • Gällivare
398 FIND OUT IF LEMMINGS LIVE UP TO THEIR REPUTATION
May to July

Relatives of hamsters and gerbils, lemmings are small furry subnivean (under snow) rodents. Their populations can boom suddenly in good years, and the resulting hordes will migrate en masse, coming down mountains and sometimes into the sea. But they don't jump off cliffs with suicide in mind: they can actually swim.

Sweden • Stockholm
399 SEE A BEAVER BUILD A DAM
All year

Once hunted locally to extinction, Eurasian beavers were reintroduced to Sweden and they now number 130,000. The dams they build are a marvel of geo-engineering.

Sweden • Sörmland
400 APPRECIATE THE POWER OF A STAG BEETLE
June

Europe's largest nonflying insect is also one of its most powerful. Just like deer, they use their "antlers" (mandibles) to fight over mates.

Sweden • Skane
401 DISCOVER SOMETHING PRICKLY YET SWEET
April to October

Hedgehog numbers are in decline around Europe as a result of loss of habitat. Famous for their spikes, they're just as noteworthy for their smiles.

Sweden • Västra Götaland
402 LET A SLEEPING DORMOUSE LIE
October to May

These rare hazelnut-brown creatures hibernate most of the year in hedges and shrubs. Don't disturb them; they'll come out when the sun is shining and there's food to eat again.

403 | *Catching the northern lights on a Finnish ski safari*

Finland • Lapland
403 GO ON A SNOW SAFARI
December to February

Cross-country skiing through the forests of Lapland is a tough proposition to resist. Add in the possibility of spotting truly memorable wildlife, and most people will be sold. Lynx, mountain hares, arctic foxes, snow grouse, and wolves and wolverines are all on offer in this snowy, unspoiled habitat of dense pine forests and frigid tundra. And if you've got children in tow, you can also press onward to catch up with one of Lapland's most famous residents, for this is where most Europeans consider to be the home of Santa Claus, and many attractions exist to capitalize on his good work.

Finland • Lapland
404 SEE REINDEER IN LAPLAND
October to March

A trip through the snow on a reindeer-drawn sled is one of the quintessential experiences you can have in this northern extremity of Finland. Reindeer in this part of the world are seldom found in the wild. They have been farmed here for centuries.

Portugal • Alentejo

405 VISIT THE HOME OF CORK

All year

Portugal is the world's largest exporter of natural cork: the bark of the cork oak tree. Until synthetic alternatives were introduced, half the world's wine corks came from here. Harvesting doesn't harm the trees, which are illegal to cut down, and the thick, spongy bark grows back in five to seven years.

Portugal • Castro Verde plains

406 WATCH A COLLECTIVE MATING DANCE

February to June

These grasslands are home to many species of bird, including the telescope-necked little bustard, which is bigger than the name suggests—around 15 in (40 cm) long. Flamboyant group displays include stamping and leaping.

Portugal • Azores

407 SURVEY WHALES AND DOLPHINS

Specific expedition dates

Biosphere Expeditions organizes scientist-led sea expeditions in which you can take part in vital research while experiencing the wonders of these sea mammals.

Portugal • Azores

408 BLINK AND MISS A MAKO

July to September

Mako sharks can reach speeds of around 60 mph (97 kmh); in fact, they can swim so fast that they can even propel themselves out of the water and into boats.

Gibraltar • Throughout

409 DISCOVER EUROPE'S ONLY WILD MONKEYS

All year

The numbers of Barbary macaques are in decline in their native North Africa, but just across the sea in Gibraltar, the population is thriving in city and country alike. The 300 or so monkeys, whose origins are ancient and unknown, have become one of the territory's top tourist attractions.

Spain • Alquézar

410 OBSERVE WALLCREEPERS

All year

The enigmatic wallcreeper is a small bird with exquisite blue-gray plumage and even more fantastic crimson wings, which are only really seen in their full glory when it takes flight. Its name comes from its ability to cling to vertical rockfaces, where it feeds on insects and often makes nests in small cracks and crevices.

405 | *The bark of a cork oak can be harvested repeatedly*

Spain • Doñana National Park
411 SEE AN IBERIAN LYNX BEFORE IT'S TOO LATE
All year

This medium-sized spotted wildcat has had its brushes with extinction. Numbers dipped as low as 100 individuals at the turn of the twentieth century, dragged down by declines in rabbit population (its main food). While numbers are currently up, they are found only in isolated pockets in the south of the country.

Spain • Extremadura
412 PROTECT CRANES
October to February

Every winter 70,000 cranes arrive in southwest Spain, drawn to its steppes and oak groves. Thanks to campaigners, these habitats are now protected.

Spain • Lanzarote
413 WATCH A STORM PETREL HOVER
All year

These tiny seabirds hold still, ready to pounce, by flapping gently into a light headwind.

Spain • Pyrenees
414 SEE A BEARDED VULTURE FEED
All year

Gasp as vultures drop their prey from a height, to break their bones and suck out the marrow!

Spain • Tarragona
415 FEEL TUNA POWER THROUGH THE BLUE
All year

Experience the thrill of snorkeling in the midst of a shoal of thousands of red tuna.

Spain • Majorca
416 SPOT A MOTH THAT LOOKS LIKE A BIRD
All year

With its long proboscis, and its technique of hovering over a flower to drink its nectar, you could easily confuse a hummingbird hawkmoth for its namesake, though it lacks its bright colors. It even hums.

Andorra
417 BE PLEASED TO SEE THE PYRENEAN CHAMOIS
All year

Hunted almost to extinction for its leather by the 1940s, the population of this goat-antelope—with the proportions of a goat but the soft brown fur of a deer—has now recovered to the tens of thousands.

France • Mediterranean
418 FIND THE BURROW OF A BEE-EATER
May to September

European bee-eaters are magnificently plumed birds that build communal summer nests—tunnels that are up to 7 ft (2.1 m) long—in the sandy soil along Mediterranean beaches. They eat bees, wasps, and hornets.

France • Provence

419 SMELL THE LAVENDER OF PROVENCE

June to August

Lavender has been farmed commercially in Provence for hundreds of years, and exploded around the start of the twentieth century, accompanied by the development of the hybrid lavandin. Take a trip to the Luberon region in the height of summer, and your senses will be bombarded by it. Long rows of purple flowers crisscross the landscape, as if they were in an oil painting. Bees buzz everywhere, collecting nectar to make exquisite lavender honey. And at harvest time you will smell a tractor coming long before you see or hear it, its trailer stacked high with freshly cut bundles of the sweet-smelling flowers on their way to the distillery for oil to be extracted. The oil is used to make perfumes and soaps, but plenty of flowers are left over to be taken home, dried or in their natural state, or else used to make cream-based desserts or countless other traditional Provençal dishes. For the rest of your life, a whiff of this unmistakable aroma will transport you straight back to these sun-drenched valleys.

France • Poitou

420 STROKE THE HAIR OF A DONKEY

All year

Once a vital part of local farm life, purebred Poitou donkeys are still considered the most valuable examples of their species. Their coats make them unmistakable, with long hair all over, making them more reminiscent of a woolly mammoth than any donkey you're likely to see elsewhere. Even an animal with one Poitou great-grandparent will possess an uncommonly long and luscious hairdo.

419 | *Rows of Provence lavender stretch for miles*

421 | *The wild horses of the Camargue*

France • Camargue
421 RIDE WITH WILD HORSES
All year

Wild horses have roamed the marshes of the Rhône delta for possibly thousands of years. This hardy breed is always gray, the effect created by being black-skinned with a covering of white hair. The sight of a herd galloping through the water has become a symbol of the region, and is breathtaking to witness in real life. The horses are also tamed and ridden by local cattle herders—known as *gardians*—and visitors can get the chance to ride alongside them to soak up the landscape.

France • Throughout
422 SEE FRANCE'S MOST VIVID REPTILE
All year

A frequent visitor to French and Italian backyards, the European green lizard is a 6 in (15 cm) long reptile, with green skin on its body, and a bright turquoise face and throat. Its tail is twice its body length, and it can regrow it if it gets caught by a predator. You'll spot them basking in the sun on rocks, slurping up insects, or catching small birds or mice. Their natural habitat is in dense vegetation in open woodland, but they also thrive in hedgerows, at the edges of fields, and in roadside embankments.

France • Alsace
423 LEARN NOT ALL HAMSTERS ARE PETS
April to September, at night

Wild Eurasian hamsters are protected by European authorities, with fines being handed out to nations that don't do their bit to protect them. These popular household pets are now critically endangered in western Europe, though they are still plentiful farther east. The best place to see them is on low-lying farmland in the Alsace region, where they emerge from their burrows in the evenings or at night in order to feed on seeds, roots, and grass.

Belgium • Throughout

424 WATCH BELGIUM'S NATIONAL BIRD HUNT

All year

Kestrels are a small, fairly common bird of prey that Belgians have adopted as their own. Kestrels like open farmland, which gives them the best chance to hunt insects, mice, lizards, and squirrels. They have the Terminator-like ability to see ultraviolet light frequencies, revealing unseen pee trails around rodent burrows. They use the wind to hover 30 to 60 ft (10 to 20 m) off the ground, then dart straight down at their target when they have it cleanly in their sights.

Belgium • Southern and central regions

425 GET DANGEROUS IN . . . BELGIUM

All year

Many people are surprised to hear that Belgium has venomous snakes; they're surprised to hear that the country has anything venomous at all, given its reputation for middle-of-the-road civility. The common adder—its only such snake—is a little shy, and if it does attack you, you're unlikely to keel over and die from the bite, but you may find yourself stricken with quite a nasty bit of swelling. A little ointment, and you'll probably be fine.

Belgium • Ardennes

426 AWAIT THE RETURN OF THE WILDCAT

All year

Though still very rare, the population of European wildcats is on the rise in certain areas of the Belgian countryside. They are slightly larger and considerably stouter in stature than domestic cats, but the two species will frequently interbreed. True wildcats, however, won't ask you for a cuddle. Sightings are still rare and precious, though, since these stealthy forest hunters are notoriously shy around humans, or anything they sense might pose a threat.

The Netherlands • Haarlem to Naaldwijk
427 CELEBRATE SPRING IN 2,500 ACRES OF FLOWERING BULBS
January to May

A road trip around the flower fields of the Netherlands provides sights and smells that you will not experience anywhere else. Time your trip to match your personal predilections, however: in January the first crocuses come up, followed by daffodils, narcissi, and hyacinths in February and March, then irises and tulips through May, followed finally by gladioli, dahlias, and fragrant lilies to see out a season that has been repeated for generations. Along the way you can visit museums dedicated to the Dutch Golden Age painters who were inspired by the same vast fields of flowers over 300 years ago, and markets where the cut flowers are sold to buyers all over the world.

The Netherlands • Texel island

428 SEE ONE OF EUROPE'S MOST CHERISHED VISITORS

October to April

Texel, the largest and westernmost island of the Wadden archipelago off the Netherlands' north coast, is a hot spot for migratory birds, and avid bird-watchers will find many species here that never set foot on the mainland. The rare waxwing is a particular treat: small and stout with red-brown feathers set off by vivid yellows and white in the wings and tail.

The Netherlands • Throughout

429 DECIDE WHETHER THE MOLE IS THE CUTEST OF ALL MAMMALS

April to July

Moles are famously blind, living most of their lives in underground tunnel systems of their own creation that constantly expand outward and feeding on worms, insects, and the odd small mammal. At some point, however, young moles must leave their mothers' tunnels. They do this in spring or summer, so that's the best time to get a glimpse of these adorable little guys.

The Netherlands • Hoge Veluwe National Park

430 LISTEN OUT FOR A CHATTY TOAD

All year

In the Netherlands' largest protected wilderness, which covers a vast 21 square miles (55 sq km) of dunes, heathlands, and woods, listen out for this particularly noisy amphibian. The natterjack toad's name literally means "nattering toad," and you'll find them calling out to each other with a rasping, rolling croak that can be heard from 1.5 miles (2 km) away on quiet nights. They're poor swimmers but surprisingly nimble when walking on their stubby legs.

Luxembourg • Throughout

431 SEE EUROPE'S SMALLEST BIRD

All year

The goldcrest is dull grayish green with a light gray belly and a black-and-yellow stripe along the top of its head. It's also tiny, weighing only 0.25 oz (6 g), and is, appropriately enough, the national bird of Luxembourg, which is itself tiny compared to most other European countries. According to Greek legend, a goldcrest hid underneath an eagle's wing and won a contest to fly the highest by launching itself just as the eagle began to tire—it's clever, as well as small.

Germany • Black Forest

432 SEE A FOREST FLOOR TURN COMPLETELY PURPLE

April

For a few short weeks of the year, a bluebell wood is a magical place, with the entire floor carpeted overnight with glorious multitudes of purple flowers. Arrive at dawn to catch the best views.

Germany • Eastern region

433 BE DEAFENED BY A CHORUS OF TOADS

April to August

The loud, melodic call of poisonous fire-bellied toads can be heard clearly during their mating season. It was copied by composer Béla Bartók in part IV of his instrumental piece *Out of Doors*.

Germany • Alps

434 TAKE IN THE BEAUTY OF BEETLES

June to September

The coloration of the *Rosalia longicorn*—a protected beetle species in Germany—is a perfect match for the bark of beech trees, but when their camouflage is blown, they suddenly stand out: blue with black spots reaching all the way up their extraordinary antennae.

Germany • Throughout

435 WATCH HARES BOX

March to April

In the country that brought us the Easter bunny (or *Osterhase*, "Easter hare"), watch these animals' "mad March hare" antics at the start of the spring mating season. At this time hares can be seen boxing in pairs—female hares that are trying their best to fight off overeager males.

Switzerland • Alps
436 WATCH A MARMOT STAND AT ATTENTION
July to September

Alpine marmots, large members of the squirrel family, spend up to nine months hibernating. Well, it *is* cold in the mountains. If you catch one out and about in summer, they may be up on their hind legs, looking right back at you.

Switzerland • Alps
437 SEE A MOUNTAIN HARE IN ITS WINTER WHITES
October to March

The mountain hare is among a small number of mammals whose coat changes with the seasons. It's brown in summer, and white in winter, for perfect camouflage. It's a great insulator, too.

Switzerland • Alps
438 SPOT THE ALPINE BLUE BUTTERFLY IN AN ALPINE MEADOW
May to August

The Alps may be ski central in winter, but for tourists and travelers, the Alpine summer brings a fresh array of enticements. Walking among these majestic peaks can be enhanced by guided nature tours, especially those focusing on one group that has a particular affinity with the clean mountain air and abundant flora: butterflies. You'll see more than 100 species on a typical week-long trip, none more elegant or striking than the Alpine blue, whose delicate lilac-blue wings add a sprinkling of magic to the meadows as they flutter past. So forget your raindrops on roses, whiskers on kittens, or schnitzel with noodles, these dainty insects are one of the true highlights of a real-life Alpine experience.

435 | *Mad March hares boxing in the snow*

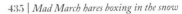

439 | *The weird and wonderful fried-egg jellyfish*

Malta • Northeastern coastline

439 FRY YOUR BRAIN WITH THE FRIED-EGG JELLYFISH

August to November

When it came to naming this peculiar animal, there was never any contest. With their smooth orange-yellow central dome and circular white bodies, they bear an uncanny resemblance to a certain breakfast favorite—fried eggs. This species is plentiful in the Mediterranean, and in the height of summer, its numbers become so overwhelming in certain areas that swimmers and water-sport enthusiasts have no option but to return to dry land and let the jellyfish do their thing.

Italy • Sardinia

440 SEARCH OUT A SUNFISH

All year

The ocean sunfish, or *Mola mola*, is the largest bony fish in the world. In fact, it's often mistaken for a shark on account of its dorsal fin, which is often spotted near the water's surface. Sunfish have been found weighing as much as 5,000 lb (2,300 kg), and they are an extraordinary sight, best seen by far with the aid of a snorkel or scuba mask, which will let you get up close and personal. Their almost circular bodies look creepily like giant floating human heads, if you squint a bit. Tip: don't squint.

Italy • Southern region

441 SOAK UP THE SOUNDS OF CICADAS
May to September

The mating song of the cicada is synonymous with balmy summer evenings around the world—wherever the climate is right for this family of large, canorous insects. You'll hear them showing up in the south of Italy, host to just a few species of the 1,300 found worldwide, where they'll add to the atmosphere of the setting Mediterranean sun.

Italy • Tuscany

442 SEE A WILD BOAR FORAGE
All year

Wild boars have the dubious honor of being both Tuscany's local emblem and an ingredient in many of its local delicacies. They have been hunted for millennia, by humans and animals alike, and are one of the ancestors of the domestic pig. Like pigs they are omnivores, with a diet consisting of everything from roots, bulbs, nuts, berries, leaves, bark, and seeds to carrion, eggs, rodents, frogs, snakes, worms, and insects. Such voracious appetites mean that they are not much loved by farmers, who consider them pests for chewing up their fields and stealing produce. You will have the best chance of seeing them at dusk, when they come out to forage for food in the undergrowth.

442 | *A wild boar, with its keen sense of smell*

Italy • Tuscany

443 SEE A PORCUPINE RAISE ITS QUILLS

All year

The crested porcupine has a strong defense. Its many quills, each up to 14 in (35 cm), raise when the animal is approached. Some smaller quills rattle and create a hiss. Go closer, and the porcupine will charge backward, to spike its attacker, then scarper back to its burrow.

Italy • Piedmont; Aosta

444 DO A DOUBLE TAKE AT A GENET

All year

The common genet might be mistaken for a cat. It has the same body, but its long, bushy tail reveals it as something rather different. Though far more wily than cuddly, they are sometimes kept as pets, and bond with their owners for life.

Italy • Cinque Terre

445 SMELL WILD HERBS IN THE MEDITERRANEAN HILLS

April to September

445 | Extravagant views from a Cinque Terre walking trail

The Cinque Terre are five once-isolated fishing villages nestled in a particularly stunning section of Italy's northeastern coastline, each with its own unique character. Though linked by train nowadays, there were once only two ways to reach them: by sea or by hiking across the hills (perhaps with a donkey or mule for company). A network of well-beaten hiking trails remains, inviting you to go exploring, weaving your way between man-made vineyards, and wild scrub that is teeming with rosemary, thyme, lavender, and oregano. Take a picnic along with you on your hike and you'll find your lunch is seasoned by the wind itself, as the aromas from all around invade your senses.

Czech Republic • Šumava National Park

446 SEE A CAPERCAILLIE IN EUROPE'S LARGEST FOREST

All year

The Western capercaillie, or wood grouse, is the largest of the grouse family, weighing up to 16 lb (7.2 kg). It also has one of the most extreme examples of sexual diamorphism (physical difference between the sexes) of all birds, with adult females only one third the size of their male counterparts. The males are dark gray, with a spectacular tail fan; the females are speckled light brown.

Austria • Danube-Auen National Park

447 SEE RED—WITH RED-CRESTED POCHARDS

April to September

These large diving ducks are particularly obsessed with dabbling for aquatic plants, upending their rears to get at the good stuff—subaquatic greenery—as often as time will allow. The male of the species is particularly striking, with a rounded orange head, red bill, black breast, and white flanks. It comes to mate and spend the summer at Danube-Auen, a massive wetland park surrounding an upland section of the mighty Danube River, which was successfully saved by protestors in 1986 from developers who planned to build a hydroelectric dam that would have destroyed this rich and valuable environment. Biodiversity studies carried out at the time of the protests led to it later being designated a national park, protecting the area for generations to come.

Austria • Throughout

448 SPOT EUROPE'S ANSWER TO THE MEERKAT

April to September

The European ground squirrel, or suslik—as its name suggests—is not a great fan of trees. Instead, it lives in large colonies underground. Standing on its hind legs, with its dirty blond fur, it bears a superficial similarity to the African meerkat, although the two are not closely related. The ground squirrel is a type of rodent.

Austria • Salzkammergut

449 SEE GREBES DANCING

April to May

Now here is a mating ritual we can relate to. These elegant waterfowl, with their smart brown-and-white plumage, seem to belong in the ballroom as much as the freshwater lakes and ponds you'll find them in as they approach each other politely to form pairs, then stand chest to chest and move in graceful circles with one another. Compared to many members of the animal kingdom (not naming any names . . .) they seem eminently civilized. Five species of grebes are found in Austrian waters: the little, great crested, red-necked, Slavonian, and black-necked.

Croatia • Northern Velebit National Park

450 SEE CROATIA'S NATIONAL ANIMAL

All year

Pine martens are cat-sized mustelids—the same family as otters, badgers, and weasels—that make their homes in hollow trees in dense woodland, creating dens for up to five infants. They feature on Croatia's coat of arms, and after reestablishing it as an independent state in 1991 (which it has been intermittently since the year 925), the Croatians designated this little critter as their national animal. Look for them in the forests of Velebit, but if you see a pair wrestling with each other on the ground, better leave them to it: pine marten copulation typically lasts over an hour.

Croatia • Dalmatian coast

451 STUDY THE SPINES OF AN URCHIN

All year

Denizens of the sea floor, sea urchins—"urchin" being an old-fashioned word for "hedgehog"— are spiky in a big way, and no fun at all to step on with bare feet. If this happens, sterilize the wound as soon as possible and remove the spike with tweezers if you can—or seek medical help if you can't. Study them closely in situ under water, however, and you can marvel peacefully at these curiously beautiful echinoderms.

451 | *Sea urchins in their ocean home*

Slovakia • Carpathian Mountains
452 MONITOR BIG PREDATORS
February

The Carpathians provide a habitat for Europe's largest populations of lynxes, wolves, and bears. What better way to become acquainted with these big predators than to join an expedition as a citizen-scientist, working alongside professional researchers? Research is ongoing into the interrelationships between these predators and their prey, and positions are available in research teams that involve tracking animals through the snow and tagging them electronically. You'll learn ancient hunters' skills like recognizing scent markings and dung, as well as cutting-edge techniques such as radio telemetry.

Hungary • Hortobágy National Park
453 SEE THE RARE AQUATIC WARBLER
April to September

An isolated population of these extremely rare birds can be found here in Hungary's oldest national park.

Hungary • Zemplén
454 SEARCH FOR A URAL OWL
All year

Similar to a tawny owl but paler in color, these owls are common in the forest of Zemplén, thanks to a nest box project.

Hungary • Aggtelek National Park
455 IDENTIFY RARE BUTTERFLIES IN HUNGARY
June to July

The butterflies that are found in this national park—such as the dusky large blue and woodland brown—are beauties, and guided tours are available for visitors.

452 | *A brown bear on the lookout in the Carpathian Mountains*

456 | *Dalmatian pelicans gather in the Danube Delta*

Montenegro • Prokletije National Park
456 UNCOVER THE SECRETS OF THE LYNX
May to September

Staying in traditional shepherds' houses, a ten-day lynx conservation trip is also a great way to survey the Montenegrin mountains.

Romania • Piatra Craiului National Park
457 HOWL WITH WOLVES IN THE CARPATHIANS
May to October

Take a trip through the mountains where a guide will escort you to a safe hide to watch Eurasian wolves hunt at night.

Romania • Danube Delta
458 SEE THE WORLD'S LARGEST FRESHWATER BIRD
March to August

Don't be too disappointed that they don't have soft fur and black spots—Dalmatian pelicans (named, like the dog, after the stretch of coastline in Croatia) are spectacular in their own right. The largest freshwater bird and one of the largest flying birds in the world, these raucous pelicans measure up to 6 ft (1.8 m) in length, 33 lb (15 kg) in weight, and 11 ft 6 in (3.5 m) in wingspan, a width equaling the record for all birds. They eat 2.6 lb (1.2 kg) of fish every day. About 400 breeding pairs persist within the Danube Delta Biosphere Reserve, one of only two populations left in Western Europe, where the birds are threatened by industry and fishing.

Romania • Transylvania
459 HELP REHABILITATE BROWN BEARS
All year

You can volunteer from one week to a month at Eastern Europe's largest bear sanctuary, just outside Braşov, and help to ensure a happy ending for the sad story of bears in this country, where they have been victims of trophy hunters, or captured and made to dance in the streets, perform tricks in circuses, or beg outside hotels. The lives of these captive animals have been awful, and they have suffered neglect, abuse, and cramped conditions. Many have now been rescued and can be found happily living out their days in sanctuaries.

Romania • Throughout
460 WATCH WATER BUFFALOES WALLOW
May to September

Water-buffalo farming is big business in Romania, where the shaggy local breed can be seen cooling off in rivers and swamps in summer. They are reared for their meat, their milk, and for pulling traditional machinery, and need to wallow to survive.

Albania • Narta Lagoon
461 SEE THE STRIKING SHELDUCK
All year

Shelducks are attractive, short-necked geese—a little larger than a mallard duck—with reddish pink bills, a white body with chestnut patches, a black belly, and a dark green head. When a family is under attack, the adult birds take off heroically as a decoy while the youngsters dive below the surface. Flocks in some places reach the tens or hundred of thousands, so watch out.

Albania • Karavasta National Park
462 VISIT A HAVEN FOR PYGMY CORMORANTS
All year

The worldwide population of this odd-looking, small brown waterfowl is concentrated in Eastern Europe, with up to 94 percent of its global population thought to occupy the relatively small area between the Danube River, the Black Sea, and the Adriatic. See them nesting in the trees around the lagoon here, from which they swoop down in large groups to hunt for fish.

Albania • Throughout
463 DISCOVER A HOST OF BUTTERFLIES
May to August

The small, former communist state of Albania is now recognized as the country with possibly the most butterflies in Europe. According to a recent estimate, there are a total of 198 species to be found here. The high numbers are probably due to the retention of traditional farming practices that have been replaced elsewhere by modern methods, and by the terrain, which is exceptionally hilly.

464 | *The aptly named tiger moths on the island of Rhodes*

Greece • Valley of
the Butterflies
464 WANDER AMONG TIGER MOTHS
May

Thanks to the presence of a clutch of rare oriental sweet-gum trees, which release a vanilla-like aroma, thousands of Jersey tiger moths are drawn to this small reserve on the island of Rhodes in late May, where they cool off in the humid air and prepare to breed. Bright orange with black-and-white striped forewings, the moths fly by day, filling the air.

Greece • Pindus National Park
465 DISCOVER BEARS AND WOLVES IN GREECE
All year

According to the Born Free Foundation, there are around 150 bears living in the forests of central and northern Pindus and the Rodope massif in the north of Greece, one of the largest populations in southern Europe; the area is known locally as "bear park." Living alongside them are large numbers of gray or western wolves, the latter a species that has been driven out of most of Europe.

Greece • Lake Kerkini
466 SEE HERONS BY DAY AND NIGHT
April to September

You can see 300 different bird species in this magnificent wetland region, one of the most important and biodiverse in Europe. In the daytime look out for both the purple (lilac gray) and the tiny squacco heron. Then at night watch the black-crested night herons come out to hunt fish by moonlight. They stand by the water's edge, still and squat, and ambush their unsuspecting prey.

Greece • Samaria National Park

467 CATCH A GLIMPSE OF A CRETAN KRI-KRI

All year

An ancient symbol of the island of Crete, and a big hitter on its tourist literature, you'll have seen a kri-kri in some form by the time you've been through the airport passport check. Head out into the great outdoors, however, and you'll see these burly light brown goats, with their huge horns, roaming wild.

Greece • Throughout

468 BRACE YOURSELF FOR THE SMELL OF A DRAGON ARUM

June to July

These small purple flowers are certainly beautiful to look at, but they are one of a number of species of flowers that have done away with the usual aromas aimed at roping in pollinators. They target a specific pollinator—flies, which they entice with the smell of rotting flesh, then consume.

Greece • Western Mediterranean coast

469 JOIN A DOLPHIN CONSERVATION PROJECT

June to September

Assist the conservation of endangered dolphin species while staying in a beautiful seaside village and making daily research excursions at sea.

Bulgaria • Danube River

470 SEE ELEGANCE EN MASSE AT AN EGRET COLONY

February to September

Egrets are a family of different sizes of beautiful white herons. Huge colonies form in spring and summer on islands in the Danube.

Bulgaria • Lowlands

471 SPOT A TORTOISE IN THE WILD

All year

The Hermann's tortoise is under threat from agricultural development, but it can be spotted here in green open spaces or hiding under bushes in the summer heat.

Turkey • Eastern Anatolia

472 SEE CROWDS OF CRIMSON-WINGED FINCHES

All year

These surprisingly hardy little birds nest in crevices on the rocky mountainsides of this elevated and sparsely populated outer region of the country.

467 | *The kri-kri, endemic to the island of Crete*

Turkey • Anatolia

473 TREAD CAREFULLY IN ANATOLIA

All year

Ancient scorpion-like creatures were among the
first to emerge from the seas and live on land.
As you venture away from the big coastal cities
and out into the arid eastern and central regions
of Turkey, you might consider that early biological
history, since you'll be sharing the way with 40
modern-day species of scorpion, including a
few that possess venom sufficiently poisonous
to harm a human.

Turkey • Anatolia

475 MINGLE WITH THE MOUFLON

All year

Modern domestic sheep were bred from long-
horned brown-fleeced wild mouflons, which still
roam the forests around the mountains of Anatolia.

Turkey • Pontic Alps

476 EXPLORE TURKEY'S VALLEYS OF COLOR

July to August

In these high mountains, wildflowers still bloom in
the height of summer—primulas, swertias, gentians,
and louseworts—bringing butterflies galore.

Turkey • Lake Tuz

474 SEE BABY FLAMINGOS EMERGE ACROSS A LAKE

June

As thousands of chicks emerge from their nests
and spread out across Lake Tuz—a huge salt lake
in central Turkey, as famous for its algal blooms that
turn the water pink as for its enormous flamingo
populations—they still have their gray, almost drab,
plumage. They soon begin to feed on the same
algae that colors the water, and their feathers
become magnificent and unmistakable.

Estonia • Throughout

477 SEE THE WORLD THROUGH BLUE-TINTED GLASSES

March to October

The barn swallow is a deep and beautiful blue, with
a yellow beak and a white breast. It is the Estonian
national bird and once graced the 500 kroon
banknote, the local currency that predated the
Euro here. This industrious little bird has an affinity
with barns, as the name suggests, preferring to
nest there, as well as in other man-made structures.
As human populations and activities here have
increased, so have the numbers of birds. Their diet
consists mostly of insects, and here, they benefit
from human activity again. You'll often see them
following farm animals and machinery, looking for
bugs kicked up in the wake of a tractor or herd.

Poland • Pine forests

478 SEE A NUTCRACKER'S STASH OF SEEDS

All year

Nutcrackers are little birds that live almost entirely on pine seeds, or pine nuts. They collect them and store them below the ground. Sometimes seeds, being seeds, start to grow. In fact, nutcrackers have been responsible for the reestablishment of trees in many deforested areas.

Poland • Białowieża Forest

479 SEE ELK IN EUROPE

All year

These animals, which are known as moose in North America and elk in Europe, are evenly spread around the northern reaches of our planet, from the west of Canada through Europe to Russia. As far south as Poland you'll see them roaming wild in the forests. They are one of the many wonders of the spectacular and ancient Białowieża Forest.

Poland • Baltic coast

480 SIGHT A WHITE-TAILED SEA EAGLE

All year

Since the banning of DDT fertilizers in the 1970s, this ancient emblem of Polish royalty and culture has come back from near extinction.

Poland • Żywkowo

481 VISIT A VILLAGE RULED BY BIRDS

April to August

Almost a quarter of the world's storks come to Poland in the summer months. They are a familiar and much-loved sight across the country, and one small village—just a stone's throw from the border with the Russian exclave of Kaliningrad—has been christened the nation's stork capital because birds here outnumber humans. In Żywkowo, about 120 storks rub shoulders with a population of only around 30 people. Each house in the village hosts several nests, and it has become justly famous.

Lithuania • Baltic coast

482 WATCH STELLER'S EIDER DUCKS AT SEA

October to March

The smallest of the eider and one of the prettiest, the males of this sea duck have a unique pattern of blue, beige, black, navy, and white feathers.

Latvia • Throughout

484 COUNT SPOTS ON A LADYBUG

All year

The two-spotted ladybug is a symbol of an ancient Latvian Earth-mother goddess, and the country's national emblem.

Lithuania • Baltic coast

483 LISTEN OUT FOR CORNCRAKES

All year

Corncrakes are birds commonly found in Lithuania and can be heard day or night, so the easiest way to find them is with your ears. Listen for a scratchy *eh! eh!*

Belarus • Braslav Lakes

485 SEE A BLACK STORK ON A "BLUE NECKLACE"

April to September

Keep a close eye out for black storks in this network of 300-odd lakes; they are much shyer than their white counterparts.

Belarus • Belovezhskaya
Pushcha National Park
486 WANDER THROUGH A PRIMEVAL WOOD
All year

Forests once covered almost all of Europe, yet after millennia of development, almost all of it has been lost or transformed by human intervention. The Belovezhskaya is an exception: a true primeval virgin forest, a UNESCO World Heritage Site, and home to thousands of free roaming wild bison.

Belarus • Belovezhskaya
Pushcha National Park
487 COUNT BIRD SPECIES IN A FOREST
All year

Among herds of wild bison, elk, and deer, over 200 species of bird can also be found in this true biodiversity hot spot. They include four types of flycatcher, five of owls, six of tits, and ten diversely colored woodpeckers, whose pecking serves several functions: communication, home-building, and feeding.

Russia • Volga Delta
488 ADMIRE A SPREAD OF CASPIAN LOTUSES
July to September

Every few years a field of floating lotus flowers springs up in the region where the Volga spreads out and flows into the Caspian Sea. An area measuring 2 miles (3 km) wide by 9 miles (15 km) long then becomes covered with these fragrant pink flowers—fragile beauties that cannot survive if picked.

Russia • Lake Baikal
489 SEE INTO THE PAST WITH THE STURGEON
All year

Fossil evidence suggests that fish very similar to modern varieties of sturgeon were present in lakes more than 200 million years ago, at the end of the Triassic and the beginning of the Jurassic period. In fact they were the first ray-finned fishes, from which many other familiar species have evolved.

486 | *The ancient world of the Belovezhskaya forest*

Russia • Ural Mountains

490 WANDER THE VIRGIN KOMI FORESTS

All year

The largest virgin forest in Europe, and a UNESCO World Heritage Site, the Virgin Komi Forests sit at the foot of the Ural mountain range dividing Europe from Asia. You'll find mostly Siberian spruce, Siberian fir, and Siberian larch trees across its 12,700 square miles (32,800 sq km). Look out for reindeer, sable (black-furred tree mammals similar to pine martens), mink, and hares, all of which are found here in abundance. (See Chapter 5 for further adventures in Russia.)

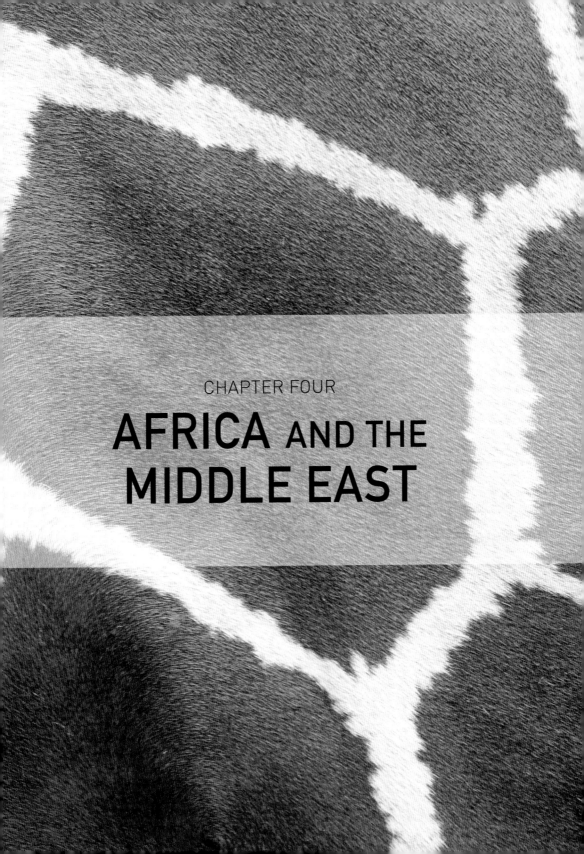

CHAPTER FOUR

AFRICA AND THE MIDDLE EAST

Morocco • Semi-arid desert with plenty of cover

491 WATCH A CARACAL LEAP

All year

This species of wildcat can be identified by its distinctive large ears, which are gray on the caracal's otherwise golden body, and have long tufts of hair sprouting from the tips. These have given rise to the caracal's alternative name of "desert lynx," although it's actually more closely related to a serval. Caracals live in the semi-arid desert savanna, where they spend the day resting under bushes or between boulders, and can be seen at dusk or at night, patrolling their territory and hunting for food. Male territories range from 9.5 to 25 square miles (31 to 65 sq km), and females have their own territories, too, but these are generally smaller.

The caracal is famed for its ability to jump up to 13 ft (4 m) in the air and pluck a bird from the sky, and it even has well-developed muscles in its hind legs, which are longer than the front ones to aid with this. However, although it makes an awesome sight, you're more likely to find a caracal stalking a small antelope or a hare, and many of the birds it catches are ground-dwellers.

Morocco • Souss-Massa-Drâa region

492 SEE THE BEST TREE-CLIMBING GOATS

June

Stumble upon some argan trees in June when the fruits are ripe, and you're also highly likely to find a troop of goats up the tree, enjoying a nice meal; they will often strip a tree bare. Argan trees are grown for their nut, which passes through the goats' digestive systems unharmed. Farmers then collect this nut (yup, from the poop) and use it to produce argan oil.

Algeria • Hoggar Mountains

493 SAY "AW" TO THE CUTEST WILD FOX

All year

The fennec fox is just 8 in (20 cm) tall from its shoulder—and its ears rise 4 in (10 cm) from its head. This has the result of making even adult fennec foxes look like small, cute cubs. This tiny fox (the smallest canid species in the world) lives in the desert, where it hides from the heat of the day by sleeping under a bush or in a den. It is well adapted to life in these harsh, dry conditions. It has fur on the soles of its feet to protect them from the heat of the sand, and its kidneys have evolved to restrict the loss of water so it can go for many days without drinking; instead, it gets its water from its food, which consists of insects, birds, and small mammals.

It is thought that fennec foxes mate for life and older siblings stay in the family group even when a new litter comes along. They are social animals and play as well as live together. The fox is the national animal of Algeria and the nickname for the country's soccer team.

Algeria • Tassili n'Ajjer National Park

494 BE AWED BY THE CUNNING SAND CAT

All year, at night

It might resemble the average domestic cat, but the sand cat has extra survival tricks on hand. The pads of its feet are covered in a wiry black fur—the rest of the cat is usually pale gold or gray, but always with a white chest and white chin—which help it to move across the burning sand and to sneak up on its underground prey unheard.

Algeria • Gouraya National Park

495 HAVE YOUR OWN DAY OF THE JACKAL

All year

As with many wild dogs, the jackal is no beauty, but that makes it no less interesting to spot in the natural confines of this national park—look out for a wolfish face; large ears; and a speckly gold, silver, and black coat. Males and females mate for life. The male has been observed taking food to his pregnant female, and they share the work of bringing up their cubs.

Egypt • Gebel Elba National Park
497 SNIFF OUT AN AFRICAN SKUNK
All year, at night

Although sometimes known as the "African skunk,"
the more common name for this species is the
"Saharan striped polecat," and it is a species of
weasel. Its body is black and white, like a skunk's,
and it can produce a nasty smell when it feels
threatened. It's usually seen at night digging around
in the earth as it hunts for amphibians and insects,
but it also eats birds, snakes, and small rodents.

Algeria • Remote coastal areas
496 SEE ONE OF ALGERIA'S MOST ENDANGERED SPECIES
All year

The monk seal gets its name from its brown
coloration, which resembles a monk's habit. It was
once common in the Mediterranean and along the
Atlantic shores of northwest Africa, but there are
now thought to be fewer than 400 left in the wild.
When once they used to live on open beaches,
they now live in caves on remote and rugged
coastlines—maybe to avoid being hunted by man.

493 | *A fennec fox's big ears dissipate heat in the desert sun*

Egypt • Sinai Peninsula

498 CHILL WITH A GENTLE GIANT

All year

Usually when you think of reef fish, you think of small, brightly colored fish of the type that you often see in an aquarium. But there's one reef fish, the Napoleon wrasse, that wouldn't fit in many aquariums—it can grow up to 7.5 ft (2.3 m) long. It is a striking fish—often bright blue or green for the males, and orange and white for the females—with very distinctive fleshy lips and a hump over its head that looks a little bit like Emperor Napoléon's hat. These huge fish appear to enjoy company and often seek out divers and nudge them like a dog wanting to be stroked.

Egypt • Sinai Peninsula
499 BE SURPRISED BY A DARTING TREVALLY
All year

When you're scuba diving and gently swimming along watching life on the reef, the world can feel slowed down. It's almost silent, apart from your breathing and the sounds of fish chipping against rocks, smoothly going about their business. Perhaps away from you, a couple of silvery trevallies are swimming off in the deep. Then before you know it, zoom, zoom . . . they have darted in with their silver sides flashing and darted back out to their patch of the deep, leaving a couple less reef fish for you to watch. These sudden maneuvers are all part of life on the reef, and it's strangely compelling to see the ecosystem in action. Experienced divers will encounter trevallies of all sizes around the world—from ones you could eat for dinner through to ones that could almost eat you.

Egypt • Sinai Peninsula
500 SEE AN EEL PEER FROM A HOLE
All year

You'll often find a moray eel poking out from the crevice of a coral reef. Just the head will be on show, but don't be deceived—behind that head its body can be anything up to 6.5 ft (2 m) long. It's probably just as well that it's hidden.

Egypt • Hurghada
501 WATCH A PUFFER FISH PUFF
All year

There are so many fish in the sea, and almost as many types of defense. Puffer fish take in water when they feel threatened to make them puff up to a bigger and boxier size. If that fails, the fact they're very poisonous usually does the trick.

Israel • Tel Aviv
502 LISTEN TO THE SOUNDS OF THE CITY
March to November

In the warmer months the soundtrack to Tel Aviv's nightlife is the sound of Egyptian fruit bats coming in to feed on the dates of the palms that line Rothschild Avenue.

Israel • Sharm El Sheikh
503 SPOT A MOLLUSK
All year

Among the corals and the fish of a coral reef, take time to look for nudibranchs. These small, shell-less mollusks come in any number of colors and patterns, some with feathery gills, others with horns, others just plain.

Iran • Abbas Abad Wildlife Refuge
504 COUNT CHEETAHS
All year

If you're going to try to tick off all five subspecies of cheetah, why not start with the Asiatic, or Iranian, cheetah. There are only 50 left alive, so urgent support is needed to safeguard them.

Yemen • Socotra

505 TOUCH THE BLOOD OF A DRAGON'S BLOOD TREE
All year

On the island of Socotra in the Arabian Sea, there grows a species
of tree with an evocative name—the dragon's blood tree. It gets its name
from the red sap it produces. Over the years, this sap has been used as
lipstick, a dye for wool, a cure for ulcers, an astringent in toothpaste, and
even as a varnish for violins. The trees themselves look fairly special. The
branches grow in a close-knit dome shape with leaves only at the ends of
them. This provides good shade for the roots beneath.

Iran • Zagros Mountains
506 TIME IT RIGHT TO SEE THE LURISTAN NEWT
September to May

This brightly colored, critically endangered newt is only found in these mountains, and only in the cooler months. When it gets hot in the summer, it burrows underground and sleeps until the temperature drops again. This is known as estivation, the opposite of hibernation.

United Arab Emirates • Dubai
507 GO ON A DESERT SAFARI
All year

You don't have to be in Africa to go on a safari. It is just as rewarding to take a 4x4 out into the dunes of Dubai on the search for wildcats, Arabian oryxes, and sand foxes.

505 | *Surveying the dragon's blood trees of Socotra*

Bahrain • Near Jebel Dukhan

508 REFLECT ON THE MIRACLE OF LIFE

All year

The desert around Jebel Dukhan is an arid land full of low-level buildings and the occasional scrubby bush. Until, that is, you come upon the only tree for miles around: the tall and sprawling Tree of Life. It is thought the tree has been growing here for around 400 years or so, and is on the site of a former military outpost. It is a *Prosopis juliflora*, and the interesting thing is, this is not a native tree to this part of the world—at some point it must have been brought here from the Americas. It almost makes its presence more miraculous. To survive in these arid conditions, the *Prosopis juliflora* grows a taproot down into the earth in search of a water source, and this root can grow as far as 115 ft (35 m). Miraculously in all this desert, just one tree found water and still survives four centuries later.

UAE • Dubai Desert Conservation Reserve

509 KEEP UP WITH THE WORLD'S FASTEST SPECIES

All year

You might have always thought it was the cheetah that was the fastest species, but that's just land mammals. The overall fastest animal on Earth is the peregrine falcon. When it dives down onto its prey, this bird can reach speeds of up to 155 mph (250 kmh). It can also catch other birds midair. This is the falcon that has historically been used by the Bedouin to hunt, but it was also able to be trained to find water. Once it found a source, it would fly high up so its masters could see it from afar.

UAE • Qasr Al Sarab Protected Area, Abu Dhabi

510 CELEBRATE THE RETURN OF THE ORYX

All year

In the 1970s the last wild Arabian oryx were shot by hunters. Fortunately there were many captive animals, and a successful reintroduction program means these stunningly elegant beasts are now back in the wild. In 2011 it became the first formerly extinct animal—in the wild—to be classed as merely "vulnerable." Not out of the woods, in other words, but still a major achievement for the conservation movement.

509 | *A peregrine falcon takes flight in Dubai*

511 | A local warden monitors hatchlings on a protected Oman beach

Oman • Ras al Jinz

511 SEE BABY TURTLES LEAVE THEIR NESTS

April to August

Baby green turtles hatch from eggs that have been safely buried underneath the sand. They clamber up to the surface and then have to make the perilous journey to the water's edge, running the gauntlet of foxes, crabs, and seagulls along the way. It's an epic journey to witness.

Oman • Al Hajar Mountains

512 WATCH GOATS SCALE ROCKFACES

All year

The Arabian tahr is a nimble-footed goat, closely related to the Himalayan and Nilgiri tahr, but smaller than both of them. It can be identified by its backward-curving horns. The Arabian tahr has been overhunted and this is now one of the last areas where this endangered animal can be seen.

Oman • Jabal Samhan Nature Reserve

513 FOLLOW THE TRAIL OF AN ARABIAN LEOPARD

All year, at night

Although extremely rare, in the Dhofar Mountains of Oman, it is possible to see this magnificent beast that once lived throughout Arabia. The mountains offer shade, trapped water, and a good variety of prey species—crucial for a creature that is now listed as critically endangered.

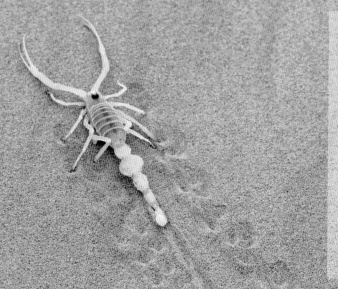

514 WATCH OUT
FOR SCORPIONS
All year

Scorpions look like they mean
business, with pincers at the front
and a curved tail at the back, coiled
and loaded to sting. Their sting
hurts, like a bee sting, but very few
of them are venomous enough
to do more damage than that to
an adult. Still, beware.

Oman • Empty Quarter

515 SMELL FRANKINCENSE AS IT GROWS

March to May; September to October

Before oil, Oman's wealth came from its trade in frankincense. The rich, spicy scent is burned all over the country—from the front of taxis to hotel foyers—and the smell is synonymous with the country. Frankincense is the resin from the *Boswellia carterii* tree. These grow in the southeast of the country, where monsoon winds bring in a mist that creates the perfect conditions for the spindly trees. The tree is cut to allow the resin to ooze out, and the harvester returns a week or two later once the resin has dried to collect it.

The Gambia • Near rivers and streams in dry savanna

516 WITNESS THE SPIT OF A COBRA

All year

As poisonous snakes go, the black-necked spitting cobra looks the part. It can raise its head and neck up from the rest of its coiled black body and has a wide, flattened neck to contain its venom. It doesn't take much to provoke a spitting cobra to spit, and it then does so liberally, projecting it toward the face of a potential threat. The venom causes a burning sensation, and if it gets in the eyes, possible blindness. Cobras spend the day hiding in tree trunks and abandoned rodent holes, but can also climb trees.

515 | *Resin oozes from a frankincense tree*

The Gambia • Abuko Nature Reserve
517 TRACK DOWN A BUSHBUCK
All year

Its name alone is enough to conjure up iconic images of African plains. The bushbuck, with its light-footed ways and large pricked-up ears, looks like it fears predators lurking behind every tree.

The Gambia • Dankunku wetlands
518 SNAP A STORK
November to June

The peculiar marabou stork is a must for any photo collection, with its bald head, hunched shoulders, and large pink throat sac. It defecates on its own legs, giving them a "whitewashed" appearance.

The Gambia • Forests of Foni
519 HUNT FOR A GOLDEN CUCKOO
All year

With rusty golden feathers and colorful skin, the rare golden cuckoo of Foni is like a trophy from a children's story. Its appeal is not lost on poachers, who sadly hunt this rare bird.

The Gambia • Abuko Nature Reserve
520 SURPRISE A GREEN TURACO
All year

Listen for the loud *cor cor* of a green turaco up in the treetops. This striking bird looks permanently surprised, due to its mohawk-esque head crest.

Ghana • Bia National Park
521 COUNT 10 PRIMATE SPECIES IN AN OUTING
All year

This dedicated biosphere reserve is among the world's most biodiverse habitats, and home to primates, including chimpanzees and several colobus monkey species.

Ghana • Kakum National Park
522 SPY ON FOREST ELEPHANTS
All year

Forest elephants are a subspecies of African elephants that live in densely forested areas. They are smaller than their savanna-dwelling relatives, with more oval-shaped ears, and tusks that point downward rather than outward. They eat fruit from the many forest trees here, as well as leaves and bark, and are sometimes visible from the park's treetop walkways, foraging at the foot of the park's tallest tree.

Ghana • Kakum National Park
523 REVEL IN A MONKEY'S BEARD
All year

If you visit Kakum, make sure you check out the fabulous long white beard of the endangered rollaway monkey—a subspecies of the Diana monkey.

Ghana • Kakum National Park

524 GET AQUAINTED WITH THE DIANA MONKEY

All year

The Diana monkey is a pretty example of its kind. It has a black body and white chest and a white stripe across its thigh. However, it earned its name from its white crescent-shaped brow that resembles the jewelry that the Roman goddess Diana wore across her forehead. There are treetop walkways in the Kakum National Park that give visitors the chance to get much closer to these canopy-dwelling primates.

Ghana • Mole National Park

525 WATCH A TROOP OF WARTHOGS ON THE RUN

All year

Warthogs are one of the more reliable African animals to spot on a safari. But that's not to say they aren't fabulous, too. They live in brushy open land and are usually seen in a family group. They are hairier than you might imagine and have distinctive tusks framing their jaws. But it is when a troop runs away that they are at their most charming—their little tails stick perpendicularly up into the air.

525 | *Warthogs on the move, tails raised*

Ghana • Dying flowers on garden plants

526 SEE THE PATTERNS OF A PICASSO BUG

November to January

Hunting down tiny insects is never an easy job, but find a Picasso bug, or Zulu hud bug, and you'll be well rewarded. This little beetle grows to around 0.7 in (1.5 cm) long and has one of the most artistically designed shells you can imagine. It looks as if it has been hand-painted, with its muted green shell featuring irregular wobbly black rings outlined in red and cream, which have evolved as a clear warning to would-be predators. It feeds on a variety of plants, but search on hibiscus, coffee, and mallow plants.

Ghana • A protected colony near the village of Bonkro

527 SMARTEN UP FOR THE PICATHARTE

October to April

The yellow-headed picatharte is a very neat-looking bird with clearly defined black wings, white body and legs, and a yellow head with black ear patches. It has picked up some names over the years such as "rock fowl" (from its habit of nesting in rock overhangs or caves) and "bald-headed crow," which seems a little unfair. "Picatharte" itself actually translates as "magpie vulture." Look for their mud nests, which are constructed on rockfaces near streams deep within tropical rain forests.

Cameroon • Around Nkongsamba; rain forest rivers

528 SEE THE WORLD'S LARGEST FROG

All year

The Goliath frog reaches 12.5 in (32 cm) in length—not including leg length—and weighs 6.25 lb (3 kg). Fortunately, with no vocal sac, it doesn't have a deafening croak to match.

Cameroon • Lake Ossa Wildlife Reserve

529 WATCH MANATEES

All year

The West African manatee is sadly a declining population. Efforts are being made here to protect and preserve its habitat.

526 | *The surreal-looking Picasso bug*

Cameroon • Douala-Edéa Reserve
530 SPOT A FABULOUS BLACK-AND-WHITE COLOBUS
All year

Colobus monkeys are unique in having no thumbs—it is thought that this enables them to swing through the canopy without fear of it getting caught in the branches.

Cameroon • Around Ntale
531 LOOK TWICE AT A HAIRY FROG
All year

Yes, a hairy frog! Mature males have hair-like structures (not actual hairs) protruding from their thighs and sides. They live on land, but breed in the water, where you might see them tending eggs on protruding rocks. They can produce claws for defense by breaking their toe bones, which then pierce through the skin.

Ethiopia • Bale Mountains National Park
532 DISCOVER THE NYALA
All year

The mountain nyala is an antelope found only in the Ethiopian highlands—and on Ethiopia's ten-cent coin. Sadly it is also now endangered due to hunting and habitat loss.

530 | *Black-and-white colobus monkeys*

Ethiopia • Bale Mountains National Park

533 STUDY THE MANE OF THE BLACK LION

All year

While most lions live in the lowland savannas, in Ethiopia there are some forest-dwelling lions that live high in the mountains. Although not genetically distinct enough to be considered a subspecies, Ethiopian lions are nonetheless smaller than regular African lions and they also have distinctive black manes. (Lions' manes vary greatly from one region to another.) The Ethiopian emperor Haile Selassie was famous for owning a private collection of black-maned lions. The descendants of these animals are now housed in the Addis Ababa zoo and they could potentially be used for a captive breeding program.

A visit to lion country is undoubtedly a thrill, but for those who live here it is more stressful than exciting, since they must remain ever vigilant in case of an attack.

Ethiopia • Around Lake Tana

534 SPOT A YELLOW-FRONTED PARROT

All year

There is only one place on Earth that you will see the yellow-fronted parrot, and that is in the Ethiopian highlands. Despite its name, the bird is actually green all over except for its head. The misleading name comes from its Latin name *Poicephalus flavifrons*, where *flavus* means "yellow" and *frons* means "forehead."

Ethiopia • Semien Mountains National Park

535 ADMIRE A HARDY IBEX

All year

The chocolate-colored walia ibex favors rugged cliffs and deep gorges—possibly because these used to give it refuge from hunters. It is now protected, but there are probably fewer than 800 individuals left in the wild.

Ethiopia • Bale Mountains National Park

536 SEE AN ETHIOPIAN WOLF STALK ITS PREY

All year

This reddish-colored wolf is only found in seven distinct sites in the Ethiopian highlands.

Ethiopia • Senkelle Swayne's Hartebeest Sanctuary

537 SAVE ETHIOPIA'S OWN HARTEBEEST

All year

Visit this dedicated hartebeest reserve and help the species to survive into the future.

Ethiopia • Bale Mountains National Park

538 SPY A VERVET

All year

If you're in the area, you have to see the endemic Bale Mountains vervet monkey. Look out for it in bamboo forests.

Ethiopia • Menz-Guassa Community Conservation Area
539 MEET THE ONLY GRASS-EATING PRIMATE
All year

The grass-eating gelada is also known as the bleeding heart monkey, due to a patch of bare red skin on its chest. It is the only species of monkey that eats just grass, and it is only found in the highlands of Ethiopia's Amhara region. The Menz-Guassa community fiercely defend their grass, which is used for all manner of purposes, such as stuffing mattresses and making thatch; they patrol the area to make sure animals graze where they should and the grass is cut by agreement. This defense has created a perfect environment for the geladas, who sleep in the craggy rockfaces below the plateau and scale up the cliffs each day to feed.

Gabon • Lope National Park

540 FALL IN LOVE WITH THE FACE OF A MANDRILL

July to October

When you look at the brightly colored blue-and-red face of a mandrill, you wouldn't think it was shy and reclusive; they look like the life and soul of the party. However, these monkeys like to hide themselves away in the rain forests. They sleep in trees, but forage on the ground for fruits, roots, and insects during the day.

Gabon • Minkébé National Park

541 DISCOVER THE BONGO THAT ISN'T A DRUM

All year, at night

There are two species of bongo (not including the drum)—the lowland, or western, bongo, which is the one in Gabon, and the mountain, or eastern, bongo, which is found in Kenya. Both species of forest antelope are beautiful chestnut-colored ungulates with thin white vertical stripes down their bodies. They are mainly nocturnal.

Democratic Republic of Congo
• Salonga National Park

542 SPOT THE DIFFERENCE WITH AFRICA'S ONLY TRUE NATIVE PHEASANT

All year

The Congo peafowl is very similar to the Indian peafowl, but bluer, with a violet tinge—and, of course, it's found in Africa.

Democratic Republic of Congo
• Virunga National Park

543 DECIPHER THE HERITAGE OF AN OKAPI

June to February

With the head of a giraffe and the back legs of a zebra, the okapi is a very unique-looking animal—and, in fact, closely related to the giraffe.

Democratic Republic of Congo
• Lomako-Yokokala Faunal Reserve

544 MEET YOUR CLOSEST RELATIVE

June to February

Similar to a chimpanzee but with longer legs and pinker lips, a bonobo is more closely related to humans than it is to gorillas.

Rwanda • Nyungwe National Park

545 WATCH THE ANTICS OF CHIMPANZEES

March to November

To truly understand the social interactions of chimpanzees, join scientists in this national park and spend a day tracking them.

543 | *There's no mistaking the rear of an okapi*

Uganda • Queen Elizabeth National Park

546 MARVEL AT SKIMMERS CATCHING FISH

All year

Watching skimmers fish makes you realize how fabulously nature has caused different species to evolve. The lower part of the skimmer's beak is larger than the upper part, and the skimmer flies low over rivers and streams with its lower beak in the water. When a fish passes over the top, the beak snaps shut. Dinner.

Uganda • Queen Elizabeth National Park (Ishasha sector)

547 WATCH A LION CLIMB A TREE

All year

Spot lions in this park climbing into fig trees during the day. This could be to enjoy cool breezes or to escape flies on the ground.

Uganda • Mabamba Swamp

548 WONDER AT THE HABITS OF THE SHOEBILL

All year

Stork-like shoebills feed by grabbing a mouthful of riverbed with their fish, then shaking their heads until all except the fish falls out.

Uganda • Bwindi Impenetrable Forest

549 FIND A RARE JEWEL OF THE JUNGLE

All year

It won't be easy, but spot a rare and beautiful African green broadbill, and it will definitely make you smile.

Uganda • Bwindi National Park

550 WATCH GORILLAS

All year (rainy season is quieter)

Creeping through the forest until you spot a troop of 10 to 20 gorillas sitting quietly, eating leaves and grooming one other, is simply unforgettable.

Uganda • Murchison Falls

551 DISCOVER A KOB— IT'S A DEER NOT A NUT

All year

This antelope—in particular, the subspecies known as the "Ugandan kob"—has such a regal appearance, it features on Uganda's coat of arms.

Uganda • Lake Mburo National Park

552 SIGHT AARDVARKS

All year, by night

The aardvark has a nose like an elongated pig's snout—and its teeth grow forever. Take a night game drive here and see if you can make a sighting.

553 | *A keeper playing with an elephant calf in Nairobi*

Kenya • David Sheldrick Wildlife Trust
553 VISIT AN ELEPHANT ORPHANAGE—AND HELP THE SPECIES SURVIVE
All year

Whether its through poaching or other circumstances, there are a number of elephants and rhinos orphaned each year, and the David Sheldrick Wildlife Trust is on hand to step in and raise them. A visit to their site is an uplifting experience, not least because of the charm of a tiny tusk on a hairy elephant baby, but also because of the numerous success stories that have come out of the trust. Orphans that are reacclimatized to live in the wild return to life as it should be, without people, and even have babies of their own. The trust also runs a program for orphaned rhinos.

Kenya • Maasai Mara National Reserve
554 WATCH A SNEAKY DWARF MONGOOSE
All year

This mongoose is considered a pest in some places—known as the "egg thief"—but find a group sheltering in a termite mound, and you will happily watch them all day. Some go off to forage while others stay put, but they all look after the lead female.

Kenya • Maasai Mara National Reserve; near water

555 APPRECIATE A SADDLE-BILLED STORK

All year

The Maasai Mara is home to more than 470 different bird species, including the majestic saddle-billed stork. Standing 5 ft (1.5 m) tall, with a striking black-and-white body, this wading bird is already impressive before you focus in on its wonderful bill: red-tipped then black, with red-and-yellow flesh where it joins the stork's black head with a striking yellow eye.

Kenya • Maasai Mara National Reserve

556 LOVE A DIK-DIK

All year

These dainty and timid-looking antelope—Maasai Mara's smallest—are higher at the back than the front, making them look as if they're always ready to run.

Kenya • Maasai Ostrich Farm, near Nairobi

557 WATCH AN OSTRICH EGG HATCH

All year

It's an amazing thing to watch a new life emerge from an egg, and an even more amazing thing if that egg is the biggest type in the world. The chances of catching the event in the wild are fairly slim, but it is possible to see it in the controlled conditions of a farm. Interestingly, although ostrich eggs are the biggest bird egg, they are proportionately the smallest relative to the size of the adult bird.

Kenya • Maasai Mara National Reserve

558 RECITE "I'M A GNU"—TO A GNU

July to October

Flanders and Swann—the 1950s and '60s musical double act—had a song about the gnu, calling him the "g-nicest work of g-nature in the zoo." You'll need to change the words when you see the gnu (or wildebeest, as it's more commonly known) on the plains of Africa rather than a zoo, but it won't be easy to find something that rhymes so well with "g-nu"! See millions arrive from Tanzania's Serengeti in the later half of the year.

Kenya • Saiwa Swamp National Park

559 SPY ON A SITATUNGA

All year

The Saiwa Swamp National Park was established purely to protect the sitatunga deer. The park is only small, but perfectly set up with platforms above the swamp, where visitors can wait patiently until they see the telltale twitch of the sitatunga deer's ears in the vegetation below. These shaggy antelopes can hide from danger by submerging underwater with just their noses showing—a handy trick to avoid both flies and predators.

560 | *The vital ecosystem of a mangrove forest*

Kenya • Gazi, along the coast
560 STUDY A KEY ECOSYSTEM
All year

Mangrove forests are distinguished by their tangled roots holding the small trees away from the water. These roots act as an essential nursery for many fish species, while the forests offer the land coastal protection. A project at Gazi, begun in 2009, is bringing its mangrove forests back to their former glory, with locals gathering regularly to plant many thousands of seedlings. Witness the benefits of the program first-hand, including the boom in local fish stocks.

Kenya • Around Lake Naivasha, even in gardens
561 KEEP YOUR DISTANCE FROM A GREEN WOOD HOOPOE
All year

The green wood hoopoe is a pretty bird: slender and a dark metallic green, with a long, gently curved red bill. However, its elegant looks conceal less elegant behavior. If the bird feels threatened, it turns its tail to the source and then lets rip with a foul-smelling odor that smells something like rotten eggs. The juvenile birds will even go one step further than this and squirt liquid feces at an attacker.

Kenya • Mount Kenya National Park
563 SEE AN ELAND FLEHMENING
All year, near a good scent

Eland's are large antelopes, and quite bovine in appearance. They like to flehmen (as many species do), which is pulling back their lips and inhaling through their nostrils for several seconds.

Kenya • Shaba National Reserve
564 SPOT BIRDS THAT FLY BY NIGHT
All year, at night

Not all nocturnal fliers are bats. The nightjar perches on trees and rocks at night, waiting for moths and other insects to fly past.

Kenya • Mount Kenya National Park
562 FIND A TINY ANIMAL WITH AN ENDEARING NAME
All year

It's the perfect oxymoron of the animal world—an elephant shrew, so called because it is shrew-like, but with a long nose. Although technically it isn't even, in fact, a shrew. They are found all over Africa in open land and forest, mountains and plains. Elephant shrews hunt in the daytime for insects, worms, and spiders, and despite their tiny size, they are incredibly fast, and have been known to reach speeds of almost 19 mph (30 kmh).

Kenya • Lake Baringo
565 IDENTIFY BIRDS ON LAKE BARINGO
October to April

Incredibly, over 470 different species of birds are known to have visited this one lake in Kenya.

Kenya • Ol Pejeta Conservancy

566 AID BLACK RHINO CONSERVATION

All year

Between 1960 and 1995, the number of black rhinos in the wild dropped by a staggering 98 percent. The shocking figure did spur some concerted conservation efforts, and the numbers are recovering, but black rhinos are still critically endangered. They live around trees since they are grazers, with a pointed lip that distinguishes them from the white rhino. The lip helps them take leaves off bushes and trees.

Kenya • Amboseli National Park

567 FIND THE WORLD'S SMALLEST KINGFISHER

All year

The world's smallest kingfisher is just 4.3 to 5 in (11 to 13 cm) long. It is the African pygmy kingfisher, although in some countries they have the nickname of "dozer" since they have a bit of a habit of nodding off—including the head jerks that go with it. They have a bright blue back and orange underparts, and are usually seen in woodlands; they eat insects rather than fish, so can be spotted away from streams.

Kenya • Lake Bogoria

568 WATCH COTTON CANDY FLAMINGOS

April to June

Seen from a distance, Lake Bogoria (famous for its hot springs and active geysers) appears to have pink silt around its edges. It is only as you get closer that you realize that the "silt" is, in fact, thousands of flamingos that come to the lake for the mineral-rich content of its waters. Both greater and lesser flamingos are found here—greater are larger with lighter pink legs. They get their color from the algae in their diet, abundant in this alkaline lake.

Kenya • Lake Victoria

569 SNORKEL
WITH CICHLIDS
All year

Cichlids encompass many
species of vibrantly beautiful
fish, all of which evolve quickly
to benefit from their environs.
There are around 200 species
in this lake alone.

Kenya • Meru National Park

570 DON'T FREAK OUT
AT A NAKED MOLE RAT
All year

The clue's in the name with this
odd-looking hairless species of
rodent. It has been referred to as
a potato with legs, or a bratwurst
with teeth—hairless and pale,
with stumpy legs.

Kenya • Meru National Park

571 OBSERVE THE
PRETTY DUIKER
All year

The common duiker is a gentle
antelope that lives in the bush of
the savanna. Its name comes
from the Dutch for "diver"; when
it feels threatened it dives into
the bush for cover.

566 | *The critically endangered black rhino*

Kenya • Tsavo East National Park
572 WATCH ELEPHANTS TURN RED
All year

It's not as surreal as it sounds. The elephants in this national park cover themselves in the red dust of the soil as a way of taking a bath. The dust acts like an exfoliator, removing dead skin and any bugs that thought they'd hop aboard for a tasty meal. All elephants indulge in the practice—the dust in Tsavo just happens to be red. There are around 10,000 elephants here, but since it's one of Kenya's biggest wildlife parks, you still have to know where to look. Many of the elephants are known by name to the wardens, and a good guide can teach you about the family connections and bring a sense of history to these fabulous animals.

Kenya • Tsavo East National Park

573 WATCH A GAZELLE REACH THE HIGHEST LEAVES

All year

The Somali name for the gerenuk means "giraffe-necked," and when you see it, you will understand why. To make even greater use of this long neck, gerenuks stand on their hind legs to browse even higher branches on the trees.

Kenya • Tsavo East National Park

574 MARVEL AT THE CONSTRUCTION OF A TERMITE MOUND

All year

It is a feat of nature that tiny termites, the size of a grape seed, can build huge, towering cathedrals of termite mounds that can be up to 16.5 ft (5 m) high. The trick is to be part of a colony one million strong—or more.

Kenya • Laikipia County

575 WATCH OSTRICH COURTSHIP

March to September

When a male ostrich wants to mate it starts rolling alternate wings forward. If the female likes what it sees, it runs in circles around the male with wings pointing downward, at which point the male winds its head in spirals until the female drops to the ground, smitten, and the male can mount it.

Tanzania • Ngorongoro Crater

576 VISIT AFRICA'S GARDEN OF EDEN

All year (less busy in winter)

The volcanic Ngorongoro Crater is the largest unbroken and unflooded crater in the world, and a true microcosm of nature. Within its natural walls you will see elephants, black rhinos, lions, leopards, buffaloes, hyenas, cheetahs, wildebeest, zebras, gazelles, and hundreds of bird species.

Tanzania • Ngorongoro Crater

577 ENJOY THE LAUGH OF A HYENA

All year

Hyenas are often depicted as lazy and greedy, but they do a great job of cleaning up old carcasses. They live together in large hierarchical groups, or clans, led by an alpha female, and several clans inhabit the Ngorongoro Crater.

Tanzania • Zanzibar

578 HEAR THE CRIES OF A BUSHBABY

All year, at night

The bushbaby got its name from the sound its cries make at night—they sound a lot like a human baby, but louder. This nocturnal primate has a very cute face with big eyes and oversized ears to help it navigate through the darkness.

575 | *A male ostrich puts on a display*

Tanzania • Zanzibar
579 HUNT FOR OCTOPUS
All year

The eastern coast of Zanzibar is protected by a coral reef, and twice a day this is exposed by the tide, creating the chance to take a rare reef walk. In the rock pools and crevices, there are sea urchins, sea cucumbers, and small stranded fish, and if you really put yourself into the mind of an octopus, you might find a small hole covered with a couple of stones, which the octopus has pulled over it as a disguise. Nudge these out the way and you might spot its purple limbs.

Tanzania • Zanzibar Island
580 TAKE A SPICE TOUR ON SPICE ISLAND
All year

A spice tour on this island, off the coast of Tanzania, leaves you feeling hyperaware of the bounty of nature. In the space of an afternoon you are taken to see where cloves, nutmeg, cinnamon, pepper, turmeric, vanilla, cardamom, and chiles grow. It reminds you of how beautiful many of these plants are—such as the nutmeg, wrapped in its waxy pink lace covering—as well as how important they are to our food.

Tanzania • Chumbe Island
581 SEE A SNEAKY COCONUT CRAB
All year

This is a phenomenal creature—not only is it the largest crab in the world, but it can also climb palm trees and open coconuts with its pincers. It has the alternative names of "robber crab" and "palm thief"—not because it will steal your valuables but because it is such an opportunistic feeder, eating anything it finds around it, from carrion to old trees. These crabs live in burrows on dry land, but females lay eggs in the sea.

Tanzania • Mount Kilimanjaro
584 CLIMB KILIMANJARO FOR THE PLANTS
June to October

Climbing Kilimanjaro is often described as crossing four seasons in four days, and it has the variety of flora to match.

584 | *Trekking toward Kilimanjaro*

Tanzania • Amani Nature Reserve
582 SEE A CHAMELEON CHANGE COLOR
All year

Tanzania has almost 100 species of chameleons, in different sizes and adornments, such as crests, horns, and spikes. They are found almost everywhere there are trees. They change color when excited, going from a light green to blue and orange, say, in milliseconds. They are easier to spot at night since they tend to turn a pale color when they sleep, so can be easily picked out in the beam of a flashlight.

Tanzania • Jozani-Chwaka National Park
583 BE CHARMED BY A COLOBUS
All year

The Zanzibar red colobus monkey looks white or gray from the front, with black bands down its arms. Its rich red back gives it its name. It has a small head surrounded by fuzzy fur, and petite facial features. The population on Zanzibar was separated from that on the mainland thousands of years ago when sea levels rose, and has evolved to be slightly smaller than its mainland cousins.

Tanzania • Arusha
585 WISE UP ABOUT BABOONS
All year

Baboons are some of the largest monkeys around. They live on the ground, not in trees, and are dangerously smart—even able to recognize written words. Combine this with their curious nature, and you have to be careful. They plan and execute raids on homes and farms, and though perhaps not intentional, a baboon once knocked out the power supply to a whole town by meddling with the wiring at the local power plant.

Tanzania • Amani Nature Reserve

586 SEE THE AFRICAN VIOLET IN SITU

October and November

This delicate and beloved indoor houseplant is an even prettier sight blooming in rocky crags in the Usambara Mountains.

Tanzania • Tarangire National Park

588 SPOT A MOUNTAIN GRAY WOODPECKER

All year

Listen out for the drumming of the mountain gray woodpecker, then identify its gray body and green wings.

Tanzania • Serengeti

590 FEEL THE LOVE FOR LOVEBIRDS

All year

These tiny parrots mate for life, mourn the loss of their partner, and feed each other if they've been apart.

Tanzania • Selous Reserve

587 SNAP AN OXPECKER ON A HIPPO

All year

An oxpecker sitting on the back of a hippo and picking off insects is one of the most iconic images of Africa, and an arrangement that seems to suit both animals. Recent research, however, has cast doubt on the true benefits to the hippos and other mammals that host the birds, since the insects they eat have already sucked up a bellyful of hippo blood.

Tanzania • Serengeti National Park

589 LOOK UP AT A GIRAFFE

All year

As you drive through the Serengeti National park in Tanzania, giraffe are animals that are a fairly reliable sighting. They tower up from the plains, standing between 14.75 and 18 ft (4.5 and 5.5 m) tall, with their neck making up at least one-third of that.

A giraffe's markings are unique, like human fingerprints, and they get darker as they mature. They also differ in style from one subspecies to another. (There are nine main subspecies of giraffe.) The Maasai giraffe that is found in Tanzania, for example, has irregularly shaped spots with wavy edges, while the reticulated giraffe has narrow, smooth-edged markings with light coloring between them, which creates a pattern that looks more like a mosaic. Giraffe tongues are famously black.

589 | *Looking up to Maasai giraffes*

Tanzania • Serengeti National Park
591 WATCH WILDEBEEST MIGRATE
April to June

Until you have seen it, the scale of the wildebeest migration is hard to fathom. Around a million animals form into rows that can reach up to 25 miles (40 km) long as they follow the rains in search of freshly growing grass. Along the way they have to contend with big cats hiding in the grass, waiting to pick off the young and the weak, and crossing rivers just swaps one predator for another as huge Nile crocodiles eye up their next meal. Be sure to check on your timings; the migration is constantly on the move, and you don't want to arrive after it has passed by.

Tanzania • Serengeti National Park

592 SEE AN AFRICAN HARE SPRINT

All year, at night

When you're the perfect meal-size for a number of ferocious African predators, it's convenient if you can run fast. Happily the African savanna hare can reach a top speed of 43 mph (69 kmh), which helps it evade capture, as does its habit of leaping sideways suddenly while in midair in order to break the scent trail it leaves behind. It's a nocturnal species, though, so it's not easy to catch it in full action mode.

593 | Grant's gazelles seen at sunrise

Tanzania • Serengeti National Park

593 WATCH A GRANT'S GAZELLE LEAP

All year

Grant's gazelles are a very beautiful example of their kind, with a delicate red coloring to the body, white underparts, and a distinctive white flash on the rump that extends up onto their back. They are fast but not fast enough to be ignored by cheetahs; as a result they tend to avoid the long grasses that cheetahs can hide in and instead browse in shorter grasses. They migrate, but in the opposite direction of the wildebeest.

Tanzania • Serengeti National Park

594 IDENTIFY A TOPI BY ITS HORNS

All year

What's lovely about the topi is its rich brown coat and the even darker patches on its legs and face mask that make its face appear almost black. This creature is a large antelope— very similar to a hartebeest— and is often seen feeding on the long grasses of the Serengeti. A male topi stands in one visible place for long stretches so that other males can see it and know that that is its territory. Spot its strong, ridged horns.

Tanzania • Ruaha National Park

595 KUDOS IF YOU SPOT A KUDU

All year

Early morning and late afternoon are the best times for spotting greater kudus since they tend to come farther out of woodland to graze on brush and grass or seek water then. Males have fabulous horns that twist around on themselves as they point toward the sky, and on their backs they have white stripes across their coats, which can range from gray to brown. Ruaha is home to both greater and lesser kudus.

Tanzania • Usambara Mountains

596 LOOK FOR A DESERT ROSE IN BLOOM

All year (spring is best)

These hardy plants, with their large bulbous stems, are a wonderful sight to see on a mountain-walking safari.

Zambia • Kasanka National Park

598 WITNESS ZAMBIA'S BAT MIGRATION

October to December

As the fruit in Kasanka ripens after the rains, ten million straw-colored fruit bats descend on the park to harvest it.

Angola • Kissama National Park

597 SEE THE RED-CRESTED TURACO

All year

Angola's national bird has a trick up its sleeve. When it's alarmed it lifts its wings to show off warning red patches underneath.

Malawi • Majete Wildlife Reserve

599 SAVE MALAWI'S LOST WILDLIFE

June to December

Visit and support Malawi's only Big Five park in its conservation work, following years of poaching and habitat loss.

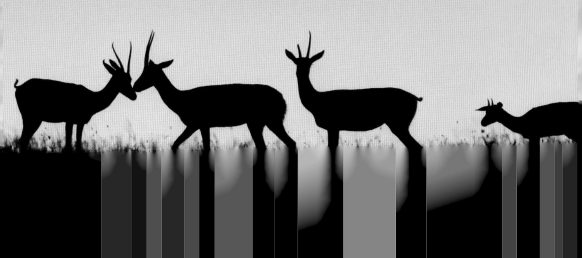

Mozambique • Riverbanks and open woodland
600 SEE SAUSAGES GROWING FROM TREES
December to June

The fruits that hang from a sausage tree—or kigelia, to give it its proper name—make you stop and look twice and wonder whether they have been put there by a person or grown from the tree. They can be from 12 in to 3 ft long (30 cm to 1 m) and are the shape of a large sausage.

Mozambique • Pinnacles Reef
601 ENCOUNTER AN UNDERWATER APEX
All year

Sharks are the apex predators of the sea. When their numbers fall, the sea's ecosystem goes out of balance. Diving with these magnifcent beasts is a way to learn more about them. The bull shark in Mozambique can be aggressive, so you're well advised to make this dive with an experienced guide.

Namibia • Spitzkoppe

602 SIT UP AND WATCH MEERKATS
All year

Watch a meerkat rush about and use its large claws to dig in the sandy desert floor as it looks for grubs. Nearby another one of the clan, which can be up to 30 strong, will be sitting up and using its tail to help it balance upright, keeping an eye out for danger. Meerkats famously take turns to be on sentry duty.

Namibia • Southern Kunene region

603 DISCOVER MORE ABOUT DESERT ELEPHANTS
All year

Namibia's desert elephants are the same species as Africa's other elephants, but they have adapted certain survival mechanisms to live in this dry semidesert environment. Most notably their feet are a little bit bigger to help them travel across sand dunes, which, on rare occasions, they have been filmed sliding down.

Namibia • Otjiwarongo region

604 SUPPORT THE CHEETAHS
All year

Volunteer at a cheetah research station for a thoroughly unique view on, and in-depth education into, African wildlife.

Namibia • Etosha National Park

605 SEE THE CAT WITH THE LONGEST LEGS
All year

The serval is smaller than a cheetah and a less fearsome predator, but still wonderful to see.

Namibia • Luderitz Island

606 MEET AN AFRICAN PENGUIN

All year

You'll probably hear an African penguin before you see one—it's also known as the "jackass penguin" because of its loud bray.

Namibia • Namib-Naukluft National Park

607 BE WOWED BY A PLANT THAT IS 1,000 YEARS OLD

All year

The welwitschia may be no higher than your desert boot, but it could have been growing since the Byzantine Empire stretched across Europe.

Namibia • Marienfluss Valley

608 PUZZLE AT NAMIBIA'S FAIRY CIRCLES

All year

For stretches of the Namib desert, there is a phenomenon of barren, circular patches of earth among the arid grassland. It could be a survival strategy of the surrounding grass to maximize water capture, or it could be unexplained and a little bit magical.

608 | *The mysterious fairy circles of Namibia*

Namibia • Southern
Namib desert
609 SEE A HALFMENS
August to October

The halfmens is a tall succulent plant—a thick, spine-covered stem that is bulbous at the bottom, leans a bit at the top, and grows in small groups. From August to October they flower around their crowns.

Namibia • Southern region; roadsides
610 DON'T MISTAKE A NEST FOR A HAYSTACK
All year

On top of utility poles, or on low branches, you'll see what look like huge haystacks. These are the communal nests of sociable weaver birds, housing 500 birds at once and lasting years.

Botswana • Chobe
National Park
611 SEE THE WORLD'S HEAVIEST FLYING BIRD
All year

You can't blame the brown-and-gray Kori bustard for not wanting to fly; it weighs 42 lb (19 kg). When it does take to the air, though, with huge wingbeats, it's a phenomenal sight.

Botswana • Okavango Delta
612 SPOT BIRDS FROM A HOUSEBOAT
All year

The Okavango Delta is a birder's paradise, offering you the chance to see hundreds of species from your deck, from cranes to hornbills and fish eagles.

Botswana • Chobe
National Park
613 BEWARE AN AFRICAN BUFFALO
April to October

In the dry season, herds of up to 1,000 buffalo can be seen on the river floodplains. Lone males can be very aggressive.

Botswana • Okavango Delta
616 SEE HIPPOS IN BOTSWANA
All year

Hippopotamuses can initially look like logs or stepping-stones in the water—until they raise their heads and noisily blow air out of their nostrils. Hippos spend their days in the water and come out at night to feed on grass; one animal can munch through as much as 150 lb (68 kg) a night. Periodically in the day, male hippos might have a territorial battle. They do this by yawning wide (they can open their huge mouths by almost 180 degrees) and crashing them into each other.

Botswana • Okavango Delta
614 ENJOY WATCHING A GAUDY ROLLER
All year

The lilac-breasted roller is not only a superbly colored bird, but it is also a good one for photos since it perches up high.

Botswana • Okavango Delta; holes in trees
615 BEWARE THE BLACK MAMBA
All year

This highly venomous snake is actually greeny gray; it's the inside of its mouth that is black.

Botswana • Okavango Delta
617 DON'T OVERLOOK SMALL CREATURES
February

As the rains restart the cycle of life, and plant life blooms, bringing butterflies and birds—remember there is more to a safari than big mammals.

Botswana • Rocky outcrops in the Tuli Block
618 LOCATE A ROCK HYRAX FAMILY
All year

This large-bodied, small-headed mammal—also called a dassie—lives in family groups that can be up to 80 strong.

Botswana • Okavango Delta
619 WATCH LIONS HUNT IN WATER
May to October

The lions of the Okavango have adapted to their home. The delta floods for six months a year, so they've learned to swim—even while on a hunt.

616 | *A hippo's head breaks the water's surface*

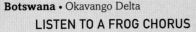

Botswana • Okavango Delta
LISTEN TO A FROG CHORUS
All year, after sunset

The sound of thousands of frogs is the nightly lullaby in the Okavango Delta. Some chirp, some cheep, others rumble and croak, and all start just after sunset and go on long into the night. Though the noise is large, the frogs are often tiny. A *mokoro* trip—in a traditional dugout canoe—around the delta can take you close enough to the reeds where many of these tiny amphibians live.

Zimbabwe • Lake Kariba
621 WATCH A BIRD SWIM LIKE A SNAKE
All year

The African darter is a cormorant-like bird with a black body and a long, reddish-brown neck. It swims with its body below water, and only its neck visible from above, looking rather like a snake.

620 | *Experiencing the sounds of the Okavango from a canoe*

Zimbabwe • Lower Zambezi National Park

622 MAKE NOTES ON A SECRETARY BIRD

All year

A secretary bird is quite unlike any other. It is a raptor, and its body resembles an eagle's, but it is perched atop a set of elegant long legs, like those of a crane. It struts around in open savanna, looking for prey in the form of mice, snakes, and lizards, but it can trap mammals as large as mongooses and hares. It uses its feet as well as its beak to stamp on prey, and can deliver a force equal to five times its bodyweight, meaning that although it's a slow runner and a reluctant flier, it remains a deadly hunter.

South Africa • Cape Floristic Region

623 SET FOOT IN A BIODIVERSITY HOT SPOT

All year

The Cape Floristic Region in the southeast corner of South Africa is one of the richest biodiversity hot spots on Earth. There are 9,000 species of plants found in these 3,860 square miles (10,000 sq km), making it more biodiverse for its size than the Amazon rain forest. The majority of species are "fynbos vegetation," characterized by being evergreen, hard-leaved shrubs. Fynbos requires fire every 10 to 14 years to thrive—to kill off both pathogens and old vegetation—and some species only grow immediately after fire.

624 | *A sea of springtime color in Namaqualand*

South Africa • Skilpad Wildflower Reserve

624 TAKE A FLOWER SAFARI

Late July to early September

Namaqualand in bloom is an amazing sight. Carpets of multicolored wildflowers spread across the usually arid landscape as far as the eye can see. They come after the rains, so timing can vary, and with more than 4,000 species of wildflower, each year's display is different, depending on the conditions that have led up to it. Vibrant orange gousbloms and pink vygies are speckled with more delicate white nemesias and lilac babianas. As you move from one land type to another, the color palette changes with you, giving rise to stunning vistas as well as intricate local finds. In many areas you can hike through the flowers, enjoying them at your leisure, or go on a driving tour with a knowledgeable guide to see the more unusual blooms and the best displays. However you seek to discover it—as long as the timing works in your favor—you'll have views that remain with you forever, and spectacular photos for the album.

South Africa • Duiker Island

625 SNORKEL WITH CAPE FUR SEALS

September to May

Cape fur seals are year-round residents on islands in the bays around Cape Town. Duiker Island is on the colder Atlantic side of the peninsula and surrounded by kelp forests and reefs that stop sharks from coming in to feed. It makes Duiker a perfect haven for snorkeling with the seals that truly come to life as they leave land and are able to move freely and nimbly under water. Larger than their Australian cousins, these seals are also deeper divers, reaching depths of 670 ft (204 m).

South Africa • Table Mountain National Park

626 CREDIT THE CRUELTY OF PLANTS

December to January

The Cape sundew is a carnivorous plant with a rosette of long, narrow leaves that are covered in hairs coated in a sticky mucus. When an insect comes in to investigate, it gets trapped in the mucus, at which point the leaves fold in, stifling any hope of escape. The mucus then starts to digest the prey. Look out for the plant's pink flowers in December and January; you'll see it along the riverbanks and in marshes.

South Africa • Hermanus

627 WATCH SOUTHERN RIGHT WHALES FROM THE CLIFFTOPS

June to November

Every year hundreds of southern right whales come to Walker Bay off Hermanus to mate and breed. A walk along the cliffs in the town can be enough to catch the fabulous sight of whales breaching and slapping their tails in the bay. At times they have been seen as close as 16 ft (5 m) to the shore. Look carefully and you might make out the two blowholes of the southern right.

South Africa • KwaZulu-Natal

628 FIND A TRUE BLUE

All year

The blue crane is South Africa's national bird. It's a fine choice—a handsome, long-legged bird that stands over 3 ft (1 m) tall and has a delicate gray-blue all-over coloring. Its wingtip feathers trail almost to the ground like an elegant ballgown and are often tipped with darker coloring. If you spot two together, stay and watch them awhile as pairs perform a courtship dance that involves running and jumping and tossing tufts of grass and even small mammals up into the air. They are usually seen on open grassland and in shallow wetlands.

South Africa • KwaZulu-Natal

629 RING THE CHRISTMAS BELLS

December

Christmas bells—or *Sandersonia aurantiaca*—is a pretty little plant that produces deep-orange, lantern-shaped flowers in December. It was once a common sight on the grasslands, all the way from the eastern Cape up into Swaziland, but is now more likely to be seen cultivated, since it's a popular garden plant. You can still find it in some national parks, however, and it'll be a joy if you do manage to locate a specimen in the wild.

South Africa • KwaZulu-Natal

630 WITNESS THE BRUTALITY OF WILD DOGS

May to September

African wild dogs have the look of animals that are not going to give anything up in a hurry. And it's true they are formidable pack hunters. They chase prey for long distances, tiring it out before going in for the kill, and then to kill it they rather savagely tear it apart (although it does apparently make for a quick death). Among their own their behavior is much more gentle. They live in sociable packs led by a monogamous breeding pair, and the whole pack helps bring up pups. If any are weak or sick, the others share their food and help them out.

South Africa • Robben Island

631 WORK WITH PENGUINS

April to August

Penguins were once numerous on this island, but over the last century their numbers have dropped by 90 percent. Help conservationists carry out surveys to monitor their populations, as well as those of other seabirds.

630 | *A pack of African wild dogs*

South Africa • Gansbaai

632 REASSESS THE GREAT WHITE

All year

They have 300 teeth arranged in rows, an exceptional sense of smell, are around 16 ft (5 m) long, and can move through the water at 15 mph (24 kmh): great white sharks certainly sound ferocious, but isn't it time we saw them as an apex predator rather than man's worst enemy? Their main diet is sea lions, seals, small whales, and carrion, and although they are guilty of between one-third and one-half of all shark attacks on humans each year, these are usually "sample bites" from a naturally curious animal rather than an attempt to get a meal.

South Africa • Richtersveld National Park

633 DON'T TREAD ON A LITHOP

All year (a guide is useful)

Lithops are succulent plants that look like a stone cleaved in two. It's a smart survival technique that stops animals from seeing them as food during a drought—but it makes them tricky to spot.

South Africa • Throughout the eastern coast

634 GAUGE IF IT'S A FLOWER OR A BIRD

May to December

There is something very uplifting about spotting a flower in the wild that you have previously only seen in a vase. The bird of paradise, or *Strelitzia reginae*, is a stunning flower with many brightly colored petals emerging from a sharply pointed pod—it could easily be a hummingbird or an actual bird-of-paradise hovering by a bush. It is pollinated by releasing pollen onto the feet of sunbirds.

South Africa • Mkuze Game Reserve

635 CHOOSE THE MOST BEAUTIFUL KINGFISHER

All year

There are ten species in South Africa to select from, but spotting any of them is a treat.

South Africa • Kruger National Park

637 SEE ANOTHER "AA"

All year

The little-known aardwolf is in the same family as hyenas, but its main diet is termites.

South Africa • Throughout

636 TICK OFF AN A TO Z OF ANIMALS

All year

From an aardvark right through to a zebra, you could complete an alphabet of wildlife in South Africa.

South Africa • Kruger National Park

638 SEE JACANAS' FEET

All year

This pretty chestnut-and-white wading bird has evolved feet that are almost as long as its body.

South Africa • Kruger National Park; near rivers

639 SEE THE WORLD'S LARGEST KINGFISHER

All year

What the giant kingfisher lacks in magnificent colorways, it makes up for in size. At 17 in (43 cm) long, this is a big bird. It is black with white spots, a distinctive shaggy crest, and a brown chest. Look for them near rivers and streams where they perch to spot prey before diving right under the water to catch it. Their nest is a long tunnel that they excavate into a riverbank using their feet and bills, laying their eggs in a chamber at the end.

South Africa • Kruger National Park

640 DISCOVER WHAT IT MEANS TO PRONK

All year

Nobody is sure why springbok "pronk," but pronk they do. It is when they strut along, then jump up several feet into the air, back arched, legs and head pointing downward, and the white hair of their rump revealed. It might be a way to let predators know that they have been spotted, or to show predators how agile they are—or to show off their fitness to herd rivals. *Pronk* itself is a Dutch and Afrikaans word, meaning "to show off."

South Africa • Kruger National Park

641 HEAR A FISH EAGLE HUNT

May to November

This beautiful, distinctive eagle has a large brown body, white head and chest, and yellow face. It usually feeds on fish that it grabs from lakes and rivers with its huge talons, and makes a distinctive *quock quock* as it carries it home. Chicks hatch between May and November, which means the adults have to go out on more hunting trips, thereby giving you a better chance of seeing—and hearing—them in action.

| *A fish eagle on the lookout for prey*

South Africa • Kruger National Park
642 SPOT THE BIG FIVE
All year

The term "Big Five" was coined in the days when African safaris were all about hunting and sticking animal-head trophies on your wall, rather than seeing animals in their natural environment. The lion, leopard, rhinoceros, elephant, and buffalo were deemed the five most difficult animals to hunt on foot, and therefore the five best trophies to collect. They are still iconic animals to see, although many on a wildlife safari would add others to the list, such as cheetahs, giraffes, zebras, hippos, and crocodiles.

Seeing these animals is often what makes a trip to Africa so special. Huge, powerful beasts seen in wide open landscapes. To watch them interact—such as sharing a waterhole or even hunting each other—is an amazing sight, and conservation of these species is essential now, so that future generations can share the same experiences. Hunting is still legal in many countries, and debate rages over whether this helps animal populations through protecting their habitat, or hinders them by making it easier for poaching to happen. For the individual animals, though, it's without doubt better to end up as a photo on someone's wall, rather than a trophy.

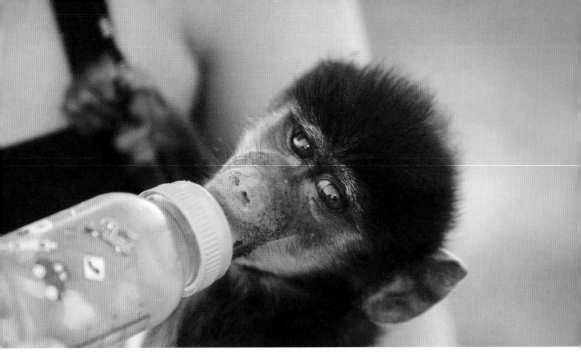

645 | *A volunteer nursing an orphaned monkey*

South Africa • Kruger National Park

643 WATCH BIRDS WALK ON WATER

All year

Technically the black crake doesn't walk on water but on vegetation floating in that water, which it grasps with its long toes. This glossy black bird with bright red legs struts around grassy marshes and ponds, feeding on fish, frogs, and tadpoles with its specially adapted bill, but is also known to eat the eggs of other bird species, and even carrion. You might also catch it perched on the rump of a hippo or warthog, snacking on parasites.

South Africa • Kruger National Park

644 FIND A DIFFERENT TYPE OF ANTELOPE

All year

The sable is an antelope that covers a fairly small range in Africa's eastern corner. It is a beautiful beast, with a dark brown, almost black, glossy coat, and white stripes on its face. Identify it by its long horns, which arch backward slightly and are fearsome enough that they can mortally wound an attacking lion. They travel in herds that change in size throughout the year as pregnant mothers separate off from the main herd.

South Africa • Riverside Wildlife Rehabilitation Centre

645 NURSE A MONKEY IN AN ORPHANAGE

All year

Hunting in South Africa leaves many orphaned primates each year, and others are injured in car accidents or by other predators. Riverside cares for these animals with the aim of reintroducing them back into nature. Since 1994, they have reintroduced 19 vervet troops, one baboon troop, and many bushbabies back into the wild. Help them out by cleaning enclosures, preparing and growing food, and bottle-feeding the babies.

647 | *A shark's fin, seen from a safe distance*

South Africa • Timbavati
Game Reserve
646 SEE A WHITE LION
All year

There have been reports of
white lions in Timbavati for
many years. Legend has it that
during Queen Numbi's reign 400
years ago, a white lion cub was
born, and the event was heralded
by a star that fell to Earth.
White lions are not albinos;
their coloring is a result of
leucism—where animals have
pigment in their eyes and skin,
but not in their pelt. It makes
the lions (which are found only
in Timbavati and surrounding
areas) a slightly mystical sight.

South Africa • Off Richards Bay
647 WATCH A FIN CUT THROUGH WATER
All year

It's an iconic image: the shark's fin slicing through the ocean. Two
currents meet off the eastern coast of South Africa, which means
there is plenty of prey for big predators, and many species of sharks
are frequent visitors here. A calm day is best for looking for shark's
fins, and—for obvious reasons—being in a boat rather than the water
is best for the search.

South Africa • Wakkerstroom Biosphere Reserve
648 BE IMPRESSED BY A WIDOW BIRD'S TAIL
October to February

For a bird that is only 7.75 in (20 cm) long, the long-tailed widow bird
has an impressive 19.75 in (50 cm) tail that blows dramatically in the
wind when the bird perches.

South Africa • Port St. Johns

649 SEE A SARDINE RUN

May to July

Take a diving expedition and share the point of view of millions of sardines following a current up Africa's east coast, with hundreds of predators in their wake.

Swaziland • Mbuluzi Game Reserve

650 WONDER AT THE MARKINGS OF A ZEBRA

All year

Zebras might be plentiful in Africa, but that doesn't diminish how intriguing their markings are. They are so perfect, and so complete, maintaining their definition and irregularity right up to the tips of the mane. A recent theory proposes that the stripes serve to ward off biting flies.

Swaziland • Hlane Royal National Park
651 TRACK AN IMPALA BY ITS SPOOR
All year

A walking safari is a fabulous way to see the African bush and feel very close to the animals. It also gives you the chance to learn about other elements of a species, such as their footprints—or spoor. Guides use spoor to track animals. Impala spoor are a distinctive elongated heart shape with a gap down the middle. The narrow end is the front of the foot.

Swaziland • Hlane Royal National Park
652 SEE THE GENTLE STRENGTH OF A RHINO
All year

In 2018, the last male northern white rhino in the wild died. The southern white was nearly as critical when, in the early 1900s, numbers were as low as 50 animals. Fortunately conservation measures have been hugely successful, and it is now the most populous of the rhino species, with around 20,000 in the wild. The "white" comes from the German *weidt*, which means "wide," referring to its mouth.

649 | *The striking coloration of zebras*

Madagascar • Avenue of the Baobabs

653 DISCOVER THE LEGEND OF THE BAOBAB TREE

All year; sunset and sunrise give the best colors

The baobab tree is one of the most iconic plants of Africa: a great bulbous trunk, bare except for the sparse branches that sprout at the top, and around 66 ft (20 m) tall. Its appearance has given rise to the legend that the baobab once angered God so much that he plucked it out of the land and turned it over so that its head became its roots and its roots were left sticking up in the air. In the wet season baobabs greedily drink in all the water they can, storing it in their huge trunks to sustain them through the dry season. And for the nine months of the dry season, they drop their leaves and live off water stored in those great round trunks.

654 | *A juicy-looking tomato frog*

Madagascar • Masoala
National Park
654 GUESS THE COLOR OF THE TOMATO FROG
All year

It's not a trick question; it really is bright red. When threatened, it inflates itself—resembling a tomato even more—but if a predator still tries to eat it, it releases a sticky white substance that numbs the predator's mouth. This is one of the 70 percent of Madagascan species that are found on this island alone. It breeds in water but travels into the forests at other times.

Madagascar • Tsingy de
Bemaraha National Park
655 SEEK OUT THE SMALLEST LIVING LEMUR
All year, at night

The pygmy mouse lemur is hard to spot. Not only is it just 5 in (13 cm) long, it's also nocturnal. However, it does give nature viewers a chance by returning to the same sleeping spots more often than once. So if a guide has found one asleep before, you could get lucky! It also freezes in light from a flashlight, so if one is heard scattering in the trees, you might see it before it dashes off.

Madagascar • Tsingy de
Bemaraha National Park
656 SEE AN OLIVE BEE-EATER
All year

The olive bee-eater, or Madagascar bee-eater, is olive green in color, with a reddish chin and reddish flashes under its wings. Its face is white with a black stripe across its eyes like a highwayman. It makes for very elegant photos as it catches insects while it's in flight. Listen out for its call: a squeaky chirp that sounds like a wonky wheel on an old piano.

Madagascar • Berenty Reserve

657 COUNT THE TAIL RINGS ON A RING-TAILED LEMUR

October to November (when the young are active)

Surely the best known of Madagascar's lemurs (perhaps because they breed well in captivity and thus have been popular attractions in zoos and safari parks for many years). There are always between 13 and 15 rings on the tail, which is no use for climbing but is used by its owner for scent marking. If you watch ring-tailed lemurs, you'll see them enjoying the charming habit of rubbing their tails on their wrists and in their armpits. Their scent gives information to female lemurs seeking a mate and also establishes dominance among males.

Madagascar • Andasibe-Mantadia National Park

658 SAY HI TO AN AYE-AYE

All year, at night

It's very rare to see an aye-aye and its nocturnal tree-dwelling habits. Look for a long skeletal middle finger to identify it.

657 | *Ring-tailed lemurs strike a pose*

Madagascar • Andasibe-Mantadia National Park

659 FEEL THE JOY OF A MOTH

May to October

The sunset moth, endemic to Madagascar, is an absolute treasure of the insect world—and the best thing is, unlike most moths, it is active in the daytime. It has shimmering yellows and oranges and greens and blues on its wings, caused by tiny clear, curved scales that reflect the light. It also has a habit of getting its nectar from plants with white flowers, adding to the visual joy.

Madagascar • Andasibe-Mantadia National Park (Perinet Reserve)

660 FIND THE LARGEST LIVING LEMUR

All year

Indri are the largest living lemur and truly fabulous to see. They have big round eyes and great pompoms for ears on the sides of their heads. They are black and white and about the size of a large toddler. They live in family groups up in the trees, and although endangered, taking an early morning walk with a guide gives you a pretty good chance of spotting them.

Madagascar • Andasibe-Mantadia National Park

661 MARVEL AT A GIRAFFE WEEVIL

April to June

You can tell from the name that the giraffe weevil of Madagascar is going to have an extraordinary neck, but that might not prepare you for just how very odd it is—the male's thin twiggy neck is the same length as its body, with a total size of 1 in (2.5 cm). It is also three times the size of the neck of the female and is used for fighting during the breeding season. The weevil's main body is a glossy red.

Madagascar • Andasibe-Mantadia National Park

662 LOVE THE COLORWAY OF THE PYGMY KINGFISHER

All year

The color of the Madagascar pygmy kingfisher come as a bit of a surprise—it is a rich reddish brown with a bill to match. Being pygmy it is only 5 in (13 cm) tall and a delight to see. Look out for it in evergreen forests, where it mainly eats frogs and insects.

Madagascar • Andasibe-Mantadia National Park; near water

663 TAME A SHREW WITH A HEDGEHOG

All year

Tenrecs are a species that look like what would happen if you mixed a hedgehog and a shrew. They can vibrate the quills on their backs to produce a sound that they use to communicate and to warn off predators. A tenrec holds the record for the mammal that has the most young in one litter: 36!

664 | *Observing the tiniest chameleon in the world*

Madagascar • Nosy Hara Island
664 SEE THE WORLD'S SMALLEST CHAMELEON
All year

To be fair the chances of seeing the world's smallest chameleon, the Brookesia, in the wild are, well, tiny. It's only slightly over 1 in (3 cm) long. It lives in leaf litter, camouflaging itself as a leaf and playing dead when predators come sniffing around. Like many other chameleons, it turns paler when it sleeps, so point a flashlight at low shrubs at night.

Madagascar • Fort Dauphin
665 HELP PRESERVE LEMURS
All year

Because lemurs are found only on the island of Madagascar, if their habitat goes, then they go. Help out by joining a project that doesn't just carry out conservation research on lemurs, but also works with local communities on practical initiatives, such as planting trees, and environmental education to help preserve this precious lemur habitat well into the future.

Madagascar • Kirindy Reserve

666 SEE THE EXOTIC SPECIES THAT LOCALS CALL VERMIN

All year

The fossa looks like a very lithe cat with an extremely long tail. It is, in fact, part of the mongoose family and is the island's top predator and found only on this island. It hunts on the ground and up trees, feeding on lemurs, wild pigs, mice, and lizards. It moves very fast through trees.

Madagascar • Ranomafana National Park

668 MARVEL AT THE TAIL OF A MOTH

All year

The comet moth is bright yellow with four eyespots, a wingspan of about 8 in (20 cm), and fabulous 6 in (15 cm) red streamer tails that end with little yellow tail-wings. Scientists think that these could be to confuse the echolocations of bats when they are trying to hunt the moths.

Madagascar • Palmarium Reserve

670 WATCH A GECKO'S MATING DANCE

All year

The Madagascan day gecko goes hunting for its diet of insects in the sunshine hours. The males are very territorial and put on a great display of sticking out tongues and head shaking if they come across one another.

Madagascar • Amber Mountain National Park

667 TRACK DOWN A FANALOKA

All year, at night

The fanaloka is Madagascar's civet—a small, fox-like nocturnal mammal with dark stripes down the length of its body.

Madagascar • Andohahela National Park

669 WATCH A SIFAKA SKIP

All year

Sifakas are a type of lemur but one that has a very distinctive manner of moving. When they are down on the ground, they skip sideways from one place to another up on their hind legs, with their forelegs out to the sides for balance. It's a fabulous sight that will have you smiling for days if you catch it.

Madagascar • Marojejy National Park

671 ADMIRE A BEAUTIFUL MANTELLA FROG

November to April

Mantella frogs are Madagascar's equivalent to the poison dart frogs of South America. They are brightly colored and excrete a toxin from their skin. Many of them feature various patterns of black and yellow, but they also come in shades of orange, green, and bronze, and their vibrant looks act as a warning to would-be predators.

673 | *The stylishly tufted crested coua*

Madagascar • Marojejy National Park

672 IDENTIFY THE BIRD WITH THE BIG BLUE BEAK

All year

Its huge curved blue beak with a black tip makes the helmet vanga a truly unmistakable bird. The rest of its body is a pretty bluish black, with a bold reddish stripe around its middle, and reddish tail feathers. The bill is truly remarkable and quite unexplained as the bird eats insects and small lizards. This bird lives deep in the forests of northeastern Madagascar and nowhere else on Earth.

Madagascar • Ankarafantsika Nature Reserve

673 ADMIRE THE HAIRSTYLE OF THE CRESTED COUA

All year

The crested coua is not a great one for flying, so look into trees to spot it. It has a greenish-gray body with a fawn-colored chest, a long tail, and a fabulous spiky crest on its head. It also has a very striking blue-and-purple patch around its eye. Listen out for its song just before sunset, when several birds seem to call to one another with a tuneful, *gway, gway, gway, gway, gwuck.* It prefers dry forests to humid ones.

CHAPTER FIVE

ASIA, AUSTRALIA, AND THE PACIFIC

674 EMBRACE THE SOLITUDE OF THE EURASIAN STEPPE

April to September

Imagine a land that stretches as far as the eye can see, as if one were looking out at an ocean, but one that consists of rough grassland, with hills rising in the distance. That is the Eurasian Steppe. It is its sheer scale that is so overwhelming—stretching from Hungary to China, it reaches almost one-fifth of the way around the world. A closer look at the grasses here will reveal a number of different species, from tall to small, feathery to spiky, and a botanist would have a field day hunting for new types. To travel out into the midst of this wasteland and wait for night to fall is a lonely adventure, but an awe-inspiring one—a night sky bright with stars, and a heavy silence all around. There are wolves, gazelles, small mammals, and birds living in the steppe, but you can go for days without seeing or hearing any.

It is still possible to have the experience of traveling through the grassland as the nomadic tribes used to. With the invention of the plow in the nineteenth century, settlements began to grow, but there is still a wide expanse of empty and magnificent landscape to explore.

Russia • Caucasus Mountains

675 SPOT A *DAREVSKIA DAHLI* LIZARD—YOU'LL KNOW IT'S A SHE

March to May; October to November

There is a wonderful phenomenon of nature, known as parthenogenesis, where females reproduce entirely on their own with no need for a male. The *Darevskia dahli* lizard is one such species—if you manage to spot it clambering around on the rocky mountainsides. It sports a soft velvety skin with a distinct brown pattern down the sides.

Russia • Caucasus Mountains

676 HELP CONSERVE THE ARGALI SHEEP

March to May or October to November

Although the argali is around the same length as many domesticated sheep, it is considerably heavier and taller, making it the largest of wild sheep breeds. The numbers of this regal-looking beast are suffering, both due to hunting and because of growing competition for grassland with domesticated sheep. Both males and females have impressive curling horns. Those of the male have been known to weigh up to 44 lb (20 kg).

Russia • Primorsky Krai

677 SEE AN AMUR LEOPARD WHILE YOU STILL CAN

All year

With only around 70 left in the wild, the Amur leopard might well be the rarest cat on Earth. But even if there were more it would still be tricky to spot one: they hunt at night, alone, in thick forest, and sleep by day.

If you're used to thinking of leopards roaming the African savannas, you might be surprised to see how this race has evolved to adapt to a very different environment—they have a thick, spotted coat (often paler than other subspecies of leopard) and a long, furry tail, which they wrap around themselves to keep warm and protected from the cold winds here, where Russia's far east meets China and Korea.

These solitary hunters mark out a territory for themselves, which they patrol for long periods of time; they will use the same hunting trails and resting spots again and again over many years. They rarely meet their neighbors, and when they do, it can often be to fight over territory, especially in areas where food is plentiful—like deer farms, to which they are understandably drawn. Deer, moose, and wild boar make up their main diet, but they sometimes take on young black bears, as well as smaller animals.

677 | *The critically endangered and elusive Amur leopard*

678 | *The semiaquatic Russian desman*

Russia • Volga

678 SCOUR THE BANKS FOR A DESMAN

April to October

Despite appearances, don't mistake this little fellow for a muskrat—the Russian desman is an entirely different species and more closely related to a mole. In fact, it's the largest species of mole known to exist. It lives in burrows around the edges of ponds and streams and, with webbed hind feet and a flattened tail, is very well suited to aquatic life. It is blind like a mole, and has a long snout with sensors that it uses instead of sight to get around.

Russia • Sikhote-Alin Mountains

679 FOLLOW THE TRACKS OF A TIGER

December to February

The beautiful Siberian tiger once roamed across the Russian Far East, northern China, and the Korean peninsula. A victim of its own beauty, it was hunted to near extinction in the 1940s, until Russia became the first country in the world to grant it full protection. There are now around 500 Siberian (or Amur) tigers in Russia. They are difficult to spot, but to follow the tracks of one through snow would be reward enough for many.

Russia • Ural Mountains

680 REVEL IN THE SURVIVAL OF THE SABLE

All year

The beautiful, dense black or dark brown fur of the sable was once almost its downfall. Fortunately this plucky little mammal has ridden out the threat of the fur trade and is now found in many Russian forests. Although not huge, it is an accomplished hunter itself and often kills hares, rodents, and even small deer for food. Despite living in burrows in the forest floor, it is good at climbing trees, where it forages for nuts, seeds, and berries.

Kazakhstan • Ustyurt Nature Reserve

681 BE IMPRESSSED BY THE NOSE OF A SAIGA

All year

A saiga antelope is a little like a goat in size, with a nose unlike any other animal's—a wonderful, wobbly, bulbous affair with two large nostrils at the end. This marvelous muzzle appears to serve two purposes: in the summer it filters out the dust kicked up by a herd of stampeding saiga, while in winter it warms the freezing air before it reaches the animal's lungs. Although saiga once roamed freely across the Eurasian steppe, they are now only found in small pockets and are one of the fastest declining mammals in the world.

Kyrgyzstan • Issyk-Kul region

682 DISCOVER THE SHEEP WITH THE LONGEST HORNS

All year

When Marco Polo was busy exploring Asia back in the thirteenth century, he became so enamored by the long, curling horns of a subspecies of the argali sheep, that he gave it his name. Male Marco Polo sheep are not only known for their size; they also have the longest horns of any sheep, with the longest recorded having measured 6.25 ft (1.9 m). Unfortunately, however, with such trophies on their heads, these sheep have fallen victim to commercial hunting and are now classified as "near threatened."

Pakistan • Chitral, Ghizar, and Hunza regions

683 FIND A MARKHOR—THE NATIONAL ANIMAL OF PAKISTAN

All year

This wild goat lives in the mountains of Pakistan. It chooses the steepest cliffs so that its predators cannot reach it easily. But any that do would need to steer clear of the male markhor's impressive horns, which grow in a series of twists up to a length of around 32 in (80 cm) and look like carved architectural sculptures. Its name comes from the Persian word for "snake," a reference to these fantastical horns.

Pakistan • Keti Bunder Wildlife Sanctuary

684 GUESS WHAT THE FISHING CAT'S BEST SKILL IS

All year

This feline wetland predator is about twice the size of a domestic cat, with small rounded ears and an uncanny ability to catch fish, either by stalking them from a riverbank or diving in to catch them. It can even swim for long distances under water. If you listen out for it, you might also hear its unique "chuckling" call, which sounds like an *eh eh eh*! On the rare occasions when they have been kept as pets, they are said to have become affectionate.

685 | *The endangered Bengal tiger*

India • Kanha National Park

685 SAVE A BENGAL TIGER AND SAVE ACRES OF FOREST

April to June

The Bengal tiger is the most numerous of the tiger subspecies. It is, however, still widely poached. Tigers roam over large distances and can travel up to 30 miles (48 km) a day. So help to conserve tigers, and in the process you'll help to look after the habitat where they live.

India • Tamil Nadu

686 LEARN HOW THE FLOWER MANTIS GOT ITS NAME

All year

When the Indian flower mantis has its wings tucked in, it is a striking insect with a white spot ringed in black on its back. However, it is when it opens those wings up that you see how it got its name—its wings unfold to reveal colors and patterns that make it look like a beautiful and delicate flower.

India • Gir Forest National Park

687 TELL AN ASIATIC AND AN AFRICAN LION APART

All year

Although Asiatic lions once roamed from India to the Mediterranean, there is now a surviving population of just 500 animals in Gujarat. Although as majestic and kingly as its African cousin, the Asiatic lion is slightly smaller, with less of a mane.

India • Northwestern region

688 COUNT THE COLORS ON A HIMALAYAN MONAL

All year

This large member of the pheasant family got far more than its share of the color palette: a metallic green head, a full rainbow of colors down its back, and striking orange tail feathers. That's the male. The female is brown with a blue eye patch.

689 | *A blackbuck on the run*

India • Blackbuck National Park
689 SEE INDIA'S FASTEST-RUNNING MAMMAL
All year

The sleek blackbuck is a large antelope with a black upper body and white lower half, and impressive twisted horns (on the male). It is not only a beautiful creature, but is also one of the world's fastest mammals, capable of reaching an incredible 50 mph (80 kmh).

India • Assam
690 IDENTIFY ORCHIDS
All year

With names as evocative as "monkey face," "angel," and "tongue orchid," these flowers are not only wonderful to look at, they also spark the imagination. There are more than 1,000 types of orchids in India, with more being discovered all the time. Go hunting and feel like a true explorer.

India • Himalayas
691 WATCH IN AWE AS A SNOW LEOPARD HUNTS
November to February

Few animals are quite as iconic as the snow leopard. These solitary beasts live high up in steep, inhospitable mountains, and it is only in this decade, with developments in camera technology, that many of us are seeing and learning about them from wildlife documentaries for the first time. They have a beautiful coat—pale yellow with black spots and horseshoes, and a white chest. They are phenomenal hunters, feeding off goats, sheep, cattle, and boars, and they can stalk their prey for many miles if they need to. They also have the longest leap of any big cat—up to 52 ft (16 m) in one almighty bound.

As well as the color of their coats, the other thing you'll notice about a snow leopard is its fat, furry tail, which is used both to shield its mouth and nose from the cold, and to help it balance on steep, narrow ledges.

692 | *The unmistakable snout of a gharial*

India • Katarniaghat Wildlife Sanctuary

692 CHECK OUT A GHARIAL'S SNOUT

November to June

There's no mistaking the snout of a gharial crocodile—it is long, narrow, and on the male, it has a peculiar bulbous end. It is designed for catching fish, which is the main diet of these critically endangered crocodiles, now found only in some of India's northern rivers. Although the gharial comes out onto land to warm up in the sun, it is far better suited to life in the water since its short legs make it a poor walker; it generally slides around, pulling itself along.

India • Thenmala Butterfly Park

693 WATCH THE MARVEL OF METAMORPHOSIS

December to March

From childhood we learn about the miracle of the earthbound caterpillar transforming into a delicate and soaring butterfly. It never stops being miraculous, and to watch a butterfly emerge from a cocoon, dry its wings for a few minutes, and then take off is a truly memorable moment. At Thenmala they have planted a utopia for butterflies— hundreds flit about the many different flowers—and in the greenhouse you can watch that miraculous moment of rebirth.

India • Karnataka forests

694 GET ALL SWEET ON A HONEY BADGER

All year

The honey badger is in a scientific genus all its own (*Mellivora*) and doesn't look much like a badger at all. It has longer legs than a badger, and a black lower body with a grayish-white top half that extends to a cap on its head. This wily creature has thick, loose, rubbery skin, which helps protect it from predators since it can writhe around within their grasp. As for the name—well, it eats pretty much anything, but disappointingly it isn't particularly drawn to honey.

India • Kabini Wildlife Sanctuary

695 FIND A REAL-LIFE BAGHEERA

All year

Although the probable setting for Rudyard Kipling's *Jungle Book* was central India, you will have more chance of seeing a black panther farther south in Kabini. This panther is actually a leopard, but with black coloring. Look closely to discover its spots.

India • Western Ghats

696 SENSE THE POWER OF THE GAUR

All year

The gaur, a type of wild cow that is also known as the "Indian bison," is an impressive beast and one of the largest of all land mammals. It stands between 5.5 and 7.25 ft (1.65 and 2.2 m) tall at the shoulder and weighs up to 1 ton.

Gaur are sometimes seen grazing in fields alongside domestic cattle, which they utterly dwarf, despite their physical resemblance and family ties. In the Indian summer, with the insufferable heat, and insects pestering them, they can get cranky, and the bulls will charge at—and sometimes kill—other cattle, apparently without provocation. Around humans, however, they are mostly timid, and a whole herd will disappear back into the thick of the jungle if they sense a threat.

696 | *A mighty gaur*

India • Nilgiri hills
697 REJOICE IN THE SURVIVAL OF THE NILGIRI TAHR
All year

Although Nilgiri tahrs are fairly plain to look at, with no distinctive colors or markings, they are still a heartwarming sight to see on the mountainsides of the Western Ghats in southern India. In the early twentieth century, there were only 100 or so animals left in the wild, but today, although they are still an endangered species, there are more than 20 times that many.

The Nilgiri tahrs live in small groups, grazing the grasslands of rocky, mountainous areas. In Tamil, their name is *varaiaadu*, which translates as "mountain goat." Unfortunately these same areas are used by man for hydroelectric plants, timber felling, and eucalyptus plantations, which is why the Nilgiri tahr remains endangered. However, it is the state animal of Tamil Nadu, and there are a number of ongoing conservation efforts to preserve this hardy beast.

India • Periyar National Park

698 SAY YOU'VE SEEN THE KING OF SNAKES

All year

The king cobra isn't perhaps something you'd want to stumble on by surprise, despite their stunning appearance (a dark brown body with light stripes). However, to see one is to be in awe. The longest of all venomous snakes, king cobras can reach up to 18 ft (5.5 m) in length, and they can raise up to one-third of their bodies off the ground to confront danger—yup, they can make themselves 6 ft (1.8 m) tall. Add in their iconic hood and a gut-wrenching hiss, and you'll get why Indians treat this reptile with the respect it deserves.

India • Tamil Nadu

699 LET A FLOWER SET YOUR MIND ON FIRE

All year

The flame lily looks just like its name. Its long, crinkled petals range from yellow to a deep orange and grow upward, resembling fire. It is a creeper and can often be found weaving its way through fences or up trees—in some places it is even considered a weed, despite its beauty. Tamil Nadu chose it as its state flower, but it is grown all over the world as a cultivar. Colchicine, a chemical extracted from the flower's seeds, is used to treat joint pains and rheumatism, so farmers in this area are encouraged to harvest the plant for export.

698 | *A king cobra lifting its head off the ground*

India • Uttar Pradesh
700 APPRECIATE THE MAJESTIC INDIAN PEACOCK
All year

It is one thing to see a peacock adorning the manicured gardens of a stately home—its excessive plumage and velvety iridescence are right at home in those opulent settings. However, to see one in its natural habitat is slightly surreal; the Indian peacock—which is the correct name for the common peacock—seems to need more space and grandeur than its forest floor provides. Those bright blues and greens, the perfect formation of each eye on its tail feathers, and the size of that tail. What was nature thinking?

India • Southwestern region
701 RENAME THE BLACK-BACKED KINGFISHER?
All year

This tiny kingfisher already has quite an impressive list of names. It's also known as the "oriental dwarf kingfisher," the "miniature kingfisher" (it is the smallest of the kingfisher species), "Malay forest kingfisher," "three-toed kingfisher," and the "pygmy kingfisher." However, none of these draw attention to the diminutive bird's large reddish-orange bill, which is by far its most notable feature. The black-backed kingfisher is often found in dense forests, on branches overhanging streams where it sits and waits for its prey to appear.

700 | *An Indian peacock in all its glory*

India • Manas National Park
702 SPOT A RARE PYGMY HOG

All year

This park in the Indian region of Assam is the last foothold that this tiny and rare wild pig has in the wild, with just a few hundred remaining. Breeding programs are hoping to reestablish it at other sites.

India • Kanha National Park
703 COUNT THE TINES ON A DEER'S ANTLER

October to June

The barasingha, or swamp deer, takes its name from the Hindi word *barasingha*, meaning "12-tined"—although these beautiful golden deer can actually have as many as 20 tines on their antlers.

India • Assam
704 WATCH A GOLDEN LANGUR LANGUISH

All year

The bright yellow fur of this primate brightens up its forest home. However, this shy and endangered animal is hard to spot. On hot days, they rest in shady spots—which is where, if you're lucky, you'll catch them.

India • Rajasthan
705 EMBRACE THE IDEA OF A BLUE BULL

All year

Technically the nilgai (or blue bull) is not a bull but an antelope. However, its body shape is fairly unique—a cross between a horse and a cow, with a small head. It is one of the most commonly seen wild animals in India—its similarity to cows has spared it from hunters—and in certain lights it does appear to be blue. It can live for several days without water as it crosses savannas to find new grassland.

India • Rajasthan
706 BE IMPRESSED BY THE INDIAN PYTHON

All year

For many the Indian python is the iconic snake. Camouflaged with light and dark patches, it conceals its huge bulk—they can grow to 20 ft (6 m)—up a tree. When this python grabs its prey, it squeezes it to death before swallowing it whole. And if the meal is big enough (a small deer, for example), the snake might not eat again for a year. Happily there are very few recorded instances of pythons attacking humans.

India • Odisha coast
707 SEE A BEACH TURN SOLID WITH TURTLES

November to January

The olive ridley sea turtle might sound like it is named after some eccentric British explorer, but, in fact, the "olive" simply refers to the color of its shell. The female turtles all arrive at their nesting sites—just a few beaches that they return to every year— around the same time. As they emerge from the sea, the beach can become so packed that it is more turtle than sand. This phenomenon is known as an *arribada*.

707 | *Olive ridley turtles congregate on a beach to lay their eggs*

India • Bhimashankar
Wildlife Sanctuary
**708 MARVEL AT THE
GIANT SQUIRREL**
All year

You will easily recognize the two-toned, tree-dwelling Indian giant squirrel when you see it—it grows to more than 1 ft (0.3 m), with a tail 2 ft (0.6 m) long.

India • Western coast
**709 BE DAZZLED BY A
COLORFUL CRAB**
All year

With a stunning yellow-orange shell covered with bright blue markings, and hues of delicate pink on its claws, the rainbow swimming crab almost lives up to its name.

India • Ganges River
**710 WATCH DOLPHINS
FROLIC IN THE GANGES**
All year

The sacred Ganges River is home to a population of around 2,000 Ganges River dolphins that battle against pollution, fishing, and dams to find a way to survive.

India • Northeastern region
**711 SPOT THE FEMALE
GREEN PEAFOWL**
All year

Although the green peafowl found in tropical forests is very closely related to the Indian peafowl, there is one crucial difference between them—the female gets to have striking, colorful plumage, and a tail that it can display as well as the male. True, the female's tail is shorter than the male's and gray rather than green, but it makes a beautiful crest when displayed. The female also has an impressive headcrest and a stunning, bright green throat.

India • Northeastern and
southern regions
712 DISCOVER LUTUNGS
All year

Lutungs are a genus of monkey comprising 16 species. They fall within the langurs group, and many of them go by that name, such as the Nilgiri langur and golden langur. All 16 species are now under threat from deforestation, and two of them are critically endangered. Some environmentalists believe their plight doesn't receive the same coverage as other primates because people haven't heard of them. Now that can no longer be your excuse.

India • Western Ghats
**713 GO IN SEARCH OF A
LION-TAILED MACAQUE**
All year

Although these macaques have a wonderful lion-like swish at the end of their tails, they also have an impressive mane and so could equally well be known as lion-faced macaques. They are black with gray manes, and are only found in the forests of the Western Ghats, where they seldom come down from the tree canopy, rich as it is with fruit and seeds. Territory still counts though—rival groups will sometimes fight over particularly well-laden trees.

716 | *A flock of sacred ibis take flight in Bundala National Park*

India • Sundarbans
714 HEAR THE POOK OF A SAMBAR DEER
All year, at night

In order to protect her young, the female sambar deer will lower her head and butt at predators while emitting a high-pitched alarm call that is known in some parts of India as a *pook*. Unlike many deer, sambar deer live in quite small herds, which are sometimes just an extended family of five or six individuals. The males are solitary for most of the year, but when rutting, they will often fight each other standing on their hind legs.

India • Nicobar Islands
715 DECLARE A PIGEON BEAUTIFUL
November to mid-May

Usually when we think of pigeons, we think of gray and purplish feathers—they're pleasant-looking birds, but they're certainly not dramatic. The Nicobar pigeon from the islands of the same name, however, is a whole different story. Its plumage consists of iridescent greens, blues, and coppers, with longer neck feathers that can be raised during courting rituals or to scare off any interlopers. It's thought that the adult birds mate for life.

Sri Lanka • Bundala National Park
716 BE FASCINATED BY BIRDLIFE
October to March

It's hard not to develop an interest in birds when you can watch 10,000 of them at once, feeding on the shoreline of the lagoons here. This park is an incredible habitat—a popular spot for waterfowl and waders to rest while on their annual migrations, and home to around 200 species, from little bee-eaters to extraordinary open-billed storks. The rare black-necked stork and great thick-knee are also highlights.

717 | *Asian elephants roam the Udawalawe National Park*

Sri Lanka • Yala National Park

718 SPOT A LEOPARD—AND ITS SPOTS

June to September

Yala National Park has one of the highest concentrations of leopards in the world, so although still never guaranteed, a sighting is highly likely, particularly if you visit during the dry season, from June to September. These beautiful big cats generally live and sleep up in the trees, but they come out into the open to hunt during the day.

Sri Lanka • Mirissa

719 BREATHE THE SAME AIR AS A WHALE

November to April

Nothing is quite as heart-stopping as seeing the world's biggest beast of all in the flesh. The seas off Mirissa are rich in plankton, so they attract a number of blue whales that, fortunately for visitors, can be seen as they surface to breathe.

Sri Lanka • Udawalawe National Park

717 DON'T LET AN ELEPHANT SURPRISE YOU

All year

Four hundred wild Asian elephants live in the scrubland of Udawalawe National Park—built to provide a home for animals displaced by the construction of the Udawalawe Dam. Listen out for them as they tear branches off trees, then be astounded by how silent their footsteps can be. Other animals to look for on your Sri Lankan safari are crocodiles, water buffalo, and monitor lizards.

Sri Lanka • Wilpattu National Park

720 LISTEN FOR THE SLURP OF A SLOTH BEAR

January to August

Loss of habitat means that only around 1,000 sloth bears survive today. They eat insects, honey, and fruit—noisily. Listen out for their giveaway slurp.

Sri Lanka • Lowlands

722 SIZE UP THE BILL OF THE STORK-BILLED KINGFISHER

All year

This bird is tall in the world of kingfishers—about 14 in (35 cm)—and it has a red bill to match. It can be spotted sitting on branches by rivers.

The Maldives • South Ari Atoll

724 SWIM WITH THE WORLD'S BIGGEST FISH

All year

The docile whale shark is the largest fish in the sea—up to 40 ft (12 m). They're happy for humans to swim alongside them, and it's a humbling experience—just keep a good distance from the tail, and don't touch them or take flash photos. Whale sharks feed almost exclusively on plankton and pose no threat to humans, despite their size. Their name refers to their size and feeding habits.

Sri Lanka • Sinharaja Forest Reserve

721 FEEL THE SHADOW OF THE SRI LANKAN BIRDWING

All year

At 6 in (15 cm) wide, the wingspan of Sri Lanka's biggest butterfly rivals that of some birds. Its black-and-yellow coloring is just as impressive.

The Maldives • Coral reefs

723 DON'T JUDGE A CRAB BY ITS SIZE

All year

The beautiful red-spotted coral crab measures less than 1 in (2.5 cm) across, but it still has a fierce nip, which it uses to drive lurking predators away from its coral home.

Nepal • Chitwan National Park

725 WATCH A MARSH MUGGER—FROM A DISTANCE

All year

Although "marsh mugger" sounds like an apt name for a crocodile that ambushes its prey, the name comes from the Hindi word for "crocodile" (*magaramachchh*). This crocodile pursues prey in water and on land, so is best viewed from afar. They've been spotted placing sticks on their heads to lure in birds looking for material to build a nest. You can guess what happens next.

Nepal • Terai grasslands
726 CELEBRATE THE SUCCESS OF A RHINO
All year

To see a greater one-horned rhino is an amazing sight. Not just
because this is the largest of the world's rhinos, or because
it looks like it is armor-plated, but also because a few decades
ago, it was nearing extinction and would have been very difficult
to spot. Now more than 3,500 animals wander between
northeast India and Nepal.

727 | *Spotted deer seen in the dappled light of the Sundarbans*

Bangladesh • Sundarbans

727 RECORD YOUR VERY OWN *BAMBI* FOOTAGE

All year

Many deer have spots when they are young, but these disappear as they reach maturity (as do Bambi's in the Disney movie). However, the spotted deer keeps its spots for life, making it one of the most endearing of the deer species. It lives on the edge of woodlands, where it can find clearings of fresh grass to graze. It is known locally as the "chital deer"—the origins coming from the Sanskrit word *citra* ("spotted"), which is also where the cheetah's name comes from.

Bangladesh • Near human habitation

728 OBSERVE A MYNA BIRD AT HOME

All year

In evolutionary terms, this bird is a huge success. It comes from the forests of Asia, but it has been introduced to many other countries, where it is now thriving. So much so, in fact, that it is often seen as a pest—it has the dubious honor of ranking on the 100 of the World's Worst Invasive Alien Species list. At home, though, it is known as the "farmer's friend" for its ability to keep insect numbers down. It is also a very talented mimic, imitating human speech, other birds' calls, and urban sounds such as sirens.

Bangladesh • Sundarbans
729 SOAK UP THE SOUNDS OF A MANGROVE FOREST
September to March

Lie back and listen to the sound of silence, birdsong, and water lapping at the roots of mangroves in this enormous UNESCO World Heritage Site—the world's largest mangrove forest.

Bangladesh • Sundarbans
730 SEE THE SEAL-LIKE FACE OF AN OTTER
All year

The smooth-coated otter is found in many parts of Asia, and in Bangladesh some fishermen have even trained them to fish: the otters are taught how to chase fish into nets.

Bangladesh • Forests and woodlands
731 IDENTIFY A PUFF-THROATED BABBLER
All year

The easiest way to identify this bird is by listening out for its babbling call—a persistent scale of ever-rising whistling notes. Its name comes from a habit of puffing its throat.

Bangladesh • Forests and woodlands
732 SPOT A GREEN-BILLED MALKOHA
All year

You will need to use all your powers of observation to spot a green-billed malkoha. With its dusty gray-and-green plumage, this bird blends in to tree canopies exceptionally well.

Bangladesh • Forests and woodlands
733 CATCH THE FLASH OF A SCARLET MINIVET
All year

As you'd expect from its name, the male of this pretty tropical bird has striking scarlet feathers on a jet-black body, so keep an eye out for a flash of red up in the forest canopies.

Bangladesh • Throughout
734 INVENT YOUR OWN JOKE ABOUT THE MAGPIE ROBIN
All year

What do you get if you cross a magpie and a robin? A magpie robin. This small black-and-white bird with an upright tail is Bangladesh's national bird.

Bangladesh • Forests
735 GET CLOSE ENOUGH TO SEE THE TAIL OF A DRONGO
All year

The greater racket-tailed drongo is famed for its elegant tail—two long streamers, tipped at the ends with feathers.

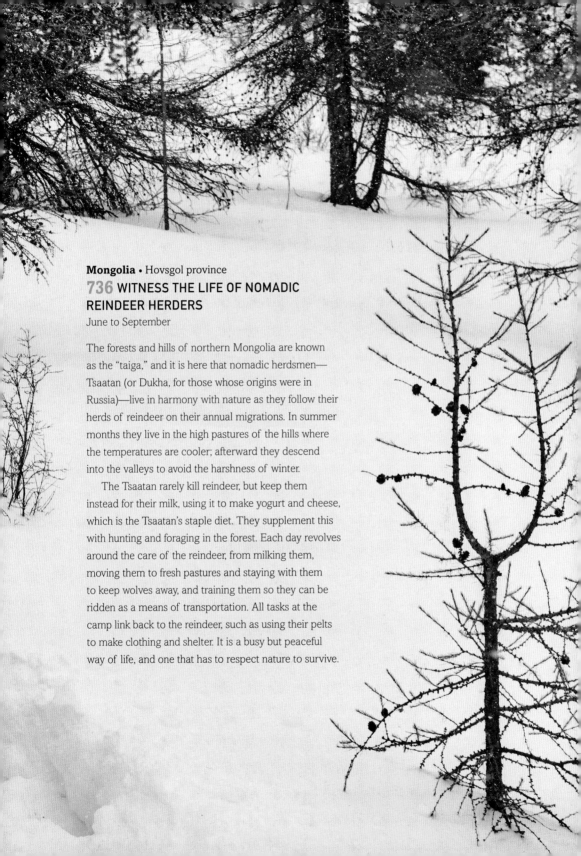

Mongolia • Hovsgol province

736 WITNESS THE LIFE OF NOMADIC REINDEER HERDERS

June to September

The forests and hills of northern Mongolia are known as the "taiga," and it is here that nomadic herdsmen—Tsaatan (or Dukha, for those whose origins were in Russia)—live in harmony with nature as they follow their herds of reindeer on their annual migrations. In summer months they live in the high pastures of the hills where the temperatures are cooler; afterward they descend into the valleys to avoid the harshness of winter.

The Tsaatan rarely kill reindeer, but keep them instead for their milk, using it to make yogurt and cheese, which is the Tsaatan's staple diet. They supplement this with hunting and foraging in the forest. Each day revolves around the care of the reindeer, from milking them, moving them to fresh pastures and staying with them to keep wolves away, and training them so they can be ridden as a means of transportation. All tasks at the camp link back to the reindeer, such as using their pelts to make clothing and shelter. It is a busy but peaceful way of life, and one that has to respect nature to survive.

737 | *The massive bill of a cinereous vulture*

Mongolia • Ikh Nart Nature Reserve
737 FOLLOW IN THE SHADOW OF A CINEREOUS VULTURE
All year

With their 10 ft (3 m) wingspan, cinereous vultures cast a shadow as they hunt for scavenged carcasses. Their blood is specially adapted to absorb oxygen at high altitudes, and they have been spotted at close to 23,000 ft (7,000 m).

China • Western Tien Shan
738 REMEMBER THAT TULIPS ARE WILDFLOWERS TOO
April to May

Although it's now usually thought of as a cultivated plant, these mountains have many magnificent tulips growing wild—including the world's largest, the *Greigii* tulip. Visit in spring to see the meadows here in full bloom.

China • Qinghai province
739 NOMINATE THE PERFECT 007 CAT
All year

Few animals would look more at home in a Bond movie than a Pallas's cat. This small wildcat has a dense and fluffy coat that makes it look larger than it is.

China • Eastern regions
740 DISCOVER THAT SNAKES CAN FLY
March to November

The flying snakes of China flatten their bodies into an S shape for their aerobatics. They are even better gliders than flying squirrels.

China • Western and central forests
741 FIND THE JEWEL OF THE PHEASANT WORLD
All year

Male golden pheasants—despite a gold head and back; red breast; and green, blue, and orange sides—are shy and hard to spot.

742 | *Tibetan antelope in their chilly habitat*

China • Tibet
742 LEAVE ANIMALS WITH THEIR FUR
All year

One animal that has the coat to cope with life on the Tibetan plateau is the Tibetan antelope, or chiru. This tall and elegant beast grows a wonderfully soft underfur—known as *shahtoosh*—which provides it with much-needed insulation. Unfortunately Tibetan antelopes have been illegally hunted for this fur, which is so fine it can make shawls that can be pulled through a wedding ring, and sell for over $1,000 each. Although numbers are thought to be recovering, this antelope is still on the endangered list.

China • Tibet
743 WISH FOR THE WARMTH OF A WILD YAK
All year

There is something wonderfully endearing about the wild yak. It looks as if it has been wearing the same long coat since the Ice Age. It's an essential coat for the weather: yaks live at altitudes of over 13,000 ft (4,000 m), and in winter, temperatures can drop to around −40°F (−40°C). Yaks form a huddled mass when they sleep, keeping their calves safe and warm at the center. Critically endangered golden wild yaks, a light-haired subspecies, are worth seeing if you can, since there are only a few hundred remaining in the wild.

China • Tibet
744 PAINT A SHEEP THAT'D PLEASE PICASSO
All year

Roaming across the Tibetan plateau are herds of Himalayan blue sheep. Their coloring is more of a subtle grayish blue than Picasso might have favored, but it works well to help them camouflage themselves among the slate outcrops on these hillsides. Both males and females have very attractive horns that curve outward from the top of their heads and then back, although the males' are larger than the females'. Approach one, and they will instinctively freeze, motionless, hoping to be mistaken for a rock.

China • Yunnan province

745 PONDER THE LOOKS OF A SNUB-NOSED MONKEY

All year

Black snub-nosed monkeys look just like their name suggests. Their nose is pushed in so that it is more like two nostrils set in their face. These monkeys live at high elevations, where winter temperatures can remain below zero for many weeks, and one primatologist has suggested that their strangely flat face has evolved as a way to avoid frostbite on a protruding nose. The monkeys spend most of their time up in the tree canopy and can move from branch to branch at impressive speeds when they need to.

China • Sichuan province

746 DISCOVER WHY THE RED PANDA IS MORE UNIQUE THAN YOU THINK

All year, at night

Despite its name the red panda doesn't have much in common with the giant panda—it doesn't even belong to the bear family. And although its ringed tail resembles that of a raccoon, it's not part of the raccoon family either. This reddish-brown creature, the size of a domestic cat, is in fact the sole surviving member of the Ailuridae family. Red pandas eat a similar diet to giant pandas, so they are often found in the same locations. However, they are nocturnal, so sightings are rare.

China • Yunnan province

747 JUDGE GARDEN PLANTS IN THEIR MOUNTAIN HOME

May

Rhododendrons have become a staple for gardeners around the world, but to see them bloom in their native environment on the slopes of the North Gaoligong Mountains is pure joy. Rich reds, purples, yellows, whites, oranges, and pinks dot the hillside in this pristine wilderness, which is a haven for many hundreds of other plant species, too.

China • Gobi Desert

748 STUDY THE HUMPS OF A BACTRIAN CAMEL

All year

It won't take long to count the humps of the Bactrian camel—it has two—but it might take a while to find the camels. A mere few hundred range across vast areas of the Gobi Desert. Their humps store energy, which enables them to cross the desert for days before they find a new source of water or food.

748 | *Camels have energy reserves that*
sustain them in the inhospitable desert

China • Mongolia

749 CAMP OUT IN THE WILDERNESS OF INNER MONGOLIA

May to September

Although the wide open lands of Inner Mongolia might look bleak, they are home to many species, and that home is vanishing. Joining an expedition to help monitor different species not only helps to look after these species for the future, it also gives you an unparalleled opportunity to camp out in nature.

China • Qingzang Plateau

750 SEE A LONG-EARED JERBOA JUMP

All year

The long-eared jerboa hops around on legs that like those of a kangaroo, but a very small one—the jerboa is less than 4 in (10 cm) tall.

749 | *Get back to nature on the vast Inner Mongolian plains*

China • Southern and central regions

751 QUESTION THE NAME OF THE TUFTED DEER

All year

The small tufted deer grows about 28 in (70 cm) tall. It is named for the tuft of black hair on its forehead, but many would say its far more distinguishing features are the tusk-like canines that protrude from its mouth like a vampire's.

China • Central and southern regions

752 WATCH A SQUIRREL FLY

All year

Technically, Chinese giant flying squirrels don't fly, they glide, but to see these 3 ft (1 m) long creatures travel distances of 150 ft (45 m) between trees is still awe-inspiring. They have flaps of skin between their front and back limbs, which they spread out like a parachute.

China • Shanghai

753 DISCOVER JUST WHAT A YELLOW RAT WOLF IS

All year

"Yellow rat wolf" is a translation of *huang shu lang*, the name that Chinese people give to the Siberian mountain weasel. It is a rusty yellowy color and a ferocious hunter, rats being a key part of its diet. It also has a foul smell like a skunk.

China • Shaanxi province

754 TAKE TIME TO FIND A TAKIN

All year

The takin is an interesting beast—it's hard to decide whether it looks more like a small cow or a large sheep. It is heavyset, dark brown, and measures up to 4.5 ft (1.4 m) tall at the shoulder. With its curved snout, it looks like an ancient beast that might have been hunted by cavemen. It lives in bamboo forests and, as such, has benefited from the habitat conservation work that has been centered around giant pandas.

In addition to the Sichuan takin found in China, there is also a Mishmi takin, which is the national animal of Bhutan. Takins are found in a number of different colors, depending on the region and subspecies. It's thought that the legend of the "golden fleece" sought by Jason and the Argonauts may have been inspired by the soft, thick coat of the golden takin found in Shaanxi.

China • Southern region

755 ENJOY THE RADIANT BEAUTY OF A CLOUDED LEOPARD

All year

These elusive beasts are expertly camouflaged—their spots are gathered together into "clouds" that blend into the dappled light of their forest homes.

China • Sichuan province

756 JOIN THE WORLD'S BEST-KNOWN CONSERVATION EFFORT
All year

The World Wildlife Fund adopted the giant panda as its logo in 1961, and since then, the panda's image has become synonymous with conserving endangered species. Although the giant panda is still endangered, measures to help conserve its habitat, and targeted breeding programs, are starting to yield results, and the number of pandas in the wild is rising. There are frequent opportunities for volunteers to help look after these members of the bear family.

Giant pandas live in China's bamboo forests and have evolved so that this plant forms the bulk of their diet—they can eat up to 66 lb (30 kg) a day. Their wrist bone has even adapted to the purpose, being much larger than in other bears and able to be used like an opposable thumb to help grab the bamboo. Despite this dependence on bamboo, it is a very inefficient diet; pandas only digest about 17 percent of what they consume, which is why they spend around 13 hours a day eating. When you come across pandas in the wild, they are invariably eating bamboo and they are always alone; they only seek out each other's company to mate, and they have a pronounced sense of smell that helps them to keep out of each other's way.

China • South of the Yangtze River

757 DISCOVER THE WORLD'S MOST TRAFFICKED ANIMAL

All year

Although internationally protected, pangolins—scaly mammals that curl up like a pine cone—are poached for their meat and for use in traditional Chinese medicine. They are the only mammals to possess hard scales made of keratin, the same substance as fingernails, hooves, and horns. They can also emit a powerful stench, just like a skunk.

China • Qinling Mountains

758 MAKE SPACE IN YOUR HEART FOR ANOTHER PANDA

All year

The giant panda certainly garners its fair share of attention, but there is a subspecies called the Qinling panda that is equally endangered and, in fact, fewer in number than its black-and-white cousin. It is similar to the giant panda in size, behavior, and diet, but it has light and dark brown coloring rather than black and white.

China • Hanzhong Crested Ibis Nature Reserve

759 TAKE HOPE FROM THE CRESTED IBIS

All year

We are lucky that we don't talk about the crested ibis and the dodo as two examples of great extinct birds. It was thought that the crested ibis—once found across Asia—was extinct till a group of seven resurfaced in the Qinling Mountains. China immediately created a nature reserve, and through careful management, there are now more than 2,000 of this beautiful red-headed, red-legged bird.

China • Gaoligongshan Nature Reserve

760 FEEL THE FORCE OF THE SKYWALKER HOOLOCK GIBBON

All year

It's no coincidence that this gibbon has a name that sounds like it's straight out of *Star Wars*. The scientists who discovered the new species were big fans of the movie so they paid homage. It's as much fun to listen to gibbons as to see them. They emit a long hooting sound that rises to a crescendo that can be heard up to half a mile away, resounding around the jungle.

760 | *A hoolock gibbon hangs from the treetops*

China • Yunnan province
761 LOVE A LORIS
All year

It's almost impossible not to love a loris, with their large and imploring round eyes—it's the same tactic babies use to make us feel protective of them! Sadly their lovable looks also make them popular (although unsuitable) as a pet, and the illegal pet trade, combined with their use in traditional medicines and a loss of habitat, has led to most loris species being classified as vulnerable. The loris is also one of very few mammals that can give a toxic bite.

China • Southeastern region
762 SEE THE SILVER PHEASANT
All year

We are so used to spectacular, brightly colored pheasants that the silver pheasant, with its monochrome plumage and bright red face, feels like a moment of calm in a sea of gaudiness. It has a glossy black underside, and is white on top, with elegant back lines running throughout and a long trailing tail. Only the males have the striking plumage—and even that takes two years to grow. The females, as so often in the bird world, are brown and don't even have the long tail feathers.

China • Yunnan province
763 SEE A SUN COME OUT AT NIGHT
All year, at night

Despite its name you won't see the sun bear in the daytime—it is nocturnal. It's also reclusive and lives in dense forest areas, so it's never easy to see. It is the smallest member of the bear family and has a distinctive golden crescent across its breast, which gives rise to its name. It is also known as the "honey bear" because it uses its extremely long tongue to dig into bees' nests to extract honey. It could equally have been the "termite bear"—it uses its exceptionally long claws to rip into trees and get to the termite nests inside.

China • Tai Po Kau Nature Reserve
764 SOAK UP BIRDSONG IN HONG KONG
All year

As one of the most densely populated places in the world, it is a surprise to learn that there is wonderful bird-watching to be enjoyed in Hong Kong. The forest of this nature reserve is home to sunbirds, minivets, leafbirds, bulbuls, nuthatches, great barbets, and more. Get up early to enjoy the full chorus at dawn and before the heat of the day sends the birds off to rest. In winter a number of migrating species can also be seen, such as flycatchers and cuckooshrikes.

China • Hong Kong
765 FIND THE PEARLS IN THE PEARL RIVER ESTUARY
All year

There are around 60 white dolphins living in the estuarine waters off Hong Kong; their presence there is recorded as far back as the 1600s. They are so beloved that in 1997, they were chosen as the symbol of Britain's handover of Hong Kong back to mainland China. They're not actually white, but a marvelous pink color. However, the many underwater construction projects around Hong Kong, and the noise pollution they create, are taking their toll on numbers and there are calls for a marine sanctuary to be created for these lovable pink mammals.

765 | *The bright flash of a white dolphin, off the Hong Kong coast*

圾 NON-RECYCLABLE LITTER

766 | *A macaque making itself at home in Monkey Hill*

China • Monkey Hill
766 MEET A MACAQUE FAMILY
All year

It's easy to find rhesus macaques in Hong Kong—in the Kam Shan Country Park, also known as Monkey Hill. Macaque families spend a lot of time sitting on the ground, which makes them easy to observe as you try to decipher their behavior. They have a variety of facial expressions, with submissive animals silently baring their teeth at the dominant ones, to dominant ones standing on four legs with their tail sticking out behind them, their mouths hanging open, as a threat to other animals. They will also sit and eat fruits and groom each other while you watch safely from a distance.

The monkeys were reintroduced here in the early twentieth century, having been almost wiped out locally. The reason? It was thought they would help control the spread of the poisonous strychnos plant. However, the plant isn't actually poisonous at all to humans. The monkeys seem to love eating its berries, though, and they have thrived here ever since.

China • Mountains
767 FIND A LITTLE BEAST WITH A BIG REP
All year

Wolverines are small and stocky mammals that nevertheless have a reputation for being extremely fierce—and they have earned it, through attacking animals far larger than themselves. They have powerful jaws that are not only good for hunting, but enable them to scavenge for carrion that has been frozen in the snow. Sadly, though, numbers of wolverines in this range of mountains are now low and possibly declining.

China • Hong Kong
768 SEE WILD BOARS ON A CITY STREET
All year

While some countries face foxes, rats, and raccoons as notorious trash-can raiders, in Hong Kong they have wild boars. These have left the safety of the woodlands to find food on the streets and are often seen at night trotting around in small family groups. Not all the human residents enjoy sharing their space, and there is great controversy over what action should be taken so pigs and humans can learn to coexist.

China • Hong Kong
769 GO ON A BAT WALK
All year, at night

An organized bat walk is a very good way to learn more about these diverse flying mammals. Pipistrelle bats in Hong Kong, for example, eat as many as 3,000 insects a night—each.

China • Bohai Gulf
770 SPOT A SPOTTED SEAL
November to May

The spotted seal isn't the only seal species found in China, but it is the only one that breeds there. It spends most of its life in the water, but it comes out on land to breed and to molt—which are the best times to see it. The numerous rivers that flow into Bohai Bay make it a rich source of food and explains its popularity with the seals.

China • Northeastern region
771 ADMIRE THE MONOGAMY OF A MANDARIN DUCK
April to September

Mandarin ducks mate for life and are often used as a symbol of conjugal love in Chinese culture. They are one of the most handsome duck species. The male has clearly defined sections of different colored feathers, from light brown to dark brown, with purples, greens, and russets, and a distinctive paler stripe around his eye. Although native to China and Japan, populations are now well established in the UK, Germany, and the US from escaped private collections.

China • Southern region
772 WAGGLE YOUR BROWS AT A MOTH
All year

Famed for centuries for the silk that it produces, the domestic silk worm moth also has another amazing feature that you might be less familiar with: two beautiful, intricate "eyebrows" that extend from the sides of its head. The domestic silk moth is also entirely colorless.

China • Yangtze River
773 HUNT FOR A VANISHING CREATURE
All year

In 2006, the Baiji dolphin was declared extinct. This freshwater dolphin, known as the "river goddess of the Yangtze," was one of two species of porpoise in the Yangtze, and its decline was entirely due to human activity. Conservationists fear that the plight of the second variety—the finless porpoise—is similarly endangered. Help conservationists educate local fishermen and prevent the extinction of this second species.

774 | *Korean cranes, symbols of luck and longevity*

South Korea • Korean Demilitarized Zone
774 LEARN TO LINK CRANES AND KOREA
November to April

The Demilitarized Zone that runs between North and South Korea is littered with tank traps, tunnels, and a million or so land mines, but that doesn't stop it from being a globally important site for white-naped cranes. It is one of the few places where these elegant birds, measuring around 4 ft (1.2 m) tall, fly for winter. The white-naped crane is classed as vulnerable by the IUCN Red List, which is sad news for a bird that represents good fortune and longevity in Korean culture.

Japan • Okinawa
775 LISTEN OUT FOR THE OKINAWA WOODPECKER
All year

This brown bird with a red cap is endemic to the forests of Okinawa, but severely threatened by the felling of its forest home. As well as its frantic hammering, listen out for its clear call—*kwe, kwe, kwe* or *pip, pip.*

Japan • Hitachi Seaside Park

776 EXPLORE A GARDEN LIKE NO OTHER
All year

Many countries have amazing botanical gardens and beautifully planted parks. Hitachi Seaside Park is both of these, but on a scale that transforms what you're looking at from pretty to amazing. In March and April, for example, its Suisen Garden is a sea of yellows, creams, and whites undulating under the trees, as more than one million narcissus flowers come into bloom. The next month the hills turn a delicate blue as 4.5 million *nemophila* (baby blue eyes) come out. As far as the eye can see, the ground is a shimmering blue, almost as if it were reflecting the sky. It's the same story throughout the year with acres and acres of colors from poppies to cosmos making a true spectacle of nature.

One of the most interesting plantings is the kochia—a shrubby plant that grows in a round ball shape. It looks fascinating enough in its green foliage when the hillsides are a surreal vista of never-ending green balls, but when this turns a fiery red in the fall months, it is like something from a Dr. Seuss book.

Japan • Kirishima
777 FEEL THE SPIRITUAL POWER OF AN ANCIENT TREE
All year

The Kirishima shrine is a holy place with a magical atmosphere. Adding to that atmosphere is the sacred tree—an 800-year-old cedar tree that is as much a beacon for pilgrims as the shrine itself.

Japan • Southwestern region
778 GUESS THE AGE OF A GIANT SALAMANDER
All year

The Japanese giant salamander is thought to live for up to 80 years. It lives in Japan's rivers, but at 5 ft (1.5 m) long, it would be a disconcerting animal to meet while taking a refreshing dip. It eats insects, frogs, and fish and can go for weeks between meals.

Japan • Ashikaga Flower Park
779 INHALE THE SCENT OF A GIANT WISTERIA
Mid-April to mid-May

Imagine if the sky turned purple. That's what it is like to wander beneath the 10,000 ft (3,000 m) wisteria canopies at Ashikaga.

Japan • Jigokudani
780 WATCH SNOW MONKEYS TAKE A SAUNA
December to March

Japanese macaques are no fools. They are the most northerly living of all primates (humans excluded) and as such have found a way to cope when the weather turns chilly—they take a warm bath. The "snow monkeys," as they are affectionately known, live in the hills around the hot springs of Jigokudani, and when temperatures plummet there (they can drop to 5°F/−15°C in the winter), the monkeys hang out in the naturally warm water. The snow monkeys are social animals, and their interactions as they play and groom each other in the pool offer lots of entertainment. Their bright red faces shine out from their light brown fur, which—if you visit in winter—is often topped off with snow or frost.

780 | *Snow monkeys bathing in a hot spring*

Japan • Honshu; Kyushu
781 BE PARTY TO A RHINOCEROS BEETLE BATTLE
April to September

The male Japanese rhinoceros beetle has a distinctive Y-shaped horn. It puts it to great use during the mating season to prove its strength and prowess by lifting lesser males off the ground and throwing them into the air.

Japan • Coasts
782 GET A THRILL FROM A FRILLED SHARK
All year

This elusive shark, long like an eel, is named for its red-fringed gills. Discovered in Tokyo Bay in the late nineteenth century, it is rarely seen since it lives deep down. It's probably best—25 rows of teeth, all pointing backward, could do some nasty damage.

Japan • Throughout
783 SMELL IT TO BELIEVE IT
April to December

Stink bugs aren't much to look at—flat brownish insects less than 0.75 in (2 cm) long. But they have a secret weapon: the ability to release a stink. When disturbed they activate stink glands, then spread the noxious odor as they fly.

Japan • Osaka
784 LOCATE A JEWEL OF THE INSECT WORLD
May to September

The tamamushi beetle, or Japanese jewel beetle, is iridescent green with blue and red stripes along its body. Its wings were used to decorate a shrine in the Horyuji Temple near Osaka.

Japan • Sensuijima Island

785 DISCOVER THE TANUKI

All year

Is it a raccoon? Is it a dog? Actually it's a raccoon dog. Technically a member of the canid family, this animal has nothing really to do with raccoons, except for sporting similar markings on its face.

Japan • Honshu; Shikoku

787 WATCH A MOON RISE—UP A TREE

April to November

"Moon bear" is the evocative alternative name for the Asian black bear, or white-chested bear; the name comes from the pale V-shaped marking found on its chest. This bear lives in broadleaf forests, and its powerful upper body makes it an extremely good tree climber. Moon bears live in family groups and apparently line up in order of size from largest to smallest when they walk through the woods.

Japan • Honshu

789 ADMIRE A GORGEOUS GREEN PHEASANT

All year

The green pheasant is found only in Japan, and the males are red-faced, blue-necked, green-bodied, brown-winged, and gorgeous.

Japan • Hokkaido

786 DECIDE HOW WILY A FOX IS

All year

Red foxes are beautiful creatures. Known as the "spirit fox," or *kitsune* in Japanese folklore, they are said to be able to shape-shift in order to deceive unwary humans.

Japan • Hokkaido

788 FEEL HAPPY WATCHING RED-CROWNED CRANES

February

The red-crowned crane—or *Grus japonensis*, to give it its scientific name—is the unofficial national bird of Japan. These stunning birds—with their white bodies, black tails, long black necks, and red crowns—stand about 5 ft (1.5 m) tall. Mating pairs perform elaborate dances, and they feature throughout Japanese culture as a symbol of happiness, good fortune, hope, and healing.

Japan • Honshu coast

790 DIVE INTO THE ALIEN WORLD OF SPIDER CRABS

March to May

The Japanese spider crab is a giant of the deep, with a claw span of up to 18 ft (5.5 m). It lives in shallower waters during the spawning season.

788 | *A pair of cranes perform a mating dance*

Japan • Kyoto
791 CONTEMPLATE CHERRY BLOSSOM
Late March to early April

Wander along the tree-lined streets of ancient Kyoto and breathe in the scent and beauty of a canopy of cherry blossoms during the brief period when the trees are in full bloom. The popular Philosopher's Path is a stone path that runs along the edge of a canal and is lined with hundreds of trees.

Japan • Amama-Oshima Island
792 DECIPHER THE PATTERNS OF PUFFER FISH
All year

Just why do male puffer fish create such fabulous patterns on the seafloor, as if the sand has been poured into a jelly mold? Could it perhaps be to attract a mate?

Japan • Nara Park
793 BOW TO A DEER
All year

Sika deer live in the hills outside Nara. They have long been thought of as sacred, due to the legend of a god who once visited the area riding on a deer. A herd of deer now live in the town's park, and they have learned to bow to humans who bow to them.

Japan • Nagano
794 SCOUT OUT A SEROW
All year

This cud-chewing animal is like a furry goat crossed with an antelope. It's one of a kind and found only in Japan, where it is also known as a *kamoshika*. It lives in forests where it grazes on various shrubs and bushes and tidily leaves its droppings in a designated "latrine" area, rather than depositing them where it stands.

Japan • Yakushima
795 PAY A VISIT TO JOMON SUGI
All year

When an individual tree is granted a name, you can get a sense of its importance to local culture and folklore. This venerable cedar (a *Cryptomeria japonica*) is said to be the oldest tree in Japan: between 2,170 and 7,200 years old—dating back to when the country was dominated by a hunter-gatherer culture, known as the Jumon period.

Burma • Irrawaddy plains
796 LOCATE A WHITE-THROATED BABBLER
March to December

See this bird in the only place you can. Note its pristine white throat and elegant long tail.

Burma • Southeastern region
797 MEET A KITTI'S HOG-NOSED BAT
All year

This tiny bat with a pig-like nose is so small that it's also known as the "bumblebee bat."

Burma • Northern region
798 SPOT A DEER THE SIZE OF A DOG
All year

The tiny leaf deer got its name because hunters could wrap it in a single leaf.

Thailand • Khao Yai National Park

799 PROVE THAT DRAGONS EXIST

All year

Although you'll find a Thai water dragon living around water, look up to find one. It will probably be on a tree branch above you. When threatened, they drop into the water where they can either swim away from predators or hide under the surface for as long as 25 minutes. Bright green in color, these dragons have a crest along the back of their heads, and long claws to help with all that tree climbing. A photosensitive spot on their foreheads enables them to sense when they are lying in the light or the shade.

Thailand • Koh Tao

800 WITNESS A HUNTING PARTY OF SEA SNAKES

All year

Banded sea snakes are very elegant to watch as they move through the sea, propelled by swift movements of their tail. They are blue with black stripes and have a very poisonous bite. Females are longer than the males, often reaching more than 4 ft (1.25 m) in length. Although they often hunt alone, these snakes do also join together to form communal hunting parties—scouring the reefs together and flushing out small fish from their hiding places.

Thailand • Coasts

801 BE FLABBERGASTED BY A FLAMBOYANT CUTTLEFISH

All year

Cuttlefish are amazing creatures, with the ability to squirt ink, change color, and create hypnotic patterns by sending color through their skin in waves. Male cuttlefish have even been seen creating one pattern on one side of their body to attract a female, while on the other side, forming a different pattern to ward off potential threats. One species—the flamboyant cuttlefish—does all this but with even more vibrant coloring. While normally dark brown, they can change color swiftly to a pattern of black, brown, white, and yellow when attacked.

Thailand • Coasts

802 DISCOVER A FISH THAT'S AS ELUSIVE AS A GHOST

April to May

Ghost pipefish are small and extremely well camouflaged, which is part of the reason it is so hard to spot them. They look like a thorny stick and come in a variety of colors, depending on the camouflage they need. Like a seahorse, they sit vertically in the water, but with their mouthparts bottommost, and they almost always travel with feather stars (or crinoids) hiding discreetly in their arms. Spotting a ghost pipefish (during the two months when the seas are warmest) gives the thrill of discovery, proving that size isn't everything.

Thailand • Coasts
803 CHOOSE YOUR FAVORITE TYPE OF FROGFISH
All year

Once you have discovered frogfish, it's hard not to want to see as many of them as possible. They come in all sizes, from smaller than a fingernail to as long as your arm, and in all sorts of colors and camouflages. There is nothing sleek about a frogfish—it is stocky and covered in bumps, which is precisely its charm. Its pectoral fins have developed into feet, and one of its dorsal fins has developed into a lure that waggles around above its mouth, attracting prey.

Thailand • Khao Sam Roi Yot National Park
804 FEEL SERENE SURROUNDED BY LOTUS FLOWERS
All year

The lotus is a sacred flower in Thailand. It is believed that when Buddha was born, he was already able to walk, and he took seven steps— and lotus flowers immediately bloomed in his footsteps to cushion his delicate feet. In Buddhism the delicate petals rising from the swampy mud of a plant's roots below are a symbol of purification and enlightenment. They are often found in ponds around temples but also occur in magnificent blooms across large wetland areas.

804 | *A tranquil expanse of pink lotuses*

Thailand • Khao Luang National Park
805 HIKE ON THE TRAIL OF THE INDOCHINESE TIGER
All year

This subspecies of tiger is slightly smaller than the Bengal tiger (the most prevalent subspecies in India), with a darker orange coat and narrower black stripes. As with all tigers they are not easy to see since they inhabit large ranges of forested hills, which only makes a sighting—or near sighting— more precious. They are endangered due to low numbers and loss of habitat from road building.

Thailand • Mekong basin
806 OBSERVE A STINGRAY BEYOND THE SEA
All year

Stingrays don't have bones (their bodies are made up of cartilage), so finding fossils—apart from those of teeth and scales—is tricky. However, scientists believe they date back to the Jurassic era, which means they have outlived the dinosaurs. Although most stingrays live in the sea, there are species that are found in fresh water. Some are small, and some are very, very large. The giant freshwater stingray, found in the Mekong and Chao Phraya Rivers, can measure up to 13 ft (4 m) across. That would be quite something to spot as you took a gentle river cruise.

Thailand • Khao Sok National Park
807 SPOT A FROG DISGUISED AS A LEAF
All year

Its name—the Thai leaf frog—gives away this amphibian's special quality: it is a frog that looks like a leaf and lives in Thailand. (It's also known as the Malayan leaf frog.) With its autumnal brown coloring, pointy edges above its eyes, and veined markings on its body, it makes you marvel once again at how brilliantly species adapt to their habitat. That's if you get to see it, of course. It's a tricky one to spot. But if you miss it, look out for its close relative, the slender-legged horned frog—its name is less catchy, but its camouflage is equally impressive.

809 | An Asiatic wild dog in search of prey

Laos • Nam Et-Phou Louey National Protected Area

809 TRACK WILD DOGS

All year

The Asiatic wild dog—or dhole—is best described as a fox, but more dog-like. Its coat is a beautiful red color, and its tail usually bushy and black. Dholes hunt in packs, usually in pursuit of deer, and live in large social groups. They are often seen at dusk at the Mo Sing To reservoir in Khao Yai.

Laos • Southern-central region

808 DISCOVER THE LAZARUS OF THE RAT WORLD

All year

The handsome Laotian rock rat is dark gray, with longish fur and a fluffy tail—hence its other name: "rat squirrel." It lives among limestone boulders and was only classified as a living mammal in 2005 (allegedly having been spotted on sale for its meat at a local market). Since it was unlike any other existing rodents, it was given a whole new scientific classification. However, a year or so later, another scientist noticed that, in fact, this "new" rat had all the features of an ancient classification of rats known from fossils. So after an 11-million-year gap in its history, the Laotian rock rat is reborn.

Laos • Savannakhet province

810 LOOK OUT FOR A WREATHED HORNBILL

All year

A trek into the Laos mountains isn't just a chance to see mind-boggling views. It is also the best way to see wildlife. In the Dong Phou Vieng National Protected Area, trekkers may be lucky enough to see—and hear—a wreathed hornbill. Hornbills are always a delight to spot, their huge and colorful bills looking like they should completely overbalance these large black birds. The wreathed hornbill gets its name because where others in the species have a horn on their bill, it has what looks like a section of a wreath carved into a bulge on its bill. The male also sports a fabulous, bulbous yellow throat.

Cambodia • Mekong River

811 RELISH THE NAME OF THE IRRAWADDY DOLPHIN

All year

This rare dolphin with such a pleasing name doesn't have the typical long beak usually associated with dolphins. It is instead snub-nosed and small-mouthed. The World Wildlife Fund estimates that there are now fewer than 100 individuals still living in the Mekong River. They don't tend to jump out of the water, either, so spotting them will require a bit of patience. But once you have, to spend an evening floating on a fishing boat watching these creatures swim and play is one of those experiences that fills your heart with smiles.

Cambodia • Phnom Penh

812 MAKE TIME FOR BEAR CARE

All year

It's a horrific fact that sun bears are all too often illegally caught for the pet trade or kept in vile farms and used for traditional medicine. Help bring an end to these cruel practices—and get up close to rescued bears in the process—by visiting or volunteering at the Phnom Tamao Wildlife Rescue Center in Phnom Penh, home to over 1,200 animals, where "no animal in need is ever turned away." Over 200,000 visitors come to see the rescued wildlife and learn about conservation efforts in Cambodia each year. When rescued animals have regained their health, they are released back into the wild.

Cambodia • Eastern region

813 UNCOVER THE LAST REMAINING KOUPREY

All year

There have been no scientific recordings of kouprey—a large wild cattle or forest ox—since 1988, although hopes are kept alive by the occasional sighting of a kouprey skull in local markets. It would be wonderful to confirm that it's not yet extinct, especially since it is Cambodia's national animal.

Cambodia • Siem Reap

814 COUNT BIRDS ON A TRANQUIL BOAT CRUISE

December to May

The fact that birds love fish means that one of the best ways to spot them is on a slow and peaceful boat trip. The Prek Toal Biosphere Reserve is probably the most important breeding ground for large birds in Southeast Asia. Here you can enjoy sightings of fish eagles, ibis, adjuncts, pelicans, and many more.

814 | *An evening paddle at the Prek Toal Biosphere Reserve*

Cambodia • Siem Reap

815 SEE THE PERFECTION OF A PAINTED STORK

December to May

One of the most memorable birds to look out for on a trip to
the Prek Toal Biosphere Reserve is the painted stork. This large
stork has a yellow beak, red face, and bright pink tail feathers.
These storks are often seen soaring on thermals. By hitching
onto these warm, rising currents of air, they are able to travel
long distances using very little energy. Rather than flapping their
wings, these majestic birds simply hang in the sky with their
wings outstretched and let the rising air do the hard work.

Cambodia • Northeastern region

816 DELIGHT IN THE COMPANY OF DOUCS

All year

Black-shanked doucs have the look of primates that have seen the world. Their large black eyes peer out from yellow rings above a gray beard. They have gray fur on their bodies, and black-furred limbs. They live up in the treetops, where their long tails help them to get around. Coming across them in Cambodia's forests is a joy since they are endangered—hunted for food and traditional medicine, and losing their habitat to logging.

Cambodia • Cardamom Mountains

817 DISCOVER AN ANIMAL YOU NEVER KNEW EXISTED

All year, at night

When you encounter an animal that you've never heard of, they're usually either very local to one area or very tricky to spot. The Cambodian spotted linsang falls into the second category. Although widespread across Asia, these small, tree-dwelling, weasel-like creatures live deep in the forest, are solitary, and only come out at night. You'll know one if you see it, though—by its distinctive spotted body and banded tail.

Cambodia • Cardamom Mountains

818 DISCOVER THE SNAKE NAMED IN CAMBODIA'S HONOR

All year

The discovery of a new species is always a poignant reminder that there is so much of this planet that hasn't yet been explored and that nature is so much greater than man. In 2012, scientists working in the Cardamom Mountains discovered a dark red snake with black-and-white rings. It was a member of the kukri family of snakes, but one that had somehow never been recorded before. Kukris get their name from the curved teeth at the back of their mouths resembling the Nepalese knife called a *kukri*. They use these teeth to puncture eggs. This new discovery was named the Cambodian kukri in honor of where it was found.

Cambodia • Cardamom Mountains

819 CELEBRATE THE SLOW RETURN OF THE ELEPHANT

All year

It is uplifting to hear good-news conservation stories, especially when they are about such magnificent beasts as elephants. Female Asian elephants don't have tusks and only about 50 percent of males do, but these animals are nonetheless hunted for their ivory. They are also hunted to be taken into domestic use and are losing their habitat to illegal logging. In 2002, the Cambodian government, with support from Conservation International, turned one million acres of these mountains into a protected forest, and footage from camera traps has revealed that herds of elephants are now breeding in the area.

820 | *The unusually shaped antlers of an Eld's deer*

Cambodia • Eastern Plains Landscape
820 TRACK AN ELD'S DEER BEFORE IT'S GONE FOR GOOD
February to April

You can tell when you're looking at an Eld's deer since they have very distinctive, bow-shaped antlers. They grow a tine almost immediately after they are born, which sticks out forward over the animal's brow; then the rest of the antler continues to grow backward before sporting more tines toward the top. As a result this endangered deer can often look as if it has four antlers. They shed these each year after the breeding season.

Cambodia • Banteay Srey Butterfly Centre
821 DELIGHT IN A MARVEL OF COLOR AND FORM
All year

There are many brightly colored butterflies, and many with beautifully shaped tails, but the emerald swallowtail butterfly combines both to stunning effect. It is large and black with a shimmering green stripe diagonally across each wing, and two delicate teardrops hanging below. The iridescent green sheen is the result of the microstructure of the tiny scales on the wings' surface, which refract light hitting the wing.

822 | An orchid mantis perches its namesake flower

Vietnam • Orchids in rain forests
822 SPOT A "WALKING FLOWER"
All year

Among those animals that have evolved a way of camouflaging themselves with their environment, very few have ended up looking as beautiful (or convincing!) as the rare orchid mantis. Also known as the "walking flower," it can even change its color from pink to yellow or brown to hide itself from prey and predators alike. Being a male mantis is never easy—the females have a habit of eating them after mating—but for this species it is especially tough. The males are only 1 in (2.5 cm) long, while the females are three times this size.

Vietnam • Ba Be National Park
823 HANG OUT WITH RHESUS MACAQUES
October to March

These are among the most common species of monkey in Asia, often trespassing into cities where they feed on what humans throw away. But where better to see them than in this gorgeous national park? You can watch them swimming in the lake that gives the park its name, surrounded by cliffs and waterfalls, and ranked among the 20 most beautiful freshwater bodies in the world. Baby macaques start swimming at a few days old, so keep your eyes open for these cute youngsters.

Vietnam • Nha Trang Bay

824 SEE BIRDS' NESTS BUILT FROM SALIVA

December to March

Colonies of edible-nest swiftlets fill the island caves in this bay. On a boat trip you'll see their translucent white nests, built almost entirely from the birds' own saliva, nestling among the rocks. Swiftlets form mating pairs, each sharing a nest all their own, which they build by adding strands of sticky saliva to the rocks, weaving a solid shell. When the nest is ready, the female will lay eggs, and her chicks will spend their first few months there. Harvesting these nests for soup has led to populations of swiftlets being threatened, yet trade in this unusual ingredient remains strong throughout Asia.

Vietnam • Ha Giang province

825 SEE ENDANGERED TONKIN MONKEYS

November to February

Conservationists have worked together with local communities to bolster the numbers of this rosy-lipped primate, but it remains critically endangered, with just a few hundred individuals in the forests around the China-Vietnam border.

Vietnam • Northern rain forests

826 PICK OUT A VIETNAMESE MOSSY FROG

All year

This bug-eyed frog hides in the rocks of caves and rivers; with its bumpy black-and-green skin, it can easily pass for a moss-covered stone.

Vietnam • Northern region

827 WATCH BUT DON'T TOUCH THE WORLD'S STINKIEST SNAKE

All year

If you try and pick up the king ratsnake, or "stinking goddess," this 8 ft (2.4 m) long cobra-eater will show you how it got its name.

Vietnam • Annamese Mountains

828 LOCATE THE DEER THAT SCIENTISTS MISSED

All year

Scientists had never seen the secretive saola till a hunter showed them a skull in 1992, and it wasn't until 1999 that the first example was caught on camera. These elegant forest animals are related to cattle, goats, and antelopes, but experts are still unsure as to which description best fits their DNA.

With their habitat under threat—and often full of traps that have been left for other species—the saola is considered critically endangered, although the Saola Working Group now exists to help save it. As of 2017, ranger patrols had removed 150,000 snares from five saola sites in Laos and Vietnam.

The Philippines • Palawan
829 SPY ON A MOUSE-EATING PLANT
All year

Attenborough's pitcher plant (named after famous fan David Attenborough) is found near the summit of a single remote mountain. Its fluid-filled "pitcher" is so big that it can digest a rodent.

The Philippines • Mindoro
830 PICK OUT A FLOWERPECKER
All year

Listen out for the call of the rare and threatened scarlet-collared flowerpecker—it's a bit like pebbles being cracked together with a triumphant *zeet zeet zeet*! This little bird is only found on the island of Mindoro.

The Philippines • Anilao
831 EXPLORE A DIVER'S PARADISE
October to June

Just hours from Manila, these waters are teeming with diversity. Divers can hope to see some 287 species of coral in the reefs that surround the bay, not to mention nudibranchs (sea slugs), fish, caves, and shipwrecks.

The Philippines • Anda
832 SEE THE BEST PALMS IN THE WORLD
All year

Palms constitute a huge family of over 2,600 species, spread across the tropics and surrounding parts of the world. They provide coconuts, dates, cooking oil, syrup, sugar, and rattan for weaving, while the sap is used to make a range of alcoholic beverages. Without the food and shelter that they provide, large parts of planet Earth might not have been colonized by humans when they were. Not all palms look alike, and while many share the characteristics of a tall, unbranched trunk with a crown of leaves at the top, there are plenty of variations to look out for. The leaves themselves come in many shapes, from feathery to flat, or spread out like hands. Some palms are actually climbers, while others break from convention completely with trunks that split into branches and limbs.

The Philippines is a great place to see some of this impressive biodiversity, with some estimates suggesting that two-thirds of its hundreds of palm species do not appear anywhere else. Many islands are still dappled with unspoiled palm forest, and energetic travelers can book mountain bike tours that will take them through the lush countryside.

The Philippines • Cordillera Central

833 ADMIRE THE LUZON PEACOCK SWALLOWTAIL BUTTERFLY

All year

This endangered butterfly can be seen only in the mountainous areas found in the north of the Philippine island of Luzon. It sports a striking design: black wings speckled with blue or green, and vivid turquoise highlights with red spots at the ends of the hind wings. The red spots, combined with the turquoise—especially on the females— really do resemble the eyes in a peacock's feathers, and the wing tips have little black tails, explaining this beautiful insect's name.

The Philippines • Southeastern islands

834 SEE THE WORLD'S TINIEST PRIMATE

All year

The Philippine tarsier doesn't grow much bigger than a human fist, yet it can jump 10 ft (3 m) between trees. Its bulging brown eyes seem almost too big for its head, and while they're fixed straight ahead in their sockets, the tarsier's neck can rotate a full 180 degrees, and its ears can move independently. This creature may look odd, but it is perfectly adapted to hunting insects at night in the forest. Analysis of their brains reveals an enlarged auditory cortex—all the better to hear you with!

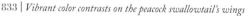
833 | *Vibrant color contrasts on the peacock swallowtail's wings*

The Philippines • Malapascua
835 DON'T STARTLE A THRESHER SHARK
All year

Divers around Malapascua might worry that they've startled some of the locals, but thresher sharks always look like that. With their wide eyes and rounded mouths seemingly fixed in a stunned expression, they look more like something from a cartoon than a disaster movie. Half of this shark's length is its tail, which is angled up behind it like a whip and used to attack prey. Threshers don't generally harm humans, but do watch out for that tail!

The Philippines • Mount Iglit-Baco National Park
836 SEE A TAMARAW
All year

Experts believe there are only 400 of these 3 ft (1 m) tall dwarf buffaloes left in the wild. They live only on the island of Mindoro, and conserving their habitat is paramount. They have thick, triangular-shaped horns and live deep in the forest, usually moving away at the sound of humans. They are among the few animals in the world to have had the dubious honor of having a vehicle named after them: the Toyota Tamaraw of the 1970s.

The Philippines • Malapascua
837 RESPECT THE MANDARIN FISH
All year

The mandarins of imperial China were respected officials who were known for their scholarly wisdom, and the name continues to inspire respect. These tiny, brightly colored— almost psychedelic—fish take their name from the extravagant robes worn by these imperial scholars. They live among the coral reefs, and at sunset, divers can watch their mating rituals, when the males perform an elaborate fighting dance to show off their prowess to the ladies.

The Philippines • Monfort Bat Sanctuary
838 VISIT BATS IN A CAVE
All year

This sanctuary on Samal Island is home to the world's largest community of Geoffroy's Rousette fruit bats—about two million and growing. Limited numbers of tourists can glimpse inside the cave through its entrances, or otherwise wait until sunset when the bats emerge in their thousands on circadian flights.

Guam • Throughout
839 CROSS YOUR FINGERS FOR A RAIL
All year

When certain island-dwelling ground birds lost the ability to fly, they hadn't foreseen that new predators might invade their territory—yes, dodo, we're looking at you. The Guam rail is smaller than the dodo but now critically endangered unless breeding programs can re-establish colonies on these islands.

Malaysia • Taman Negara National Park
840 LINGER IN AN ANCIENT RAIN FOREST
All year

The forests that make up this national park are estimated to have been there for 130 million years. The park's claim to having the world's oldest forest is disputed, but its breathtaking beauty is not. You can explore parts of the 1,677 square miles (4,343 sq km) of virgin forest by trekking the forest floor or adventuring through the treetops on the world's longest canopy walkway. Boat trips will also take you out into the jungle, from where you can set off with a backpack and a guide.

Peninsular Malaysia's tallest mountain, Mount Tahan, is within the park and is a draw for serious climbers. A return trip to the summit along its most scenic trail takes seven days, and it's a trip few people who take it ever forget. Cave systems can be explored, too. But before you pitch your tent for the night, you might like to know that the park is also home to wild tigers, gaurs (a type of bison), elephants, and birds, including the Malayan peacock pheasant and the wild chicken known as a junglefowl.

Malaysia • Coasts (particularly off Sabah)
841 HELP PRESERVE MALAYSIA'S CORAL REEFS
All year

As elsewhere in the world, climate change and pollution are causing bleaching of coral reefs in Malaysia. In attempt to keep tabs on this increasingly serious situation, the World Wildlife Fund now deploys volunteer divers to check on the health of reefs around the country's 2,900 miles (4,600 km) of coastline.

Malaysia • Taman Negara National Park
842 BE WOWED BY A GREAT HORNBILL'S BILL
All year

Spotting a great hornbill is a magical experience for bird-watchers in the Taman Negara National Park. You can't miss its massive, bright yellow bill, topped with an orange horn or "casque" that juts along the top of its head like a mohawk hairdo. These extravagant birds are also very long-living, surviving for up to 50 years.

Malaysia • Central Malay Peninsula
843 TRY TO FIND A MALAYAN TIGER
All year

Poaching and habitat loss mean this national animal is now critically endangered; the Malaysian Conservation Alliance for Tigers estimates that only a few hundred remain.

Malaysia • Western region
844 SEEK OUT THE COLORFUL PITTA
All year

A tiny perching songbird, the pitta comes in dozens of vibrant colors and patterns, from black, green, and orange (the hooded) to yellow, blue, and white (the Javan banded).

Malaysia • Western rain forests
845 SEE GIANT BUTTERFLIES
All year

Birdwing butterflies are among the largest there are. Look out for the common, or yellow, birdwing, notable for its vibrant yellow-and-black wings, and the stunning Rajah Brooke's birdwing, which congregates in large groups around sulfur springs.

Malaysia • Western region
846 LEARN ABOUT BATS
All year

Not all bats echolocate. Many fruit bats—such as the large flying fox, or "megabat"—rely on superior eyesight to get around. As their name suggests, they eat fruit (as well as insects and flowers) and can have a wingspan of up to 6 ft (1.8 m).

Malaysia • Coasts
847 SPOT A MINIATURE MASTER OF DISGUISE
All year

Hiding among coral reefs you might just spot this little guy if you try. Depending on the color of the coral around it, the perfectly camouflaged candy crab can be white, pink, yellow, or red, with spines on its tiny 1 in (2.5 cm) body and real coral polyps on its back, which it attaches by itself to complete the effect. All these efforts make it look just as bejeweled as the coral itself.

Malaysia • Forests and shrubland
848 SEE THE MASSIVE ATLAS MOTH
All year

With a wingspan approaching the 12 in (30 cm) mark, the Atlas moth is a long-standing contender for the title of world's largest moth (despite some heavy competition). Their cocoons are so big that they are sometimes used as purses, but this magnificent winged beast has no mouth and only lives for a few days as an adult—the final brief culmination of a life cycle that begins months earlier as a voracious caterpillar.

Malaysia • Shallow sandy waters
849 HEAR A SHRIMP THAT GOES *BANG*
All year

By clicking its pincer, the tiger pistol shrimp sends out a bubble of air that creates a 60 mph (100 kmh) shock wave that can kill or stun its prey.

Malaysia • Lowland forests and swamps
850 MEET A REBEL CUCKOO
All year

The chestnut-breasted malkoha is a cuckoo that breaks the mold: it builds its own nest and rears its own young.

Malaysia • Malay Peninsula
851 SEE A MONKEY WITH GLASSES
All year

The spectacled langur, or dusky leaf monkey, is a quirky little monkey with cartoonish white rings around its eyes that give it its name. Look up to spot them clambering about in the canopy.

Singapore • Throughout
852 GIVE THE EYE TO THE PEACOCK PANSY
March to August

This orange butterfly is perfectly named. The wings resemble delicate flower petals with amazing eye patterns, just like a peacock's.

Singapore • Throughout

853 WAKE UP TO A CRIMSON SUNBIRD

All year

The crimson sunbird was first documented in 1822 by Sir Stamford Raffles, the founder of Singapore. Nearly two centuries later, at a nature society dinner, it was voted the nation's national bird. And why not? This beautiful bright red fellow, with its curved nectar-swilling beak and straw-like tongue, is a cheerful sight across the prosperous city-state.

Borneo • Gunung Mulu National Park

854 CATCH A NIGHTLY BAT EXODUS

All year, at night

Every evening around 6 p.m., a colony of over three million bats leaves Deer Cave en masse for a nightly insect binge.

Borneo • Sarawak

855 PICK OUT A RARE MONKEY CALL

All year

Camping in Bako National Park? Expect to be tormented by macaques, but listen for the rare proboscis monkey's squawking call.

Borneo • Rivers and swamps

856 SEE THE DRAMATIC ASIAN BONYTONGUE

All year

A symbol of good luck and prosperity, these colorful freshwater fish are prized by collectors, but are also an endangered species.

Borneo • Rain forests

857 ADMIRE A PAINTED TERRAPIN

June to August

During breeding season the head of the male of these pretty (but critically endangered) turtles turns white, and a red stripe appears between his eyes.

Borneo • Sipadan Island

858 SWIM AMONG SHOALS OF FISH

April to December

Witness the remarkable sight of huge jackfish shoals that swarm around you in perfect synchronicity and never collide.

Borneo • Rain forests

859 PICK OUT FROGS ON THE FOREST FLOOR

All year

Be careful where you tread—with its curious angular features, the long-nosed horned frog looks just like a dead leaf.

Borneo • Forest hillsides

860 BE IMPRESSED BY A SQUIRREL'S TAIL

All year

Borneo's reputedly carnivorous tufted ground squirrel has the largest tail-to-body ratio of any mammal in existence.

Borneo • Forests near Sabangau River

861 SEE ORANGUTANS IN BORNEO

All year

The orangutans of Borneo are a separate species to those in Sumatra, and they are larger and more solitary than their cousins. About the same size as a human, they hold the crown of being the largest tree-dwelling animal in the world, and are expert climbers. Travelers can get to know the individual personalities of the animals by staying in lodges at orangutan sanctuaries, from where they can also set out into the forest to see these charming and empathic great apes living in the wild.

Brunei • Forests

862 FEEL PEACE WITH A PRAYING MANTIS

All year

The mantis, with its front legs raised as if in prayer, usually inspires feelings of serenity. But in the jungles of Brunei, mantises have been found that can eat small mammals, so beware!

Brunei • Forests by rivers

863 BE POLITE ABOUT THE PROBOSCIS

All year

As a species, these monkeys are unlikely to win any beauty contests. With their potbelly and the male's long drooping nose, they are a bit weird-looking—by human standards anyway. Take a river safari with a local guide through the dense forest around Brunei's capital and see them swimming, leaping between trees, or simply perching, looking after their young.

Brunei • Lowland rain forests

864 GLIMPSE A SUNDA CLOUDED LEOPARD

All year

The largest cat on Borneo is nevertheless one of its most elusive species. A beige-and-black, deadly forest hunter, its oval markings form the shapes of clouds. Despite their size—up to 57 lb (27 kg) in weight and 3.5 ft (1 m) in length—they are remarkably agile climbers, and have been seen in captivity climbing headfirst down vertical tree trunks.

Indonesia • Mentawai Islands

865 SEE A MONKEY WITH A PIG'S TAIL

All year

One of the world's most endangered primates lives only on a few islands off the west coast of Sumatra. Pig-tailed langurs never leave the treetops, and have short hairless tails that seem to belong on another animal entirely. Most are dark gray, but rarer still are the creamy browns. They are polygynous, with one male taking several female partners.

A juvenile orangutan swinging from a vine

Indonesia • Sumatra

866 ENCOUNTER THE WORLD'S LARGEST FLOWER

All year

The flowers of the parasitic rafflesia flower, or "corpse lily," are the biggest of any plant on Earth, at up to 3 ft (1 m) in diameter. The plant has no leaves at all; all of its energy is siphoned off a host plant. And if you're wondering how it got its common name, you'll have to walk up to one in person. They bear the fragrance of rotting flesh, which attracts flies, who pollinate them, and curious humans, who like to marvel at these grotesque cabbage-like monsters. In the interests of conservation, locals are encouraged to charge tourists money to see them, rather than chop them down.

Indonesia • Sumatra; pockets throughout

867 STALK SUMATRAN TIGERS

All year

Sumatra hosts the only wild tigers within the islands that make up Indonesia—a population that was cut off from mainland Asia many thousands of years ago. Sumatra's tigers are smaller than those found on the mainland, and they have denser stripes. The island remains the only place where tigers, rhinos, orangutans, and elephants all live together. Tigers once lived on the neighboring island of Java as well, but they have been extinct there since the 1970s. Sadly, due to deforestation and poaching, the Sumatran population is in decline too, since they rarely venture out of their traditional forest habitat into the man-made plantations that have replaced it.

Indonesia • Northwestern coast of Sumatra

868 ESCAPE THE CLUTCHES OF THE GIANT CLAM

February to August

Legends tell of man-eating giant clams, snapping their shells around unsuspecting divers and holding them in their grips until their prey expire. Giant clams off the coast of Sumatra have been found that are 4.5 ft (137 cm) across, but if they do snap on you, it's probably only to protect themselves, and despite their size, they probably won't hold you for very long.

Indonesia • Way Kambas National Park

869 SHARE YOUR HOPES FOR THE SUMATRAN RHINO

All year

Small and hairy (for a rhinoceros), the Sumatran version is not what you might expect. Once found all over Asia, this stubby-horned and hirsute redhead is now confined to small pockets of Indonesia, such as the Way Kambas National Park. But extensive conservation efforts do mean that its numbers are growing slowly, so there is hope for this unique creature.

866 | *Investigating the odor of the well-named corpse lily*

Indonesia • Western rain forests

870 WATCH FROGS FLY IN THE CANOPY

All year

The rain forest floor is a dangerous place, so the Wallace's flying frog has adapted to life in the treetops, where insects are plentiful and only the occasional snake might slither up to try to attack it. This unconventional life is only interrupted when they descend, as frogs must, to mate and to spawn in water. But they don't just jump between trees, they glide—or they parachute all the way down to the ground by spreading out their giant webbed feet and the interconnecting membrane of skin between their legs to form a sort of wing suit. A single leap may span as far as 50 ft (15 m).

With their vibrant green-and-yellow bodies and bulging black eyes, these frogs surely qualify as true rain forest eye candy.

Indonesia • Ujung Kulon National Park

871 SEE EVERY SPECIES OF RHINO

All year

Even those who've spotted a black, white, Indian, and Sumatran rhino will be lucky to land their eyes on the exceptionally rare and critically endangered Javan rhinoceros.

Indonesia • Bali

872 WATCH DAMSELFISH GUARD THEIR PATCH

May to November

Male damselfish mark out their territory among the coral reefs, and jealously guard it against competitors. Only roving females are allowed in to lay their eggs.

870 | *A Wallace's flying frog in full glide*

873 | *Mantis shrimp eyes—a wonder of nature*

Indonesia • Bali
873 SEE WHAT A MANTIS SHRIMP SEES
May to November

A mantis shrimp's eyes are unlike any other animal's. With 16 color receptors instead of three, they can tune each receptor to the wavelengths of their environment, a system that has evolved independently in parallel to ours—one of the many features that makes these creatures truly alien.

Indonesia • Bali
874 ENTER A SACRED MONKEY FOREST
All year

Three Hindu temples share a space with some 700 so-called crab-eating macaques, who are fed fruit and sweet potatoes by visitors and park-keepers. The forest is owned by the local village, and is an important spiritual, conservation, and education center. It attracts 10,000 visitors a year.

Indonesia • Bali
875 CONTEMPLATE THE STRANGE POPEYED SCORPION FISH
May to November

It's important sometimes to simply be thankful for animals as bizarre as this scorpion fish. These "weed fish" have bright red, purple, or yellow bodies covered in hundreds of seaweed-like appendages—a disguise that they use to creep up on their prey along the seafloor at night.

Indonesia • Lembeh Strait
876 SEE AN OCTOPUS CONTORT ITSELF
July to December

The mimic octopus takes the familiar chameleon's technique of changing its color for camouflage a step further. Sure, it changes color (and pattern), from white to black and everything in between, but this ingenious cephalopod can also shape-shift to impersonate sea snakes, jellyfish, lionfish, flatfish, and crabs.

877 | *Rambutan fruit hanging from a tree*

Indonesia • Gunung Pati
877 APPRECIATE WILD RAMBUTAN
July to March

Across Indonesia you will see the fragrant and exotic rambutan tree growing in orchards and gardens, but the biggest treat is to encounter one in the wild, laden with clusters of ripe-red fruits. Peel away the hairy skins (*rambutan* translates to "hair") and you'll find the sweet inner fruit, with a taste somewhere between a grape and a lychee (to which it's closely related). Rambutan roots, bark, and leaves are all used in local traditional medicine.

Indonesia • Sulawesi
878 HEAD TO THE HILLS FOR THE WORLD'S SMALLEST BUFFALO
All year

Not many species of buffalo really qualify as cute, but the tropical island of Sulawesi has two: a lowland and a highland anoa. The highland incarnation is the smallest of all. At just 28 in (70 cm) at the shoulder, it has a stature more like a deer, and is smaller than some dogs. Unlike most cattle, they move in ones and twos, so you'll never see them in a herd.

Indonesia • Seram; Sulawesi
879 ADMIRE RAINBOW EUCALYPTUS TREES
All year

If you're out exploring the forests of Seram or Sulawesi with young children, you might think they've gone AWOL with a box of crayons when you see the rainbow-colored bark of this surreal-looking gum tree. However, the effect is 100 percent natural. As the smooth outer bark of the tree peels off throughout the year, it reveals an inner layer of bark that is at first green, then cascades through shades of blue, purple, orange, and maroon.

Indonesia • Buton
880 ASK YOURSELF, DOES A DRAGON OWN THIS TREE?
All year

While the Komodo might be Indonesia's most famous dragon, it's not the only local lizard to take its name from the mythical beasts. The relatively tiny *Draco volans*, or flying dragon, uses the flaps of skin on either side of its body like wings to glide between the trees. It can travel as far as 30 ft (9 m) in a single glide. These dragons are also fiercely territorial, each laying claim to around three trees, so remember whose property you might be leaning against in the forest.

Indonesia • Sulawesi
881 SEARCH FOR A LIVING FOSSIL
All year

Rediscovered in 1938, 66 million years after
it was believed to have become extinct, the
coelacanth is a remnant of an order of fish that
has more in common with four-legged animals,
like reptiles and mammals, than modern fish.
Two species are known to exist, the most recently
discovered being found in 1999 in Indonesian
waters. Yet trawlers who catch this missing link
to our evolutionary past just throw them back
in the sea.

883 | *A psychedelic frogfish with "fingerprint" swirls*

Indonesia • Sulawesi
882 TAKE LIFE LESSONS FROM A HARLEQUIN SHRIMP
July to December

In among the reefs around Indonesia, you're likely
to spot these cheerfully attired, peachy-cream
shrimps, adorned with intricate purple-and-blue
spots and about 2 in (5 cm) in length. They live in
pairs and, heaping extravagance on extravagance,
eat nothing but starfish. So many positive life
choices for such a tiny creature! The couples can
be seen cooperating to flip and maneuver the
starfish before they dine on its insides. Eating all
that starfish is believed to make them poisonous
to predators, so they are free to spend the rest of
the time wandering around the reefs.

Indonesia • Ambon Island
883 TRIP OUT WITH THE PSYCHEDELIC FROGFISH
July to December

If you had to pick a favorite frogfish, this would
have to be the one. Either beige or peach in
color, these fish get their name from the fantastic
pink-and-white stripes that cover their bodies
in random swirls. Unusually for a fish, their eyes,
which are intense and blue, are on the front of
their heads, giving them depth perception much
like that of a human. When they need to get from
A to B, they don't swim. Instead they puff into a
ball and use their fins to walk along the seabed.
Watching them move like a lost beach ball drifting
away in slow motion is a surreal sight.

884 | *The deceptively beautiful triggerfish*

Indonesia • Hoga Island
884 DON'T TEMPT A TRIGGERFISH
April to May

Triggerfish are very beautiful, and from a distance appear delicate and elegant, but they are also said to be responsible for more bites, cuts, bruises, and permanent injuries among divers than any other animal. Certainly more than sharks—angels by comparison. The reason is that at certain times of the year, the males' jaws, which are adapted to crushing shells, become weapons that will crush just about anything that comes near their nests and mating sites. Their cone-shaped territory extends upward from the nest, so swimming to the surface won't help you. The best tactic is to move away sideways, fast.

Indonesia • Coastal shallows
885 SEE A SHARK GO FOR A WALK
All year

Epaulette sharks are long—typically about 3.3 ft (1 m)—and thin, and their bodies are most often seen draped languidly in shallow coral pools or deeper, on the reefs. But it's in the shallows that they come into their own: using their fins they can literally walk from pool to pool in search of food, a sight that seems to replay the evolution of sea life onto land. It's often said that sharks need to keep moving to stay alive, but the epaulette is an exception. Their habit of hanging around in the shallows means they are sometimes left with no option but to lie still, shut down nonessential functions, and wait for the tide.

886 SEE THE SMALL AND SWEET SUGAR GLIDER
All year

These tiny gliding possums feed on nectar and sap when they can, and insects when they can't.

Indonesia • Sumatra; Java
887 SEE A CORPSE FLOWER BLOOM
All year

The Guinness World Record holder for the tallest floral bloom emerges about as often as a summer Olympics. When it does, however, it's magnificent. The bloom consists of a central spadix, a warm and very fragrant prong much like a French baguette, that hides a ring of tiny flowers at its base. Fanning out around this is a spathe, a green-and-burgundy wraparound (like a giant leaf or petal). The whole structure can be over 10 ft (3 m) in height and shaped like a calla lily, but smelling exactly like rotten flesh (hence the name), which attracts insects. This plant is not to be confused with the corpse lily, which has a similar smell but a very different shape.

887 | *A towering corpse flower*

Indonesia • Lesser Sunda
Islands
888 WATCH CRABS
AT WORK
All year

The many species of decorator
crabs attach any debris they
encounter to their Velcro-like
shells to use as camouflage.

Indonesia • Lesser Sunda Islands
889 BEWARE OF DRAGONS ON KOMODO
All year

The 29 islands, including Komodo, that make up
Komodo National Park are a haven for wildlife, none
more special than the famous Komodo dragon. These
10 ft (3 m) long lizards roam wild here in their natural
habitat, where they hunt Timor deer, their main prey,
and sometimes attack humans.

889 | *The fierce and fast-moving Komodo dragon*

Indonesia • Throughout
890 CURL UP WITH A COLUGO
All year

The two things to know about a Sunda flying lemur are that it's not a lemur and it doesn't fly (and from the forever-startled look on its face, you'd think it has only just heard the news). In fact, it's a colugo, and like many tree dwellers, it has evolved membranes of skin (a patagium) around its body that help it glide between branches. It can travel an impressive 230 ft (70 m) in one leap, but its excess skin makes it clumsy on foot. By day you'll see them curled up, hanging from trees, while you'll catch them feeding on leaves and fruit.

East Timor • Tropical savanna
891 SEE THE TIMOR DEER
All year

Large herds of native deer are a feature of the tropical savannas of East Timor. Timor deer are notable for their large antlers—a sign they are a social creature, and that the rutting season plays a significant role in their lives. Fun fact: these deer don't drink water; they get all their fluid from food.

890 | *She's not startled—a colugo always looks like this*

Papua New Guinea • South
892 CHECK OUT A NATIONAL BIRD
All year

A silhouette of the Raggiana bird-of-paradise is proudly displayed on the Papua New Guinean flag. The species is widespread throughout the region, and the males really stand out, with their striking yellow crown, blue beak surrounded with emerald green, orange belly, and flowing red-brown plumage. While they stand out on an average day, during mating they become unmissable. The males take turns to outdo one other with loud calls, songs, and displays of hopping, flapping, and swirling their feathers. After copulation the males hold a static pose, their hind feathers spread in the air for the females to inspect.

892 | The bird-of-paradise named after Count Raggi of Genoa

Papua New Guinea • Lowlands
893 BOW TO THE VICTORIA CROWNED PIGEON
All year

With their deep blue feathers and a white-tipped crest around their heads, these relatives of common pigeons inspired naturalists to name them after Queen Victoria herself.

Papua New Guinea • Vogelkop
894 LEARN DEN BUILDING FROM A BOWERBIRD
All year

The Vogelkop bowerbird's twig hut can be up to 40 in (100 cm) high, with an ornamental front lawn decorated with flowers and beetles.

Papua New Guinea • Waigeo
895 BE STUNNED BY A BALD BIRD-OF-PARADISE
All year, at night

With its heart-shaped tail feathers and bright blue bald head (visible at night), Wilson's bird-of-paradise is a sight you won't forget.

Papua New Guinea • Forests

896 MARVEL AT AN ASTRAPIA'S TAIL

All year

The spectacular tail feathers of the male ribbon-tailed astrapia can be three times the length of its 21 in (30.5 cm) body.

Papua New Guinea • Throughout

897 DISCOVER THE TREE KANGAROO

All year

With their large, flat back feet, these cat-sized marsupials are unmistakably related to their Australian cousins, even though they have adapted to life in forests rather than the plains. Walking on flat ground they are pretty slow, clumsy, and unbalanced, but up in the trees they come into their own, employing the familiar hopping action to propel themselves up branches, gripping and controlling their motion with their arms.

Papua New Guinea • Forests

898 SEE A BIRD PUT ON A SHOW

All year

The mating display of a male blue bird-of-paradise involves hanging upside down, fanning out its violet-blue plumes.

Papua New Guinea • Throughout

899 ADMIRE THE COLOR CONTRASTS OF THE CRESTED SATINBIRD

All year

Almost like a yin and yang, the crested satinbird has a demure dark brown breast and an unabashed riot of yellow and orange on its back.

Papua New Guinea
• Huon Peninsula

900 SEE AN EMPEROR

All year

The emperor bird-of-paradise is a striking inhabitant of the hill forests of the Huon Peninsula—its plumage cascades around its yellow-and-green body in an extravagant golden array.

Papua New Guinea
• Throughout

901 ADMIRE A PARROT

All year

The dusky lory, or banded lory, is a type of parrot. It has a hooked orange beak, and bands of autumnal orange, yellow, and black along its body. It's also a skilled mimic of sounds.

Papua New Guinea
• Throughout

902 TICK OFF ANOTHER EGG-LAYING MAMMAL

All year

The spiny, short-beaked echidna is a lesser-known relative of the platypus. It lives on land and feeds on ants using its long, sticky tongue.

Papua New Guinea • Throughout; mountains

903 MEASURE THE KING OF SAXONY'S
HEAD FEATHERS

All year

It's hard not to notice something extraordinary about
this species of bird-of-paradise. Emerging from the male's
head and at least twice the length of his whole body are
two long, thin plumes of feathers. They can move these
feathers independently, which they do to great effect
in their seldom-seen but elaborate mating ritual.

Papua New Guinea • Highland forests
904 COUNT THE SPOTS OF A QUOLL
All year, at night

The New Guinean quoll is a small nocturnal
marsupial with a hairy tail, blotchy white spots, gray
coat, and a fine snout. It is known as a scavenger,
often stealing chickens and other domestic animals.

Micronesia • Yap
905 WITNESS WATERS THAT ARE TEEMING WITH RAYS
December to April

The tiny isolated island of Yap is a mecca for
divers, who come to experience the dramatic
sight of manta rays in mating season.

Solomon Islands • Throughout
906 SEE AN OVERLOOKED SEAHORSE
All year

Pygmy seahorses are so small and so well
camouflaged against the soft coral, sea fans,
and sea grasses that they're often missed.

Solomon Islands • Throughout
907 LOOK UP AT THE SOLOMON EAGLE
All year

The only major predator on these remote islands,
the majestic Solomon sea eagle soars above the
turquoise waters.

908 | *The mighty migration of millions of crabs*

Australia • Christmas Island
908 ENCOUNTER 43 MILLION RED CRABS
October to November

Each year, as the wet season begins and the moon is sufficiently bright, the entire red crab population of Christmas Island uproots itself from the forests and returns to the coasts to mate and spawn in the wet sand. They must cross roads and rough terrain, and at some points locals build special bridges and barriers for the crabs to guarantee their safety in a world where their biggest threat is the motor vehicle. The males move first, and dig burrows on the beach, where they are later joined by females. The females then stay behind for 12 to 13 days, buried in the sand, looking after the eggs.

Australia • Christmas Island
909 VILLIFY THE CRAZY YELLOW ANT
All year

Since this ant was introduced to Christmas Island it has wreaked havoc on local species, causing many to decline and some to become extinct.

Australia • Northwestern coast
910 FIND NEMO
All year

The Australian clownfish was the inspiration for this popular Pixar hero. Conservationists, however, have warned against overcollection as aquarium pets, so that Nemo can continue to be found on reefs.

Australia • Southern and western coasts
911 LOOK PAST THE CAMOUFLAGE OF A LEAFY SEADRAGON
All year

With its leafy protrusions branching off its spindly body, you'll easily mistake these for exotic seaweed.

Australia • Southern parts of Western Australia
912 HIGH-FIVE A KANGAROO PAW
October to February

Sounds exciting? Dangerous? Actually, this is the name of a beautiful ornamental flower that comes in many colors.

Australia • Southern and southwestern coasts
913 OBSERVE A VERY RARE MARINE MAMMAL
All year

The endangered Australian sea lion lives only on a few island groups off the southern and southwestern coasts, and mothers return to the same colony throughout their lives. One of the best places to see them is on Kangaroo Island, where a guided tour around the Seal Bay Conservation Park will take you as close as you can get to these social animals. Their breeding season takes place on a complex 18-month cycle, and each colony follows its own schedule. This results in their populations being somewhat volatile and sensitive to disruption.

913 | *The affable Australian sea lion*

914 | *One of the sociable kangaroos of Lucky Bay*

Australia • Lucky Bay, Western Australia

914 CHILL OUT ON A BEACH WITH KANGAROOS

All year

The kangaroos of Lucky Bay, a perfect horseshoe of protected white sand nestled within a national park, are known to be very friendly. They hop freely along the beach in groups, and curious individuals frequently approach sunbathers and surfers out getting their boards ready. Sometimes they just need to relax, and it's not unusual to see them lying right there next to you in the sand.

Australia • Southern coast of Western Australia

915 EXPERIENCE WILDFLOWERS ON THE RAINBOW COAST

August to December

From the first crack of spring, this area of Western Australia springs forth with flora like an irrepressible waterfall of color, stretching from the beaches back into the forests. There are more than 4,000 species of flower here, 80 percent of which do not grow anywhere else on Earth. Look out for the grandeur of wisteria alongside smaller specimens like the vanilla lily and black kennedia.

Australia • Rottnest Island, Western Australia
916 BEFRIEND A HAPPY MARSUPIAL
All year

Meet the quokka, Australia's friendliest native animal, with a reputation as the happiest animal on the planet. Dutch explorers once unfairly mistook these cuddly critters for rats, naming the island that is home to so many of them a "rat's nest." Rottnest today is a popular spot for day-trippers escaping the city life of nearby Perth. Some residents make the crossing in organized swimming events, but most hop on a ferry.

Quokka are extremely rare on the mainland, but they have thrived on the island in the absence of dogs, cats, foxes, or other predators. There are thought to be as many as 12,000 of them on the island's 7.3 square miles (19 sq km), all with zero fear of humans and infinite curiosity, especially for anyone holding a camera. It's no surprise that in the age of social media they've risen to become the island's biggest tourist attraction.

Feeding or petting the quokkas is strictly banned, though, so it's a case of look but don't touch. The maximum penalty for quokka cruelty is five years in prison, so consider yourself warned.

Australia • Western Australia
917 SEE AN OLD LADY
September to April

The old lady moth, or granny moth, is an attractive brown moth with blue "owl eyes" on its wings. Its name apparently comes from the fact that its markings look like a shawl.

Australia • Western Australia
918 BE CLEAR ABOUT THE TURTLE FROG
October to February

A muscular red-brown mini colossus, you might think a turtle has lost its shell, but this is a frog for sure, adapted to digging deep in the sand for termites.

916 | *Say hello to a quokka*

Australia • Western Australia

919 MAKE A WISH ON AN ALBINO KANGAROO
All year

Sightings of albino kangaroos are rare and always cause a stir. Many kangaroos are pale, but a true albino—with its fur the color of freshly laid snow, and bright red eyes—is something else. Their color makes them a target for predators, so if you see a lucky full-grown adult, you'd better hope a little bit of their luck will rub off on you.

Australia • Northern coast

920 IDENTIFY A LESSER-KNOWN TURTLE
October to February

The flatback sea turtle has a flatter shell than other turtles. It basks in shallow waters with a seabird perched on its back.

Australia • Mataranka Springs, Northern Territory

921 RELAX . . . IF BATS ARE YOUR THING
All year

Enjoy a dip in a hot thermal pool while watching the sky overhead fill with swarms of little red bats known as flying foxes.

Australia • Mary River, Northern Territory

922 STAY SAFE AROUND THE SALTIES
All year

There are more saltwater crocodiles concentrated in this national park than anywhere else you'll ever go.

Australia • Eastern and western coasts

923 FEEL THE FEAR OF A HUNTING SHARK
All year

The oceanic white tip shark is one of the sea's top predators. Make sure you're watching from a boat.

Australia • New South Wales

924 LEARN ABOUT OZ'S LESSER-KNOWN JUMPER
All year

Often found alongside kangaroos, wallabies are smaller, which may explain why they frequently get overlooked. In fact, "wallaby" refers to any member of the kangaroo family other than the six largest species, and they are many and varied, from ones so small you could fit them in your pocket (though you shouldn't) up to those that are 3 ft (1 m) tall.

Australia • Kakadu National Park, Northern Territory

925 GET UP HIGH TO SEE CROCODILES
August to November

See both of Australia's croc species in one place—the freshwater and the more aggressive saltwater kinds.

931 | *A plague of locusts sweep through ground crops*

Australia • Western and South Australia

926 LEARN ABOUT THE NUMBAT'S TONGUE

All year

An animal with a name like this could only be found in Australia. Also known as a banded anteater, it stands under 11 in (30 cm) high. Its most amazing feature is its tongue, which is about 4 in (10 cm) long, and thin enough to needle its way into termite holes. Because it only eats termites, the numbat has no need for teeth; it has small pegs instead. Increasingly endangered, only a lucky few see a numbat in the wild.

Australia • Adelaide River, Darwin

927 SEE CROCS JUMP FROM THE WATER

All year

Usually when you catch sight of a crocodile, which is a cold-blooded creature, it is lying on a riverbank, soaking up the sunshine to stay warm. But on a stretch of the Adelaide River just east of Darwin, crocodiles can be seen all year as they jump out of the water to grab at hunks of meat hung from lines by locals. As alarming as this might sound, it is definitely one way to see a crocodile's hunting technique in action.

Australia • Northern Territory; tropical forests

928 SPOT A WEAVER ANT NEST—IN A TREE

All year

Australian weaver ants live in trees and have a clever technique for creating nests by joining leaves together using larval silk. The ants use their legendary social groups to work together to pull the leaves into a cocoon shape and then to pick up a larva in their mandibles and manipulate it to excrete silk where it is needed—a little like a glue gun. The result is a well-constructed and well-protected cavern of leaves.

Australia • Arid and semi-arid areas
929 READ THE SMILE OF A BEARDED DRAGON
All year

These prehistoric-looking creatures have a spiky beard that they puff up to make themselves appear larger and scarier when faced with predators. Not that they don't start off looking fairly alarming, with their long, low bodies—about 20 in (50 cm) long—scaly skin, and fixed, wide smiles. Usually low to the ground, when they run, they push their bodies up high and can reach quite a surprising and impressive speed.

Australia • Central regions
930 FIND CAMELS IN THE OUTBACK
All year

Camels are not native to Australia—they were imported in the nineteenth century as working beasts that could take on the crucial duties of transportation and heavy lifting. However, these animals turned out to be perfectly suited to the climate. Once no longer needed, they were turned out into the wild, where they formed the world's largest herd of camels, though with devastating consequences to many of the country's native species.

Australia • Queensland
931 STEEL YOURSELF FOR A LOCUST SWARM
September to January

Locusts are legendary for forming huge swarms that can be devastating to both crops and countryside. The swarms occur as juveniles hatch from nests in the ground and they can easily be 2 square miles (5 sq km) wide. The spectacle is unnerving yet breathtaking— the sky darkens and the locusts cover everything before them, and as they move along, fields are left stripped bare. A swarm of these pests can travel as far as 12 miles (20 km) in a day.

Australia • Victoria

932 MEASURE UP TO AN EMU

All year

Only found in Australia, the emu is one of the world's tallest birds—up to 6 ft (1.8 m) tall. Unsurprisingly for its size, it cannot fly, but it is a fast runner. Its body is covered in long, shaggy, brown feathers. The female emu lays a clutch of around 12 speckled green eggs that it then leaves for the male to incubate and care for once hatched.

Australia • Shrublands

933 ADMIRE THE PAPER WASP'S NEST

November to March

The paper wasp gets its name from the way it constructs its nest. It takes plant material and combines it with its saliva to create a nest that looks as if it were made from paper. Sometimes the nest is open, and you can see the cells within where the wasps lay their eggs and rear their young.

932 | *Emus grow to the height of a human*

Australia • Urban areas

934 WELCOME THE FESTIVE SEASON WITH A BEETLE

December

Christmas beetles are drawn to lights and can be found in many urban areas during Australia's summer months—they tend to hatch just before Christmas and then feed on eucalyptus leaves. They are about 0.75 in (2 cm) long, usually a golden brown—although some species are green or black—and always glossy. And they make plenty of noise when they fly.

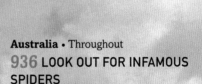

Australia • Queensland

935 DECIDE IF THE BLACK-THROATED BUTCHER DESERVES ITS NAME

All year

This bird earns its name through its habit of impaling captured prey on spikes and thorns so that it can eat it. It's not a pretty sight, but close your eyes and listen instead—it is a heavenly singer.

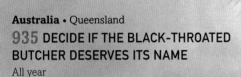

Australia • Throughout

936 LOOK OUT FOR INFAMOUS SPIDERS

All year

Although Australia's spiders have a fearsome reputation, there has only been one death from a spider bite in the last 30 years. The Sydney funnel web is the most venomous at 0.75 in (2 cm). The huntsman (hardly poisonous) is a more impressive 6 in (15 cm) across.

937 | *A tiny dunnart in the hands of a wildlife biologist*

Australia • Southern regions
937 DISCOVER THAT NOT ALL MARSUPIALS JUMP
All year

Marsupials come in any number of different shapes and sizes. One of the smallest is the dunnart. There are many species of dunnart, from the hairy-footed to the fat-tailed, and while some are bigger than others, they are all around the size of a house mouse. When their young are born, they're smaller than a grain of rice, and tuck themselves into a fold on the mother's stomach while they grow. In times of plenty, dunnarts can store fat in their tails, making it slightly carrot-shaped. They are then able to draw on this reserve in leaner times.

Australia • Kangaroo Island, South Australia
938 HAVE AN AUSSIE ISLAND ADVENTURE
All year

More than one-third of this island (Austalia's third largest) is designated as a national park. It is the perfect place to see much of the country's iconic wildlife— plus more that you might not expect to find. The island has its own subspecies of kangaroo (the Kangaroo Island kangaroo, of course) as well as wallabies, possums, koalas, bandicoots, and echidnas. You can also find seals resting on beaches, pelicans swimming in small bays, and all manner of underwater attractions if you choose to go for a dive.

Australia • Central semi-arid regions
939 LEARN NESTING FROM A MALLEEFOWL
October to February

This large ground-dwelling bird is found in many areas of Australia. Its nesting habits are fascinating. Rather than sitting on eggs to incubate them— during a five-month incubation period—the male bird builds a nest of leaf litter that generates heat as it decays, topped with sand. The male uses its bill to test how much heat is being created; if it's too much, it removes sand to allow heat to escape. In the summer months, when the nest is warmed by sun, the male applies more sand to act as a heat shield.

Australia • Southern regions

940 SEE A SPIDER'S MATING DANCE

All year

There are many species of peacock spiders—all are only about 0.2 in (5 mm) across but each displays a fabulous mating dance. The male first waggles its stripy black-and-white legs at a female, as if to attract its attention. If this works, the male lifts its abdomen to reveal an intricate pattern of orange and blue while performing a dance. (It's these colors that give the spider its name.) Abdomen patterns and dance moves vary between species.

Australia • Southern regions

941 HEAR THE REPTILE THAT BARKS LIKE A DOG

All year

On rocky outcrops throughout southern Australia, you could be forgiven for thinking that a wild dog had its beady eyes on you as you heard a low, rasping bark. However, this could actually be the sound of a gecko barking. Yes, the *Underwoodisaurus milii*, or barking gecko, is a reddish-brown species of gecko with white stripes. The gecko arches its back and barks just like a dog when it's threatened. These geckoes live in colonies, often huddled in rocky crevices.

Australia • Queensland

942 SEE THE FLASH OF A ULYSSES BUTTERFLY

All year

The iridescent blue on this butterfly's jet-black wings catches sunlight beautifully.

Australia • Nullabor Plain

943 BE CHARMED BY A HAIRY-NOSED WOMBAT

All year

The southern hairy-nosed wombat—state animal of South Australia—is a stocky marsupial with pig-like facial features.

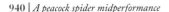

940 | *A peacock spider midperformance*

Australia • Queensland

944 IMMERSE YOURSELF IN THE GREAT BARRIER REEF

All year

The beautiful caves and the corals of the Great Barrier Reef are among the world's greatest sights and have earned the reef a UNESCO World Heritage listing. The reef runs for 1,600 miles (2,575 km) along the northeastern coast of Australia. To dive into its depths is to enter a world of fabulous shapes, colors, and marine life, but it's equally impressive to snorkel around on the surface. The Low Isles near Port Douglas offer unforgettable snorkeling—and the chance to see turtles munching on the sea grass.

Australia • Great Barrier Reef

945 BELIEVE IN UNICORNS—OR AT LEAST THE UNICORN FISH

All year

It is a wonderful thing to study the different fish that might swim by you on a coral reef and compare their many different features. The unicorn fish, for example, is a silvery fish about 20 in (50 cm) long that sports a "horn" growing out from between its eyes. Marine biologists are not entirely sure of the purpose of this horn—the fish has spikes on its tail for defense, so it's not needed for that—although some believe it may be like a rudder, helping the fish navigate through the water. Or perhaps it's just something they like the look of!

Australia • Great Barrier Reef

946 SPOT THE SHARK THAT LOOKS LIKE A CARPET

All year

The wobbegong shark is also known as the carpet shark. It blends into the seafloor like a carpet, and it even has a frilled edge around its upper lip.

Australia • Great Barrier Reef

947 PHOTOGRAPH A LIONFISH

All year

It's poisonous, but with showy fins and long spikes, it's rather lovely to look at.

Australia • Great Barrier Reef

948 SEE THE FISH WITH A BEAK

All year

Parrotfish are remarkable for many different reasons. First their name—which could be down to the many bright and varied colors of parrotfish, but is actually because where other fish have lips, parrotfish have a beak like a … well, like a parrot's. They use this beak to tear off branches of coral that they then grind up to get at the algae inside. The beautiful white sand found in the same reefs is quite often made up of this undigested coral. And finally, parrotfish can change sex and color many times throughout their lives. Remarkable.

Australia • Great Barrier Reef

949 FIND—AND AVOID—THE WORLD'S ONLY POISONOUS OCTOPUS

All year

Beautiful as the blue-ringed octopus might be—yellow skin covered with striking black-and-blue blotches—one bite from this tiny creature can paralyze a human.

944 | *The Great Barrier Reef—host to a diverse world of underwater life*

950 | *A tiny joey in the care of a rescue worker*

Australia • New South Wales

950 HELP OUT IN AN ORPHANAGE

All year

In New South Wales alone, 7,000 animals are killed or injured each day in traffic accidents. This leaves an awful lot of orphaned animals for wildlife rescue centers to look after. When a mother kangaroo is hit, there can be a baby joey hidden in its pouch. These joeys need the warmth and nurturing of their mother for a full year, which is why they can be so dependent on kangaroo orphanages. Volunteering at a remote site in the outback is a wonderful way to observe kangaroo life and to help babies make it to adulthood.

Australia • Cape York, Queensland

953 MAKE EYE CONTACT WITH A CUSCUS

All year, at night

The common spotted cuscus is a fluffy nocturnal tree dweller, famed for its round, bright eyes.

Australia • Eungella National Park, Queensland

951 MAKE UP YOUR MIND ABOUT A PLATYPUS

All year

The platypus—or duck-billed platypus, to give it its full title—is such a wonderful mix-up of features that when it was first seen, scientists thought it was a hoax created by skilled taxidermists. It has a wide rubbery bill, a flat tail, webbed feet, and is covered in fur, so is perfectly suited to a semi-aquatic life. The platypus is one of only two monotremes (mammals that lay eggs rather than giving birth to live young), the other being the echidna. To see one is to believe just how unique it is.

Australia • Cairns, Queensland

954 SPOT A BIG BIRD WITH A BLUE NECK

All year

A cassowary is almost as tall as an emu, but with a stunning blue neck, red wattle, and lavish crest.

Australia • Heron Island, Queensland

952 STUDY TWO TURTLE SPECIES ON ONE ISLAND

October to April

Both the green turtle and the loggerhead turtle come to Heron Island to breed. They wait until an overnight high tide, and then, under cover of darkness, they pull themselves up onto the beach—the same one where their life began around 30 years earlier. Making sure they are beyond the high-water mark, they then dig a hole and lay up to 120 eggs in the sand, covering it over again before they leave. Then, two months later the nest comes alive again as tiny baby turtles hatch, dig their way out of the sand, and instinctively make their way to the ocean, and the cycle of life begins again.

Numbers for both turtle species are in decline, so make sure you do everything possible not to disturb these precious breeding moments.

Australia • Queensland
955 FIND A WALKING STICK ON A TREE
All year

The leaf and twig-like disguise of this stick insect makes it tricky to discern, but if you get a whiff of toffee, you might have disturbed the male, who releases the scent when threatened. Both the male and the female, when under threat, will lift their abdomens up into the air in the manner of a scorpion.

Australia • Queensland
956 FEEL THE FLUFF ON A FLOWER CHAFER
All year

Flower chafers are beautiful, brightly colored scarab beetles with a soft hairiness to their underside. These hairs catch pollen as they visit flowers, making the beetles excellent pollinators. At just 0.5 in (12 mm) long, it's handy for observers that they come in such brilliant shades.

Australia • Raine Island, Queensland
957 SWIM WITH TURTLES
December to January

When 30,000 turtles descend on this tiny island to lay their eggs, you can dive among them as they wait for the high tide, which is when they come ashore. It is thrilling to find yourself swimming at the speed of a turtle, able to look it in the eye as you do so.

Australia • Queensland
958 SPOT A KOOKABURRA IN AN OLD GUM TREE
All year

The kookaburra is the archetypal bird of Australia—so much so that it was chosen as a mascot for the 2000 Sydney Olympic Games. It inspired the famous Australian song "Kookaburra Sits in the Old Gum Tree," which is usually sung in a round. And the wonderful sound of the laughing kookaburra has formed the backdrop to many movie scenes that want to create an instantly Australian atmosphere.

Although it is a member of the kingfisher family, it does not make its home around water, and instead of a diet of fish, it favors small mice, snakes, insects, and even other birds. There are four subspecies of kookaburra. The blue-winged and the spangled varieties have bright blue wings, but the rufous-bellied and the laughing varieties are less spectacular. All have impressively strong-looking bills.

Australia • Granite Gorge
959 ENCOURAGE ROCK WALLABY NUMBERS
All year

Rock wallabies are like the mountain goats of the marsupial world, leaping from boulder to boulder and finding footholds on impossible cliffs. Despite these survival skills, some species are now threatened due to a loss of habitat, an invasion of weeds, and because of competition from other species. Help to raise awareness.

Australia • Queensland
960 STUDY CLIMATE CHANGE IN A RAIN FOREST
All year

With so many different species living in the rain forests of Queensland, it's important to monitor what effect climate change is having on this important habitat. Don't leave the monitoring up to others—instead, get stuck into species surveys and be part of the investigations. It's important work for our times, and it also affords a unique opportunity for wildlife watching.

961 QUESTION THE COLORS OF A RAINBOW LORIKEET

All year

The colors on the rainbow lorikeet are so bright and so flashy you could be forgiven for wondering if they are natural. The birds have an unmistakable blue head, orange breast, blue stomach, and green back. If you see one, you're likely to see several as they tend to live in noisy and fast-moving flocks wherever there are trees—including urban gardens.

962 GO COCK-A-HOOP FOR THE SULPHUR-CRESTED COCKATOO

All year

This is one of those animals that is so often seen in captivity, so it's a true pleasure to be able to see it in the wild.

961 | *Gregarious and colorful lorikeets*

Australia • Eastern coastal regions

963 JUDGE WHETHER A BANDICOOT IS AS WONDERFUL AS IT SOUNDS

All year, at night

The name "bandicoot" sounds like an animal that Walt Disney might have created, but this nocturnal marsupial is entirely real. There are seven species in Australia. They look a little like a large rat but with a much longer snout. You can tell where a bandicoot has been foraging as it digs in the ground for insects and its snout leaves deep conical-shaped holes behind.

Australia • Northern and eastern regions

964 SEEK OUT THE LONG-TAILED PLANIGALE

All year

When you're in the land of the marsupials, it's only right to seek out the smallest one.

Australia • Northern and central regions

965 HEAR A DINGO HOWL

All year

Dingoes are feral dogs that can, however, be trained to live with humans. They live in packs led by an alpha male and female, and they howl like wolves to communicate.

Australia • Phillip Island, Victoria

966 ENJOY AUSTRALIA'S ONLY YEAR-ROUND PENGUINS

September to May

At only 13 in (33 cm) tall, the little penguin is the smallest of the penguin species. And being small, it works hard to protect itself from predators—both those in the air and those in the ocean. Its back is dark blue so that it blends in with the sea when seen from above; its stomach is white so it blends with the sky when seen from below.

Little penguins spend as much as 80 percent of their time at sea, and they can spend a month in the water without coming back to land. When they do come ashore, it is always after sunset, when their land-based predators have gone to sleep. Then they waddle up the beaches and into burrows in the sand dunes. Between February and April each year, little penguins molt their old set of feathers and have to wait on land while a new set grows—which takes around 17 days. As they can't go out to fish during this time, they have to ramp up their body fat beforehand to have enough in storage to keep them going.

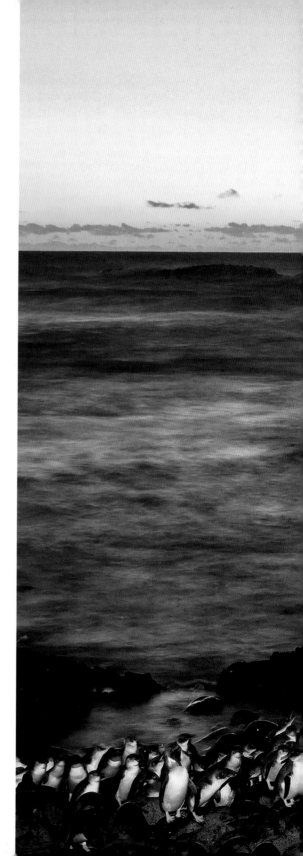

Australia • Apollo Bay, Great Ocean Road

967 SPOT A KOALA UP A TREE
All year

Seeing a koala in a tree while driving the Great Ocean Road is an iconic image of Australian wildlife. It's not easy, though, since they spend most of the day asleep. When they are awake, you'll find them slowly munching eucalyptus leaves and looking very lovable with their fuzzy ears and distinctive black noses.

Australia • Eastern states

968 DISCOVER WHAT A GREEN GROCER IS
December to February

You would be right to think that a green grocer was green. But would you have guessed that it was a cicada? Its name comes from its color. It's one of the loudest insects in the world—it can reach a similar volume to a chainsaw—and up close can hurt the human ear.

967 | *A koala in a rare waking moment*

Australia • Southeastern forests

969 SEE HOW SUPERB THE TAIL OF A LYREBIRD CAN BE

All year

Not only is the superb lyrebird a renowned songbird, it also has a tail shaped like a lyre: does that make it the most musical of birds? This pheasant-sized bird lives in eucalyptus forests where its constant rummaging through the forest floor for grubs helps to speed up the decay of leaf litter. It is an excellent mimic and can imitate other birds' songs, car alarms, and chainsaws.

Australia • Southeastern region

970 LISTEN FOR THE CREAK OF A GANG-GANG COCKATOO

All year

This attractive cockatoo is a lush gray with a bright red, crested head. Although not a noisy bird, it makes a very distinctive sound, like a creaky door hinge blowing in the wind. Sadly due to land clearing, the gang-gang is losing its natural habitat and is now listed as a vulnerable species.

Australia • Albatross Island, Tasmania

971 BE AWED BY AN ALBATROSS'S TRAVELS

All year

Famed for their lonely migrations across the ocean, a wandering albatross can travel up to 10,000 miles (16,000 km) in one trip to search for a meal for its growing infant. The albatross that breeds in Tasmania is known as the shy albatross and flies from its nesting site all the way to South Africa.

Australia • Eastern coasts

972 FIND BEAUTY IN A JELLYFISH

All year

It might leave you with a nasty sting, but that's no reason not to admire the delicate beauty of the white spotted jellyfish.

Australia • Tasmania

973 LEARN WHAT INSPIRED THE TASMANIAN DEVIL'S NAME

All year

This cat-sized black marsupial makes a ferocious sound as it fights for food—like a devil in the bush.

New Caledonia • Throughout
974 DISCOVER A PLANT THAT IS ONE OF A KIND
All year

The corail (or *Parasitaxus usta*) is a rare species of conifer— and the only conifer that doesn't grow roots, but lives as a parasite on a host plant.

Fiji • Coastal waters
975 WATCH A JET-PROPELLED NAUTILUS
All year

The beautiful brown-and-white shell of the nautilus is famed for featuring a perfect Fibonacci spiral on the inside, but the mollusk that creates this shell is equally fascinating. It lives in the shell's main chamber and fills and empties other smaller chambers with water to jet-propel it forward. It trawls reefs looking for crustaceans to devour.

Fiji • Throughout
976 WATCH SPONGES SWAY ON A REEF
All year

Hang in the water and wash away your cares by watching sponges blooming like flowers on Fiji's spectacular reefs.

Fiji • Beqa Lagoon
977 DIVE WITH EIGHT SHARK SPECIES IN A DAY
All year

Experience these magnificent fish in close quarters in the comfort of the protected Shark Reef Marine Reserve.

Fiji • Northwestern islands
978 DECIDE ON AN IGUANA'S BEST SHADE
All year

The Fijian crested iguana is a critically endangered subspecies that is found only on certain islands in the Fijian archipelago. It is a wonderful green color, with three narrow white bands across its back—although it quickly changes from green to black when it gets bothered. Fully grown adults usually reach around 30 in (75 cm) in length and have a row of stubby spines down their back. They are generally found in trees in dry forests where they dine on leaves, flowers, and fruits.

Fiji • Throughout
979 FIND FIJI'S ONLY NATIVE LAND MAMMAL
All year

For an island twice the size of Cyprus, it is surprising to learn that the only native land mammals are bats. Six different kinds can be seen here.

Fiji • Taveuni
980 ASK WHAT A TAGIMOUCIA IS . . .
October to December

. . . and you will discover a beautiful crimson-and-white flower that is only found on one island in Fiji—as well as on the country's $50 bill.

978 | *A crested iguana in the Fiji islands*

981 | *The fearsome fangs of a barracuda*

Fiji • Coastal waters

981 STARE A BARRACUDA IN THE EYES
All year

It is lucky for the snake-like barracuda that it is not a tasty fish, for at 3 to 6 ft (1 to 2 m) long, it is a prime catch for fishermen. It is, however, hugely prized in the diving world, where underwater photographers like to catch schools of these long, sleek, striped creatures chasing smaller fish and bearing their vicious-looking sets of teeth, which often feature a distinctive underbite. They don't tend to turn these fearsome jaws on humans, thankfully.

Fiji • Gau

982 SEE FIJI'S ONLY ENDEMIC SEABIRD
All year

Despite being an island surrounded by miles of South Pacific Sea, Fiji has only one endemic seabird—the Fijian petrel. It is an elegant seabird with long, tapering black wings with a silvery underside. Very little is known about the Fijian petrel's habits, since it nests deep in the island's rocky crags and is then thought to spend long periods out at sea. If you see one, though, make a note and become part of its conservation plan.

Fiji • Throughout

983 BRING A LORIKEET BACK FROM THE BRINK
All year

The red-throated lorikeet is a pretty little songbird—bright green with a red throat and cheeks, and red feathers at the tops of its thighs. Tragically, though, recent surveys on some of Fiji's islands have failed to spot any of this species, leading many ornithologists to believe it is extinct. If individuals were spotted, the bird would have a reprieve in its status, and conservation efforts could help to save yet another species from being lost.

984 | *A zebra crab lurking among the spines of a fire urchin*

Fiji • Coastal waters

984 SPOT A CRAB IN THE SPINES OF AN URCHIN

All year

The zebra crab is a tiny wonder of nature. It is around 0.75 in (2 cm) wide, with a shell and legs beautifully decorated with black-and-white markings, and long, projecting spines. Despite its unmistakable appearance, you'll have to look closely to find one, peering into the spines of a sea urchin, where the crab likes to live. The urchin's spines no doubt provide great protection for the crab, but scientists aren't quite so sure what the urchin gets out of the relationship.

Fiji • Coastal waters

985 DISCOVER ANOTHER DOLPHIN SPECIES

All year

You're unlikely to get the opportunity to check at close range why the rough-toothed dolphin got its name—from the ridges on its teeth—but it's always a joy to see a subspecies you haven't seen before. This dolphin has a less pronounced beak than other subspecies—its head has more of a gentle slope into a long nose—and its body is long with large flippers, a small tail, and blotchy black, white, and gray coloring. It's often seen in pods with other dolphin species.

New Zealand • Kapiti Island

986 WONDER AT THE UNBIRD-LIKE KIWI

All year

The first time you see a kiwi you can't help but wonder if it really is a bird; it looks more like a snuffling mammal as it picks through the topsoil on the hunt for grubs and insects. The little spotted kiwi that is found on Kapiti Island is about 14 in (35 cm) long and, like all kiwis, has a long narrow bill but no tail feathers or wings. Choose to stay overnight on this island, and you will be able to enjoy watching the birds at length in their natural habitat.

New Zealand • Waitomo Caves
987 ENTER A CAVE LIT BY GLOWWORMS
All year

It's a magical feeling to venture into a cave system, leaving the light of the sun behind you, only to find hundreds of tiny lights on the ceiling. These are the lights of glowworms. Here they are the larval form of a particular species of gnat, and without the glowing tail, they'd look a lot like a maggot. Their light is caused by bioluminescence—a secretion of chemicals that reacts with the oxygen in the air to cause the glow. The reason for this isn't to delight cave visitors, but to attract small flying insects that are then caught on sticky threads produced by the worms that hang down from the ceiling.

If you think this all sounds rather spider-like, you'll be interested to hear that the glowworm's scientific name is *Arachnocampa luminosa*, or "light-producing spider larva." The cave produces the perfect conditions for the worms—a river flows through it, bringing a constant supply of insects; the darkness means insects can see their lights; and it is sheltered, so their web-like threads don't dry out in a breeze.

988 | *The ancient and mighty presence of Tane Mahuta*

New Zealand • Waipoua

988 FEEL THE POWER OF THE KAURI

All year

The Waipoua Forest is home to Tane Mahuta ("Lord of the Forest"), New Zealand's largest kauri tree. Its girth is almost 46 ft (14 m), it stands about 168 ft (51 m) high, and it is around 2,000 years old. The tree is imbued with Maori legend, and said to be the father of all the living creatures in the surrounding forest.

New Zealand • Throughout; lakes and estuaries

989 DANCE WITH A BLACK SWAN

All year

We are so used to swans being white that the Antipodean black swans make a beautiful, exotic alternative. They are graceful birds, like their white cousins, with a dramatic contrasting red bill. They were once extinct in New Zealand, but a deliberate reintroduction in the 1860s coincided with a natural recolonization, and they are now plentiful.

New Zealand • Throughout; forests

990 IDENTIFY LIVING FOSSILS

All year

Cycads are a form of fern found widely in New Zealand. They look a bit like palms, but actually belong to a group of plants that has changed very little since the time of the dinosaurs.

New Zealand • Offshore islands

991 MEET NEW ZEALAND'S HEFTIEST LIZARD

All year

The tuatara is certainly no beauty. In fact, at 20 in (50 cm) long, and with spines all down its back, it's quite fearsome.

New Zealand • North Island's western coast

992 APPRECIATE THE WORLD'S RAREST DOLPHIN

All year

Maui's dolphin is a black-and-white dolphin with a rounded dorsal fin, and this is the only place in the world where you can see it.

New Zealand • Kaikoura

993 SWIM WITH FUR SEALS

October to May

New Zealand fur seals, or kekeno, are found along rocky shorelines. Get in the water with them to see their endearing faces and aquadynamic swimming style up close.

New Zealand • South Island
994 SAY HELLO TO A HOIHO
All year

One of the world's rarest penguins, the endangered hoiho—also known as the yellow-eyed penguin—is only found in New Zealand, where it is a popular draw for tourists. It has a pale yellow band around the back of its head, and its eyes are, as you'd imagine, yellow. It also takes pride of place on the New Zealand five-dollar bill.

New Zealand • North Island
995 WORSHIP THE SACRED KINGFISHER
All year

The sacred kingfisher is so-called because Polynesian Islanders believed it could control the ocean and worshiped it accordingly. It is a beautiful bird with a cream breast and dark turquoise head, back, and wings; it is an insect eater rather than a fisher. Listen out for its distinctive *kee-kee-kee* call.

Tahiti • Throughout
996 FEEL UTTERLY SOUTH PACIFIC WATCHING A GARDENIA BLOOM
All year

This pure white flower with waxy petals is the national flower of Tahiti—a country that embraces flowers as a strong part of its culture. Many islanders will have one flower or another tucked behind their ear, and the Tahitian gardenia with its delicate scent is a popular choice.

Antarctica • Coastal waters
997 ENTER A FOREIGN WORLD— DIVING UNDER ICE
January to March

Under the surface, ice takes on sculpted shapes, and every hue of blue, creating a beautiful and unique world. You have to be experienced and organized to dive into this world, but the sights—and the accompanying seals and penguins—will make it unforgettable.

Antarctica • Throughout

998 PAY SOME RESPECT TO A WEDDELL SEAL

November to March

The Weddell seal is the only species of seal that toughs it out year-round in Antarctica, staying throughout the winter when temperatures can reach −22°F (−30°C). They can also dive to depths of 2,000 ft (610 m) and stay under water for 45 minutes. Respect is due.

Antarctica • Antarctic Peninsula

1000 DISCOVER THE GIFTS GENTOO PENGUINS GIVE

November to March

Each year when gentoo penguins meet up again for the breeding season, they build new nests of stones, moss, grass, and feathers, and it all starts with a gift of a pebble from one to the other.

Antarctica • Weddell Sea

999 ADMIRE THE COMMITMENT OF A PENGUIN COUPLE

November to March

Emperor penguins are truly magnificent and devoted birds. In winter they form huge colonies to breed. The male stays on the ice, the egg resting on its feet and incubated by a brood pouch of feathers and flesh, while the female treks back to the sea to fish. Two months later the female is back and they swap roles. Within the huge colony, the female quickly finds its male by the distinctive call they have established. Emperor penguins mate for life, but they still perform a mating dance each year.

999 | *A colony of emperor penguins in Antarctica*

INDEX

INDEX

INDEX

INDEX

PICTURE CREDITS

AUTHOR ACKNOWLEDGMENTS

Selecting the 1,000 entries for this book was not a job that
happened quickly. There were many conversations with many
people that all contributed toward the final list. So to all the
friends, family members, taxi drivers, shopkeepers, opticians,
and school teachers who helped, thank you. Inspiration also
came from the World Wildlife Fund, the International Union
for Conservation of Nature (IUCN) Red List, *National
Geographic*, and the inspirational BBC series *Blue Planet*.

In researching the individual entries and where to find them,
many websites offered valuable insights, but the following
in particular came up trumps again and again: arkive.org,
allaboutbirds.org, and audubon.org.

I'd also like to thank Angela, Jane, and Katie, who have
made the book look so beautiful. And I owe a special debt
of gratitude to conservation biologist Dr. Simon G. Dures
for casting his knowledgeable eye over everything.

And finally, to my husband Steve, whose endless supplies
of patience, support, and love make everything possible.
Thank you.